The CD that accompanied this book has been replaced by a web site that can be found at the following address: http://www.phptr.com

Note that all references to the CD in the book now pertain to the web site.

Streamlined
OBJECT
MODELING
PATTERNS,
RULES, AND
IMPLEMENTATION

ISBN 0-13-066839-7

90000

9 780130 668394

The Coad Series

Peter Coad, *Series Editor*

———■———

About the Series

The Coad Series' mission statement is: Improving the ways people work together. Each book in the series delivers practical keys for building better businesses (or for building better systems that support growing businesses) faster, better, easier.

Peter Coad personally selects authors and books for this series—and works on a strategic level with each author during the development of his book.

About the Series Editor

Peter Coad is a business builder, model builder, and thought leader. As business builder, Peter has taken TogetherSoft Corporation (www.togethersoft.com) from 35 to 450+ employees in 24 months—profitably. As a model builder, Peter has built hundreds of models for nearly every business imaginable, with special focus on building competitive advantages into businesses. As a thought leader, Peter writes (six books to date) and speaks at events worldwide. You can contact Peter at peter.coad@togethersoft.com

- Dave Astels, Granville Miller, Miroslav Novak
  A Practical Guide to eXtreme Programming

- Andy Carmichael, Dan Haywood
  Better Software Faster

- Donald Kranz, Ronald J. Norman
  A Practical Guide to Unified Process

- Jill Nicola, Mark Mayfield, Michael Abney
  Streamlined Object Modeling: Patterns, Rules, and Implementation

- Steve Palmer, Mac Felsing
  A Practical Guide to Feature-Driven Development

- Jo Ellen Perry, Jeff Micke
  How to Get the Most Out of the Together ControlCenter

Streamlined OBJECT MODELING

PATTERNS, RULES, AND IMPLEMENTATION

JILL NICOLA • MARK MAYFIELD • MIKE ABNEY

THE COAD SERIES

PRENTICE HALL PTR
UPPER SADDLE RIVER, NJ 07458
WWW.PHPTR.COM

Library of Congress Cataloging-in-Publication Data

Nicola, Jill
   Streamlined object modeling : patterns, rules, and implementation / Jill Nicola, Mark Mayfield, Mike Abney.
      p. cm.
   Includes bibliographical references and index.
   ISBN 0-13-066839-7 (alk. paper)
      1. Object-oriented methods (Computer science) I. Mayfield, Mark. II. Abney, Mike. III. Title.

QA76.9.O35 N53 2001
005.12--dc21

20001045919

Production Supervisor: Wil Mara
Acquisitions Editor: Paul Petralia
Editorial Assistant: Justin Somma
Marketing Manager: Bryan Gambrel
Manufacturing Manager: Alexis Heydt
Cover Designer: Talar Boorujy
Composition: Aurelia Scharnhorst

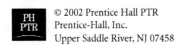

© 2002 Prentice Hall PTR
Prentice-Hall, Inc.
Upper Saddle River, NJ 07458

The publisher offers discounts on this book when ordered in bulk quantities. For more information contact: Corporate Sales Department, Prentice Hall PTR, One Lake Street, Upper Saddle River, NJ 07458. Phone: 800-382-3419; FAX: 201-236-7141; E-mail: corpsales@prenhall.com.

Printed in the United States of America

ISBN 0-13-066839-7

Pearson Education LTD.
Pearson Education Australia PTY, Limited
Pearson Education Singapore, Pte. Ltd
Pearson Education North Asia Ltd
Pearson Education Canada, Ltd.
Pearson Educación de Mexico, S.A. de C.V.
Pearson Education—Japan
Pearson Education Malaysia, Pte. Ltd
Pearson Education, Upper Saddle River, New Jersey

A message from Peter Coad…

Why read this book

Hidden behind effective model shapes are the interactions of all the parts with each other.

Some of the best model builders I work with know those interactions in a very deep way—relating to them visually, musically, and kinesthetically.

Yet the classic problem has been: how do expert ones communicate this keen intuitive sense to others?

In books, so much is left unsaid, unseen, and unheard.

Somehow, Jill, Mark, and Mike have closed the gap, by inventing, advancing, and describing a set of twelve irreducible design molecules—including, and perhaps most significantly—the interaction rules, the secrets that expert model-builders know yet are largely unable to verbalize.

If you are a newcomer to modeling, this book will help you become effective. If you are good at modeling, this book will make you better. If you are an expert at modeling, this book may fill in some gaps in understanding and most definitely will help you in helping others build better models.

Enjoy!

Peter Coad
The Coad Series
peter@coad.com

Peter Coad is a business builder, model builder, and thought leader. As a business builder, Peter has taken TogetherSoft Corporation (www.togethersoft.com) from 35 to 450+ employees in 24 months—profitably. As a model builder, Peter has built hundreds of models for nearly every business imaginable, with special focus on building competitive advantages into businesses. As a thought leader, Peter writes (six books to date) and speaks at events worldwide.

About the cover art

"Midnight Zephyr," by digital artist M. Kungl, was inspired by the masters of streamline design, Raymond Lowey and Henry Dreyfuss. Reflecting the glory days of travel, this original digital artwork was created for limited-edition, fine-art prints using Adobe Photoshop® and Painter®. This image has become popular in all realms of decor for its stylized design simplicity, period color tones, and rough texturing.

For additional information about the artist and his work please visit *www.mkungl.com*

To Dixie, Jacque, and Larry,

My inspiration for everything I do.

Love, Jill

— Jill Nicola

To Stephen Alexander Mayfield,

So much energy, so much fun!

Love, Dad

— Mark Mayfield

To my parents, Joyce and Don,

my siblings, Candise and Matthew,

and especially my wife, Michelle.

Love, Mike

— Mike Abney.

Contents

CHAPTER   3
Collaboration Patterns

CHAPTER 4
Collaboration Rules

CHAPTER 9
Combining Collaboration Patterns

CHAPTER 10
Object Model Documentation

APPENDIX A
Streamlined Object Modeling Principles

Preface

This book started as a guide for how to apply object modeling to real-world problems. Our plan was to apply existing patterns and principles to real-world examples and write about the results. However, while working on real-world applications, we uncovered inadequacies in the existing patterns and the associated information-gathering processes. We found two things especially troubling: first, the existing patterns showed only structure and simple behavior; second, there was no method for capturing business rules in terms of objects. Also bothersome was our inability to justify the use of one set of existing patterns over another.

Our consulting and development work gave us the opportunity to experiment with patterns, make refinements, and consider the results. We became particularly interested in finding the primary patterns for representing people, places, things, and events. From those we knew, we could derive all other patterns for modeling business domains. Over time, we distilled a set of 12 patterns and were successfully applying these patterns to many diverse domains. This convinced us that those patterns were the core set of irreducible patterns from which all other patterns could be derived.

Our work also revealed that business rules are encapsulated behaviors of collaborating objects. Just as similar objects appearing in different object models suggested patterns, similar business rules occurring around our core patterns suggested strategies for discovering and organizing business rules around objects. Now we knew we had something powerful. Indeed, once we determined the core patterns and based the business rules organization around them, we made other discoveries: new principles for distributing behaviors and rule-checking among the objects, new modeling techniques utilizing "object inheritance," and new strategies for implementing patterns and business rules.

Together, our discoveries, which are presented in this book, form a methodology that addresses the problems we saw inherent in earlier methods. We are presently applying this method to commercial applications. We are also looking to expand it in two ways: back into business and technical strategies, and further into design and implementation. But, this expansion is a story for another day. This book describes our object methodology and its uses in modeling business domains and implementing business rules. We call this methodology "streamlined object modeling" because its foundation rests on a streamlined set of patterns that organize and accelerate the modeling and implementation process.

The Value of This Book

The dot-com frenzy encouraged software development trends that put action ahead of thought. Advocates of these techniques were extremely harsh to object modeling, labeling it as an elitist, time-consuming, impractical activity. Well, we beg to differ. We believe in thought before action, and any activity that increases understanding of a problem and decreases the effort of reaching a solution is hardly impractical.

You should read this book if you like thinking through a problem and getting an insightful understanding of it before you try hacking up a solution. This requires some up-front time and effort. But it is not nearly as time-consuming as the trial-and-error programming we observe programmers routinely undertaking to produce code with no apparent organization and that is understandable only to them. With streamlined object modeling, once a problem is modeled in the core patterns, and the business rules described, the implementation is a straightforward application of our strategies and templates. The resulting code reflects the organization of the object model and follows naming standards set in the implementation strategies and templates.

With our core set of patterns, we have moved object modeling from a guru practice closer to a disciplined science. Principles guide object selection, object collaboration, business rule description, behavior placement, and property specification. While it still requires analytical thinking to object model, we have eliminated much of the guesswork for newcomers to object modeling, and provided experienced object modelers with tools for more precise organization and implementation of objects.

What Is in This Book?

When defining any software system, there are three important questions to be answered: why, what, and how. "Why" explains the overall goals and purpose of the system. "What" defines the information, rules, and processes necessary for the system to achieve its goals and purposes. "How" refines each aspect of "what" and creates a blueprint for assembling those aspects into a working system. In short, "why" means discovery of motivation (often called strategy), "what" means requirements analysis, and "how" means application design.

Leaving one or more of these three questions unanswered or incompletely answered increases the difficulty of successfully creating a system. Without motivation (why), it is difficult to weigh the value of features to be analyzed (what). Without knowledge of requirements (what), it is impossible to guess which technologies and design strategies (how) will be best for the final system. While all three questions are important, what is in this book is a great deal about "what."

More specifically, this book describes a method for modeling and implementing information, rules, and processes with object-oriented concepts. While other methodologies cover modeling information and processes with objects, this methodology goes further than most by modeling the rules governing the information and processes. These rules, which are commonly known as "business rules," are a major component of any complete requirements analysis. This book shows not only how to organize business rules around objects, but also provides guidelines for implementing business rules. Examples are provided in Java and Squeak.

Our simple, strong motivation for spending so much time on system business rules is this: they are the rules that make the business work. To put it another way, business rules are the foundation of what businesses will and will not allow. Your bank allows you to deposit money into a checking account and withdraw it when you need it, but it will not allow you to withdraw more than you deposit—at least not without charging you a fee. The rules that define who can put money into your account, who can take it out, and what happens when money moves, are what make the checking account behave the way the bank wants checking accounts to behave. A larger group of these rules, including rules about checking accounts, savings accounts, loans, and what the bank is allowed to do with the money while it is in their hands, is what makes the bank behave the way the bank thinks it should.

A key object-oriented concept is encapsulation: keeping related things together. Business rules make objects behave correctly: they keep the interactions legal, and safe, thereby keeping the system together. We encapsulate business rules inside the business objects they govern so that the mechanisms that bind the system together and keep it from coming apart are held within the business objects. We want the herd of cattle to herd itself; we want the heart to regulate its rhythm; we want the product to track its own inventory. We don't want to have to hire wranglers, wear pacemakers, or build "inventory manager" objects. Too many existing methods proscribe the externalization of business rules. Business rules enforced externally by user interfaces and databases that work across entity objects tend to be more problematic over the life of the system. Such rules are not encapsulated; they are kept in many places, but not necessarily in a logical place, and certainly not with the objects they govern.

Together the business objects and their encapsulated business rules are referred to as the business domain. While the business domain is the major component of the system analysis, requirements for other components are important, too. Part of the "what" of a system includes its user interface analysis and its technical requirements such as load factors, availability, and system scalability. No system analysis is complete without these other aspects. However, without knowing the business rules, the interface design might allow something to happen that it shouldn't. Also, requirements such as load factors, availability, and system scalability are closely tied to business rules. For example, system availability requirements might vary according to company policies preventing system access after business hours. For these reasons, we do not cover user interface analysis or technical requirements gathering. We do, however, encourage you to take whatever you can from this book and apply it in those areas.

How to Read This Book

This book emphasizes communication and "object" thinking. Just as you tailor your words for your audience, so we tailor our object models. With streamlined object modeling, our primary audience comprises the clients of the analysis. To ensure accuracy of the model, clients must be able to understand it and validate it. For this reason, the models produced use simplified notation and are verbose. When you read the models in this book, remember that these models are not the final design of the system. They are not refined into reusable components, optimized for efficiency, or heavily annotated. They do not include "stereotypes" in any of the diagrams, and class inheritance is not used until the later chapters that deal with prototyping. These concepts, while useful, detract from the client's ability to understand the model.

While reading this book, it will help to imagine you are building a model for a business client. Although you may be tempted to collapse related objects into one generalization, or pull out a reusable policy object, keep in mind that you must explain that generalization or reusable object to your client. Go ahead and make that generalization or policy object in your design, but keep the business object model verbose and simple for the client's sake. Also, there is a difference between verbose and cluttered. Limit the model to only those objects, services, and attributes that are necessary to understand the business rules.

Who Should Read This Book?

This is not an introductory software development book. While much of the book is non-technical, it does assume a working knowledge of the Unified Modeling Language (the UML) and general object-oriented development terminology. That being said, this book has three primary audiences: business analysts, system analysts, and software developers who receive system requirements and translate them into system designs. Those who belong to more than one of these groups should get added benefits.

For business and systems analysts, this book offers a new method for gathering and organizing business requirements. This method is significant for incorporating business rules into the object model, and for organizing objects in patterns that communicate with the client. A secondary goal is learning how to prototype a modeled system in one of two programming languages: Java or Squeak.

For software developers, this book offers two benefits. First, since the patterns in this book address modeling business requirements in object-oriented terms, the patterns structure business requirements in a format understandable by most developers. When receiving a business object model, developers will better appreciate the meanings behind the objects. When receiving a functional requirements document, developers can use the patterns to transform it into a more object-oriented representation. Second, once the developers understand the 12 patterns and the ways in which the pattern objects interact, the developers can quickly take the business rules of a domain and apply the prototyping guidelines provided in the later chapters. This effectively jump-starts the development process.

Outline of This Book

The first six chapters of this book outline the activities of streamlined object modeling. These chapters are required reading for business analysts and software developers. Don't skip these chapters if you want a solid understanding of the methodology.

Chapter 1 is a general discussion about the use of object modeling for analysis.

Chapter 2 discusses principles for finding and categorizing objects.

Chapter 3 applies the principles from Chapter 2 to derive the core set of patterns. There are 12 patterns consisting of collaborating pairs of objects. Therefore, we call them collaboration patterns.

Chapter 4 discusses how to organize business rules around objects using the 12 collaboration patterns.

Chapter 5 covers modeling information and business processes and uses the 12 collaboration patterns to distribute processing among the objects.

Chapter 6 explains "object inheritance," a powerful modeling technique for sharing information among objects. Object inheritance underlies several of the collaboration patterns.

Chapters 7 and 8 are geared more toward software developers. They provide guidelines for realizing objects, collaborations, services, and business rules in code. These guidelines are intended to aid understanding of how the methodology translates into a working system, and to validate the business rules through a working implementation. Because they follow from a business object model, and not a refined, optimized system design, the guidelines are not the final story in a coding methodology. We offer them here as a starting point and organizational framework.

Chapter 7 presents an implementation template for translating business objects into programming code. The objective here is to put the code for each object into a common template and establish naming standards and practices to be used later when coding business rules.

Chapter 8 shows how to implement the business rules modeled in Chapter 4 within the templates established in Chapter 7.

Chapters 9 and 10 are for both business analysts and software developers. These chapters examine how collaboration patterns form the basis for new patterns, and structure documentation for business object models.

Chapter 9 presents a "periodic table" of the objects involved in the collaboration patterns. By examining the "chemical properties" of the pattern objects, new patterns can be created by snapping together collaboration patterns through shared objects and by overlaying pattern objects to create new patterns.

Chapter 10 presents documentation outlines we have used to describe streamlined object models. They are by no means the final word on documentation, but show two ways to augment the relationships and rules displayed in the object model diagrams with textual descriptions.

Appendix A lists important principles of streamlined object modeling. It is organized around the core activities and concepts. Each principle refers back to the chapter text where it was first described. Use these principles to guide your object modeling efforts.

Appendix B summarizes the core patterns and concepts of streamlined object modeling in a convenient reference format. Each summary includes hints and examples to assist understanding and application of the pattern or concept. Use these summaries as a quick refresher.

A Quick Note About the Fonts

The ambiguity of written language was a nasty obstacle for us while writing this book. The problem was trying to describe, on different levels, how to object model real-world domains. On one level there are the real-world things we are modeling, on the next level are the pattern objects we use to represent them, and on the final level there are the data structures we make in programming code to implement them. So the same word can refer to a real-world thing, an object abstraction, or Java or Squeak classes.

To help clear up this ambiguity we used different fonts to indicate what a word represents. For example, to indicate when a word refers to a pattern object (as opposed to simply the common meaning of the word), we put it in a special font—`pattern player`.

We used another font to write about Java classes and show Java code listings—`Java code`.

And we used yet another font to write about Squeak classes and show Squeak code listings—**Squeak code**.

We hope these contentions make the text and its inherent meaning clearer for you.

Acknowledgements

This book would not have been possible without the many clients and customers who shared with us their business domains, practices, and visions. Their willingness to think big, plan for the future, and do it right, made this book possible by providing the raw material for crafting and refining our object modeling methodology. For helping us transform that raw material into a finished book we thank our executive editor, Paul Petralia, our tireless production editor, Wil Mara, and our talented compositor, Aurelia Scharnhorst, from Prentice Hall PTR. For their valuable comments and feedback we thank our friends at TogetherSoft: Peter Coad and Eric Lefebvre. For support, encouragement, and ideas during the early days of this book we thank Richard Kelman, Louis Pelikan, Janice Dorr, and Chris Jarzombek. For ideas and assistance in getting this book to completion we thank John Gray and Andrew Reed of Chelsea Marketing Systems and Jay Williams of The Concours Group. Also, we thank the many developers and co-workers who offered ideas and support for this book, especially: Henry Cooper, Jeff Miller, Chris Murphy, and Corby Page. For keeping us full of caffeine and allowing us to monopolize the corner table during peak hours we give a "venti" thanks to the afternoon and evening crew of the coffee shop at West Gray and Shepherd. For rejuvenating us late at night with seafood pad thai, we thank Greg and the staff of Mo Mong's on Westheimer at Montrose. Most importantly, we thank our families for understanding and enduring the many long hours away.

Object Modeling

The mother art is architecture. Without an architecture of our own we have no soul of our own civilization

Frank Lloyd Wright

The Soul of an Application

Long before the flashy graphics, the power keystrokes, the server-side back-end, and the wireless interface, an application develops a soul of its own indicating its purpose, personality, and promise. Applications slammed together using the latest, most-buzzword–compliant, off-the-shelf technology never have any purpose other than to solve an immediate need. Such a hurried application takes on the multiple personalities of its constituent off-the-shelf solutions, and its promise for the future lies only with those features in its package solutions not yet exploited. By contrast, a well-planned application creates new markets and opportunities and evolves its capabilities in response to market needs. Such a thought-out application takes on the singular personality of the vision driving its development, and its promise for the future is limited only by the scope of this vision.

This book is for people who seek elegance, beauty, and soul in software architecture. Such people care about understanding the problem before selecting the solution, and believe in finding the correct solution instead of the first one that works. Popular stereotypes suggest that elegant, beautiful software emerges from the sudden, extreme inspirations of highly-caffeinated hackers, and perhaps occasionally it does; however, the vast majority of elegant software results from careful planning and thorough understanding. By taking the time to understand the market being served, the good software architect produces a model of the architecture that is obvious to the non-technical client, and that communicates the business terminology and requirements to other developers joining the project.

For understanding a problem and modeling it in a form that supports software development, there is no better technique than object modeling. Object modeling, when done properly, extracts client knowledge and represents it in a format that is recognizable to the client and profoundly informative to the developer. This book teaches an object modeling approach distilled from many years of experience working on commercial applications. The sum of our experiences is this: the more we learned, the less we needed to know. Today, we need only a few simple ideas and techniques to object model even the largest and most complex business domains. We present these ideas here as both a statement and a challenge for simplicity. We state that from this simplicity we can model complexity, and we challenge the reader to seek simplicity beyond what we present here.

Object Modeling a Business

Every computerized system from simple e-commerce to full-scale factory management incorporates data, rules, and processes characteristic of the particular business being automated. A successful company knows how to rapidly adapt the data, rules, and processes driving its business as soon as market conditions change; however, these rapid changes are futile if the company's computerized systems are not similarly adept at quickly altering their data, rules, and processes. Keeping computerized systems in sync with the business is easier to accomplish when the two share a common underlying model. This is true whether you are maintaining an existing system, customizing an off-the-shelf framework, or building from scratch.[1]

---

1. This means that our approach to maintenance and customization projects is also to start by object modeling the business and then doing the gap analysis between existing functionality and the desired system.

Organized Around the Business

Object modeling produces a useful model for system developers that is also closely aligned with the organization of the business model. Business data, rules, and processes are organized around conceptual objects representing the people, places, things, and events involved in the business. The resulting object model is a graphical and textual document that businesspeople can verify because it presents familiar objects within their business. System developers can understand it because its notation and symbols map into the object-oriented software languages and packages that most development shops use. What sets object modeling apart from traditional entity modeling is that each object includes both the data and information concerning a business entity *as well as* the rules and processes governing its use.

Growing with the Business

As a business grows, it not only handles larger volumes of data, but also new kinds of data, with new rules and processes. Evolving the data, rules, and processes simultaneously leads to catastrophic results if they are not in sync. Object modeling helps here in two ways. First, it recasts the business in natural terms by focusing on the people, places, things, and events involved in the business, and it expresses growth as it incorporates more events involving more people participating with more things at more places. This representation is easy to understand and easy to document by adding and updating objects in the object model. Second, it synchronizes the data, rules, and processes by encapsulating them together in the objects they represent and regulate. Changing the data inside an object does not "automagically" update the rules and processes inside it; however, it does localize where the changes need to be applied, which is half the battle of synchronization.

Benefits of Object Modeling

Systems built without a sound understanding of the business requirements are difficult to explain, difficult to modify, difficult to expand, and difficult to maintain; on top of that, they generally do not meet all the requirements in the first place. Pre-packaged solutions can hurt rather than help if they predispose the development team to neglect the business and technical requirements before coding begins. Object modeling offers a practical technique for rapidly capturing business requirements while simultaneously planning for future growth and evolution. Object modeling is practical because it represents business requirements in a notation that translates directly into programming code. Object modeling is rapid because it incorporates past solutions and generalizes them for use in future systems, thus no system is ever built from scratch. Lastly, object modeling is adaptable and extensible because it organizes the requirements in a model that mirrors the business and allows the model to grow and evolve in sync with the business.

Object Modeling with Clients

Object modeling is not just for programmers and analysts. It is also a very effective tool for communicating with clients, especially clients who are trying to articulate their vision of a new business, improved process, or future system. Most clients love talking about their vision or their business. Object modeling taps into that client enthusiasm, and channels it by asking focused questions about the business entities, rules, and processes. Organizing questions around the objects gives direction and purpose to the discussion, and the group sees the progress as the model grows.

Planning the Business Endeavor

Object modeling requires the involvement of domain experts, people who know the business thoroughly, and who can either make decisions about it or get an answer from someone else who can. Modeling sessions with these people, who are inquisitive, curious, and well-informed, can easily digress into side issues ranging from marketing strategies to database reports. Gathering that kind of information is important, but in its own time and place. Conceptual planning for a business goes through three phases: why, what, and how.

During the "why," or business strategy, phase, the business entrepreneurs flesh out the purpose of the business endeavor and answer questions such as: Why undertake this endeavor? Why will it succeed? Why will customers come to it, use it, or buy it? Why will they return to it, continue to use it, or buy more of it? Answers to the "why" questions contribute to the business strategy for the endeavor.

During the "what," or business requirements, phase, business domain experts plan the particulars of the business and answer questions such as: What kinds of people, places, things, and events are involved in the business? What information about them is important? What is their involvement in the various business processes and service offerings? What business rules govern their participations in the business processes and service offerings? Answers to the "what" questions contribute to the business plan, the organizational chart, and become the inputs for the "how" stage.

During the "how," or technical requirements, phase, technical and business experts plan the mechanisms for enabling and tracking the business processes and service offerings. Questions answered include: How does the business enable interactions with people or other businesses? How are their interactions recorded? How are available things and places described or presented to them? How are their individual events described or presented to them? How is summary information about past events extracted? How is information stored, retrieved, and distributed? How is information made secure and private? Answers to the "how" questions contribute to the technical strategy, technical architecture, and the user interface, business logic, and database designs.

Object modeling addresses the "what" of the business; its concern is only with what is to be built, never why or how. Prior to the object modeling session, a good object architect inquires about the "why" questions, and raises a red flag if no one at the client site knows the answers. Clients not clear on their strategy are not ready to discuss what they want to build. On the other hand, clients too focused on "how" are likely to choose inadequate solutions because they do not fully understand what is involved in the endeavor. It is only natural that "how" questions arise during the object modeling session; the best response is to punt, and wait until the requirements are known. To minimize the time between "what" and "how," use iterative development technique.[2]

PRINCIPLE 1
THE HOW OF WHY IS WHAT

> Conceptual planning for an endeavor goes through three stages: why build, what to build, and how to build. How needs what to define its scope, and what needs why to define its purpose.*

* See Appendix A for a complete listing of streamlined object modeling principles.

New Business Endeavors

With new companies, the object modeling session is often the first time many of the executives sit in the same room and talk to each other about the business. Centering the discussion on business entities such as customers, products, discounts, procurement schedules, work flow, and supply chains keeps domineering personalities at bay and power trips to a minimum.

---

2. For more on iterative development, see "Object Modeling and Iterative Development," in Chapter 10.

Modeling the business entities as objects, and working to extract their responsibilities, gets the executives away from high-level market-speak and down into the details. Often, object modeling brings out details and issues not yet considered, and the client has to defer answering until a later time.

Process Re-engineering

Other clients are using technology to re-engineer a process, probably taking it off the mainframe and to a client/server or Internet-based architecture. These clients are intimately familiar with details, but are stuck in how it is done now, overlooking potential improvements. The worst thing to do with these people is to talk about users and user scenarios, because that tends to bring focus on how the old system worked, not what the real underlying business process should be.[3] To get them out of the trees and seeing the forest requires modeling the process and its goals. Only by concentrating on the objects involved and the goals of a process can clients see the flaws in the process and possible solutions.

Some clients try to skip business modeling and use a vendor's framework to implement their processes. This can work, but if the processes are documented only in the code generated by the product, clients will have a difficult time predicting how changes in one process will affect others. As a result, updating one process can break or seriously impact other processes. Also, it is difficult to tell whether a particular framework is an appropriate solution without doing some up-front analysis. At a minimum, clients need some form of gap analysis between their processes and a framework's functionality, and that is simplified for clients who have invested time in building an accurate model of their own processes. Finally, clients who have a model independent of a technology or vendor framework are better equipped to redefine their processes beyond the features offered by the vendor.

Common Viewpoint

For all clients, object modeling succeeds because it focuses on the domain objects and forces everyone in the group to take the object's viewpoint. Putting people into the same viewpoint is a powerful technique for gaining group consensus. By contrast, building scenarios around users compels every participant to consider the system from his own personal viewpoint,

---

3. User scenarios are frequently called "use cases." Building use cases before object modeling focuses attention on how things are done now instead of what needs to be accomplished. The result is often a continuation of poor processes and a missed opportunity for process re-engineering.

and how he[4] wants it to work. Not surprisingly, getting group consensus on "what" with use cases is considerably harder. Once the object model is created, then user scenarios are helpful in fleshing out the "how." Specifically, user scenarios are helpful in walking through the object model and bringing out preferred interaction flows.

PRINCIPLE 2
THE OBJECT MODELING VIEWPOINT

Use object modeling to build group consensus by focusing on impersonal objects, not subjective users.

PRINCIPLE 3
OBJECT MODELING A NEW BUSINESS

Use object modeling with clients building a new business to flesh out details and issues, and document the proposed business in an impartial and objective manner.

PRINCIPLE 4
OBJECT MODELING FOR PROCESS RE-ENGINEERING

Use object modeling with clients who are re-engineering a business process to get them out of the current way of doing things and to help them see the big picture, so they can discover a better solution.

PRINCIPLE 5
OBJECT MODELING BEFORE USE CASES

For understanding a complex business process, use object modeling to bring out what needs to happen. Consider use cases afterward to illustrate how users interact with the objects in the system.

---

4. Use of the pronoun "he" and all its variations should be understood as a generic pronoun representing both male and female persons. One of the authors is a female, and she passionately hates writing "he or she."

Object Modeling and Complexity _____

"[C]omplex systems will evolve from simple systems much more rapidly if there are stable intermediate forms than if there are not."[5]

Cognitive psychology and computer science teach us that the trick to solving a complex and difficult problem is to decompose it into smaller tractable ones. Learning a new skill or writing a large computer program is made easier by solving many small problems, and applying these solutions as steps contributing to the ultimate goal. While a novice golf player must consciously consider his hands, feet, and club placement before driving off the tee, an advanced player does these unconsciously, focusing his attention more on the wind, the course layout, and his next shot. Skills, once mastered, and software programs, once debugged, become stable intermediate forms upon which more complex solutions can be built.

Before a complex problem can be decomposed into smaller tractable problems, it must first be described in a representation that can be partitioned. For software applications, this means gathering the requirements in a format that reveals the big picture, and remains meaningful when subdivided into smaller chunks. Object modeling excels in this regard; it captures the details of the overall business and retains its integrity and structure when partitioned into smaller chunks.

Stability Through Encapsulation

Object models are stable and decomposable because they are created through successive layers of encapsulation. The smallest unit of an object model, an object, encapsulates information and behaviors behind a message interface. Changes in how the information is represented and how the behaviors are coded remain hidden from the outside world, which only considers the object in terms of its interface. The next layer of encapsulation, a group of collaborating objects, is stable because it reflects relationships among people, places, things, and events in the real world.[6] Although the technology and service offerings of a business may change, the set of people, places, things, and events involved in it rarely do. A bookstore is still a bookstore, whether it is a brick-and-mortar or an online variety; it still has customers looking for and purchasing books.

---

5. *Sciences of the Artificial*, Herb Simon, 1998, MIT Press, p. 196.
6. For more on collaborating objects, see Chapter 3.

The final layer of encapsulation, a component, is a group of objects performing a common task. Account billing, document workflow, and product procurement are examples of object model components. The simplest component implements a business scenario, which in the object world starts by messaging a single object that then distributes the work among its collaborating objects; thus the entire component, containing many objects, becomes identifiable with the message interface of its starter object, and external objects and components can ignore its internal structure and communicate with it using these few messages. Moreover, because it performs a specific task, a component can be independently implemented, debugged, and tested, thus becoming a stable, working building block for constructing larger components.

PRINCIPLE 6
MANAGING COMPLEXITY WITH OBJECT MODELING

Object modeling handles complexity by encapsulating information, rules, and behaviors within successive layers of objects. Each layer provides a stable intermediate form for building a larger system.

Object Modeling Patterns

Modeling complex systems depends heavily on finding the right objects—constructs that represent people, places, events, and things or parts of them—and placing them into collaborating groups. Furthermore, it depends on selecting properties for these objects from the real world and encapsulating within these objects behaviors that work on those properties. Because collaborating objects represent real-world relationships, and these relationships appear in many diverse domains, similar groups of collaborating objects appear in object models, again and again. Patterns generalize these recurring groups of collaborating objects into templates that can be filled in with domain-specific objects to quickly model common real world relationships.

Why Use Patterns?

Modeling with patterns has several advantages; the most obvious is speed. Once a real-world relationship is identified, it can be quickly modeled by filling in its corresponding pattern with domain-specific objects. In this manner, patterns not only build the object model by connecting known objects, they also help find new objects needed to fill in an identified pattern.

Models built with patterns rest on a foundation of previous success. Patterns evolved because various people consistently arrived at the same solutions for modeling the same real-world relationship. This common solution did not happen by luck or magic; these people were using similar strategies for finding objects and establishing object responsibilities. These strategies applied consistently yielded patterns.

Models exhibiting regular patterns are more easily understood. Organizing objects with patterns accentuates how each object contributes to the overall model. Understanding the role an object plays in the object model factors heavily into how the object is realized into program code, and how that code handles the object's business rules, behaviors, and collaborations.

Types of Patterns

Object-oriented patterns occur throughout the software development lifecycle. This book considers object modeling patterns and analysis patterns as the same. There are other object-oriented patterns for design and implementation, but since those patterns apply after the object modeling activity, this book does not treat them as object modeling patterns. Their contributions are to turn the object model into software designs and programs, whereas object modeling patterns are for modeling a real-world domain in a form the domain expert can recognize and understand.

Design patterns work on an object model to make its objects efficient, reusable, and pluggable. This book does not discuss design patterns because its focus is on representing business requirements, especially modeling domain relationships and capturing business rules. Implementation patterns focus on code elegance, style, readability, and efficiency. Books and guides on these topics abound; however, this book does provide implementation templates and strategies for coding the patterns discussed here. Our implementation patterns show how to code collaborating objects, and how to distribute business rule checking between them. Examples are included in Java and Squeak Smalltalk.[7]

---

7. To learn more about Java and to download its software developer's kit (SDK), go to *http://java.sun.com/*. To learn more about Squeak and to download its free development environment, go to *http://www.squeak.org/*. Java SDK 1.3.1 and Squeak 3.0 are provided on the CD-ROM in the back of this book.

Streamlined Object Modeling _____

This book teaches an object modeling methodology we call "streamlined object modeling." The theme underlying streamlined object modeling is that from a very small set of irreducible object modeling patterns, which represent all the possible people, place, thing, and event relationships in a real-world domain, any object model can be created. The authors have applied streamlined object modeling successfully over the past several years for a number of commercial applications. Through testing and refining, we have whittled the methodology down to what we believe are the bare essentials necessary to completely and accurately object model the data, information, processes, and rules behind any real-world domain. Streamlined object modeling consists of 12 irreducible object modeling patterns, five types of business rules, and three types of business services.

Fundamentals of Streamlined Object Modeling

At its core, streamlined object modeling includes 12 irreducible patterns that cover all the people, place, thing, and event relationships needed to model any real-world domain. They are irreducible because they cannot be decomposed into smaller constituent patterns. Each pattern consists of two template objects called pattern players, and each pattern player has a unique meaning that determines how it handles business rules, participates in business scenarios, and is implemented in code.

Streamlined object modeling also includes a precise process for mapping business rules into an object model. Two types of business rules are identified: those that regulate data values and those that regulate real-world relationships. The data regulation rules largely become internal rules for checking object property values. More interesting are the rules for regulating relationships; streamlined object modeling recasts these rules as preconditions for creating or dissolving the relationships modeled by its core set of patterns. With this formulation, each business rule is a test between two pattern players and falls into one of five categories: (1) type, (2) multiplicity, (3) property, (4) state, and (5) conflict rules. For each pair of pattern players, streamlined object modeling specifies which category of rules each pattern player has the responsibility of checking.

Lastly, streamlined object modeling recognizes three types of business services: (1) determining current information, (2) determining historical information, and (3) initiating business actions. As with business rules, how to distribute the work of performing business services among objects depends on the pattern player roles each object plays, so that knowing what patterns an object participates in determines how much work it undertakes and how much it delegates to its collaborating objects.

Finding Objects

2

Point of view is worth 80 IQ points.

Alan Kay

Modeling Knowledge

Some people ask us if we build object models because we program in object-oriented languages. That's not why. We don't object model to write object-oriented code, we write object-oriented code because we object model. We're used to thinking that way.[1] Other ways of thinking about and writing code look very unattractive once you grasp the object-oriented way of thinking and its benefits. Success in object modeling requires two abilities: (1) good object think, and (2) good object selection. This chapter briefly discusses object think and introduces categories for consistently and accurately selecting objects. It is important to recognize that the informa-

---

1. One theory of cognition, cited by Peter Coad in his books, claims that people organize information about the real world into objects and attributes, wholes and parts, and general and specific classes. Such theories support the naturalness of object thinking. *Object-Oriented Analysis* (2nd ed.), Peter Coad and Edward Yourdon, 1990, Prentice Hall. pp. 16 – 17 (A great book!). *Object Models: Strategies, Patterns, & Applications* (2nd ed.), Peter Coad, David North, and Mark Mayfield, 1997, Prentice Hall. p. 1n (Another great book!).

tion gathered through object modeling is not the only set of requirements gathered. Some requirements are more subjective and have to do with user experience and user interactions. Other requirements are more technical and specify the operating environment of the system. These are captured by methods other than object modeling, but are driven by the domain defined in the object model.

Object Think

Object think is key to properly encapsulating data and functionality within objects. Poor object thinkers put data and functions into objects haphazardly. At best, they use a set of guidelines they find difficult to explain. This makes their models and code difficult to understand and brittle to changes in requirements and system growth. When requirements change, a brittle object model must significantly alter its structure by redefining objects, rearranging collaborations, and shuffling responsibilities between objects. Object models built through functional analysis are filled with objects representing functions, which makes them notoriously brittle as changes in functional requirements render objects obsolete, and reorder collaborations among them.

Good object thinkers apply consistent principles for distributing data and functions; they can explain and justify the results in their object models by relating them back to the objects in the business domain. Object models built with object think remain stable as the requirements and the system evolve because the model mirrors real-world objects and their relationships. New requirements mean more of the domain is being modeled or more responsibilities are being given to the objects that are already modeled. These changes are neatly encapsulated in a stable object model by adding new objects and expanding objects' responsibilities. Objects do not change their meaning or lose collaborators, so the underlying structure of the model remains intact even as new layers are snapped on top of it.

Rule one of object think is to personify objects and conceive of them as active, knowledgeable entities.[2] From the object personification point of view, a domain of entities and processes becomes a collection of active objects capable of undertaking complex actions in response to outside requests. A model produced by object personification has an organization that reflects the natural structure of the domain. The opposite of object personification is the functional perspective that models a domain as a collection of functions working on data.

---

2. This book uses the word "entity" to mean a real-world something; it uses the word "object" to mean an abstraction or representation of something in the real world.

Rule two of object think is to adopt the "first-person" voice when discussing objects. Under the first-person perspective, all statements about an object are expressed using the pronoun "I." Speaking of objects in the first-person voice is useful for determining precisely what responsibilities an object needs, along the lines of "If I am this object, do I really need to know about X, or really need to be able to do Y?"

Rule three of object think is to transform knowledge about an object and the functions performed on it into responsibilities of the object. Under the responsible objects perspective, functions performed on an object become services the object performs; data recorded about an object become properties the object maintains; and links to other things become collaborations with other objects, formed according to business rules.

> EXAMPLE—A fruit juice bottling plant keeps statistics on all of its bottling lines that include the theoretical cases per hour it can produce under 24/7 operation, and the actual number of cases it produces in a month. These statistics are used to calculate each bottling line's monthly efficiency.

> Applying object think:

> I'm a fruit juice bottling line. I know my theoretical cases-per-hour limit and how many cases I produce in a given month. I know how to calculate my theoretical limit for each month, and I know how to calculate my case efficiency for each month.

PRINCIPLE 7
PERSONIFY OBJECTS

Object model a domain by imagining its entities as active, knowing objects, capable of performing complex actions.

PRINCIPLE 8
GIVE OBJECTS RESPONSIBILITIES

Turn information about a real-world entity and the actions performed on it into responsibilities of the object representing the entity.

PRINCIPLE 9
OBJECT'S RESPONSIBILITIES

An object's responsibilities are: whom I know—my collaborations with others; what I do—my services; and what I know—my properties.[*]

[*] We use the word "property" to mean both stored data, such as date of birth, and derived or calculated data, such as age.

PRINCIPLE 10
TALK LIKE AN OBJECT

To scope an object's responsibilities, imagine yourself as the object, and adopt the first-person voice when discussing it.[*]

[*] To use a sports analogy, "Be the ball!"

Object Selection

Finding objects is easy if you know how and where to look for them. How to look is simple; use object think to ask questions of domain experts. Where to look is straightforward, too; look for objects in the following four categories: people, places, things, and events.

Coad's Categories and Patterns

Listening to domain experts and probing for people, places, things, and events are simple, yet powerful activities in the object modeling methodology. They direct attention away from users, screens, and technologies and toward understanding the underlying business domain. We learned this methodology from Peter Coad, the author of one of the very first books on object-oriented analysis.[3] While working with Peter, object modeling complex domains all over the world, one of us co-authored a book[4] with him on object modeling and patterns. In this book were 31 object modeling patterns. Over the past several years, we have, through practical application on commercial systems, whittled and transformed these patterns down to 12 pairs of players.[5] As

---

3. *Object-Oriented Analysis* (2nd ed.), Peter Coad and Edward Yourdon, 1990, Prentice Hall.
4. *Object Models: Strategies, Patterns, & Applications* (2nd ed.), Peter Coad, David North, and Mark Mayfield, 1997, Prentice Hall.
5. See page 11, "Fundamentals of Streamlined Object Modeling." A pattern player is a template object within a pattern. A domain object can participate as many pattern players. More on this later.

expected, each object in these 12 pairs belongs to one of the four domain categories. When you know the objects in the domain categories and are able to recognize them in the responses of domain experts, then you will be well on your way toward becoming a very effective object modeler. The remainder of this chapter introduces the domain objects, and the next chapter shows how these objects form the 12 object patterns we use for modeling.

People

People play a big part in nearly all domains. Information to capture about people includes details identifying individuals, the different contexts in which they can participate, their privileges and duties in those contexts, and records of their interactions. Often people participate not on their own behalf, but on behalf of a company or agency; however, object think dictates that it is the organization that is bidding, buying, and selling, and otherwise acting like a single individual. To model a person or an organization that can participate in the system, use an actor object. Model the participation and actions of the person or organization with separate objects.

A simple rule of object modeling is that every action by a person or an organization happens within a context. A context is a focused piece of the business domain that concentrates on the information and rules necessary to reach a single goal. Putting an action within a context helps ensure the action is only undertaken by those able to participate in that context, and that the action only involves other people, places, and things within that context.

> EXAMPLE—In an e-commerce system for ordering office supplies, a person can participate as an individual customer, as a buyer for a business, as a supplier agent, and as a system administrator. The same person may be able to participate in more than one of these roles. Fred is both a customer and a business buyer. When Fred logs in as a business buyer, he enters a different context than when he logs in as an individual customer. Prices and discounts may differ, and he can use a purchase order to acquire supplies, something he cannot do as an individual customer. Peggy Sue, acting as a supplier agent, can update inventory for her company's products on the site. Billy Bob, acting as a system administrator, can update pricing and discounts.

Whenever a person or organization participates in a context, two things inevitably happen. First, the system endows the person or organization with permissions, IDs, and passwords necessary to distinguish and track that person or organization within that context. Second, the person or organization's participation acquires its own history, recording the events undertaken within that context. Objectify the obvious. For each context a person or organization participates in, create a `role` object that has the permissions, IDs, and passwords necessary to participate in the context, and that has associated to it the records of interactions within the context.

> EXAMPLE—In the above e-commerce system, create separate `role` objects for each goal-based action: customer orders products; business buyer orders products for organization; supplier agent sells products; and system administrator creates and manages the accounts and other information in the system. Fred has two `role` objects: a customer `role` for his personal orders, and a business buyer `role` for his company orders. His personal billing and shipping information is held with his customer `role`, along with his personal orders. His company billing and shipping information, along with his company orders, are held with his business buyer **role**. Both `roles` are associated to the person object representing Fred; this common object allows Fred to get to both `roles` through a single login.

We often say a person like Fred is "taking on many `roles`." Organizations take on `roles`, too, possibly many. In general, use a `role` object to model how a person appears and what a person does in a given context. Ditto for organizations. They're people, too.

PRINCIPLE 11
THE PEOPLE PRINCIPLE

> Use an `actor` object to model individual people participating in a system. Also use an `actor` object to model an organization of people participating in a system as a single entity.

PRINCIPLE 12
THE CONTEXT PRINCIPLE

> A context of participation exists whenever a person or organization undertakes actions that are tracked and recorded. Actions that require different permissions or information from the person or organization belong in different contexts.

PRINCIPLE 13
THE ROLE PRINCIPLE

> For each context an entity participates in, create a separate `role` object. Put the information and permissions needed for that context into the `role`.

Places

Another simple rule of object modeling is that every recorded action by a person or organization happens in a given place.[6] In a simple system where all actions occur at the same location, having an explicit place object maybe be redundant; however, adding it now simplifies expansion to a system with multiple locations later.

> EXAMPLE—A retail clothing store seeks to consolidate all its orders in one database, but wants to be able to distinguish those that were purchased online from those that occurred in a physical store or were catalog telephone orders. In the model, an order can occur in one of three places: physical store, online store, or telephone catalog store.

Places are often hierarchical for the following reasons: (1) a position for a localized place cannot be fully specified without putting it inside a larger place,[7] and (2) recorded actions in localized places are rolled up into larger places for auditing or statistical comparison. The smallest place of interest is where recorded actions occur. A location that merely contains things, but is not a location for recorded actions, is not a place, but a container (see Section 2.2.6). To model a location where recorded actions occur, use a `place` object; to model a location that contains `places`, use an `outer place` object.

> EXAMPLE—In the retail clothing store example, each physical store is assigned to a geographical region overseen by a regional supervisor. The performance of each geographical region is determined by rolling up the orders placed at the physical stores within it.

In the retail clothing store example, there are only two levels, and the geographical region is acting as an `outer place`; however, if the nesting of levels was greater, then the geographical region might itself be a `place` contained within an `outer place`.

A `place`, just like a person or organization, can take on different `roles` depending on the context in which the `place` is viewed. To model the appearance and participation of `places` in different contexts, use `role` objects.

---

6. An example of a non-recorded action is a search. While it generates results that may be modeled as objects, the search is typically discarded after the user logs out, so it is not permanent history stored with the user `role`.
7. An example of this is a gate at an airport; its position is within a particular terminal that is within a particular airport.

EXAMPLE—An airport can be either or both a civilian airport and a military airport. An airport gate can be possibly one or more of the following gate roles: international, interstate, or intra-state.

PRINCIPLE 14
THE PLACE PRINCIPLE

Model a location where recorded actions occur with a `place` object. Model a hierarchical location with an `outer place` containing a `place`. Model the uses of a `place` or `outer place` in different contexts with `role` objects.

Things

Every real-world action involves a subject that is the entity being acted upon. A tangible entity that can be the subject of an action is considered a thing. When people and places are the subjects of actions, they are acting like things.[8]

To describe a real-world thing requires two objects. The first object provides a general, high-level description of the thing that is abstract enough to be shared with other similar things. In effect, this general description defines a set of related things. The second object is a specific description that extends the general description and distinguishes the thing from others in the set.

Decomposing a thing into general and specific descriptions resembles a data modeling technique called normalization; but this is not normalization, because the goal of normalization is to avoid replicating data. Objects are more than just data; they have behaviors, too. Having one general description for many specific descriptions allows data sharing, but it also allows for behaviors within the general description that work across all the specific objects, for instance, rank them from best to worst.

To model the general description of a set of things, use an `item` object, which is a reusable description for many particular things. Use a `specific item` to model the properties that distinguish a particular thing from other things with the same `item` description.

EXAMPLE—An automobile belongs to a set that is defined as all cars with a certain manufacturer, make, model, and production year, but it also has unique characteristics, such as its color, options, and vehicle identification number. Model the automobile with two objects: an

---

8. Examples include selecting a particular individual as your insurance agent, or reserving a particular cabin at a ski lodge.

automobile description containing the general characteristics, and an automobile object containing its unique characteristics. The automobile description object is reusable for all similar automobiles.

Use `role` objects for things that can participate in multiple contexts or have multiple uses.

> EXAMPLE—A master videotape is stored within a storage library and has a storage `role` that participates in the checking-in and checking-out events. The same videotape is also converted to a digital file so that segments can be extracted into online videos. The videotape has a digital master `role` that participates with the editing events to track the history of the videotape's usage in online videos and the number of minutes involved.

PRINCIPLE 15
THE THING PRINCIPLE

Model a thing with two objects: an `item` that acts as a description defining a set containing similar things, and a `specific item` that distinguishes a particular thing from others in the set. Model the uses of a thing in different contexts with `role` objects.

Aggregate Things

As with places, a thing can be tracked at different hierarchical levels of scale. Going up the scale, a thing can be placed within a container, classified within one or more groups, or fitted as a part into an assembly; going down the scale, a thing can act as a container, a group, or an assembly. It is quite common for a thing to exist at both levels; for example, a part in an assembly may itself be assembled out of smaller parts.

To model a thing that is a receptacle or storage place for other things, use a `container` object. Use a `content` object to represent a thing that is placed in a `container`. A `content` object can only be in at most one `container` at a given time, although its `container` may be a `content` object in another `container`.

> EXAMPLE—A television network sends its master videotapes to a videotape storage library. Each videotape is bar-coded and assigned a storage location. When the network recalls the videotape, and later returns it to the library, the videotape is again assigned a storage location that may or may not be the same as its previous location.

To categorize a collection of things, use a `group` object. A `group` is different from a `container`, because it denotes categorization, not physical containment. A `group` is also different from an `item`. Recall that an `item` acts a common description for all things in a set, whereas the things belonging to a `group` need not be related other than by their inclusion in the `group`. Use a `member` object to represent a thing that belongs to one or more `groups`.

> EXAMPLE—The television network has a classification scheme for its videotapes that includes categories such as news, sports, documentary, comedy, drama, children's, and talk show. A videotape is classified into one or more of the categories.

To model a thing constructed from other things, use an `assembly` object. Unlike a `container` and a `group`, an `assembly` cannot exist without its constituent parts. Use a `part` object to represent the component things that make up an `assembly`.

> EXAMPLE—A made-to-order computer workstation is assembled from components selected by online by a customer.

PRINCIPLE 16
THE AGGREGATE THING PRINCIPLE

> Model a receptacle of things as a `container` with `content` objects. Model a classification of things as a `group` with `member` objects. Model an ensemble of things with an `assembly` of `part` objects.

Events

An event is an interaction between people, places and things. Because they tie together the other three categories of objects, events are considered the historical glue in the object model. A simple event involves people interacting at a place with only one thing. Complex events involve multiple things and are discussed in the next section.

> EXAMPLE—A mechanic inspects an automobile on a given date and time and records the results and success or failure of the inspection.

To model simple events involving only one thing, use a `transaction` object. `Transactions` are either point-in-time events that represent a momentary interaction, or they are time-interval events that occur over a long-term duration.

EXAMPLE—Common point-in-time events are orders, purchases, returns, deposits, withdrawals, arrivals, departures, shipments, and deliveries. Common time-interval events are leases, rentals, job assignments, memberships, and itineraries.

To model a point-in-time event, use a `transaction` that knows about a single timestamp. For a time-interval event, use a `transaction` that knows about the starting and the ending timestamps. History events are a special kind of time-interval event. A history event knows information about a person, place, or thing during a specified time span.

EXAMPLE—An e-commerce system assigns each of its products a price with an effective date range; for legal reasons, the price history must be retained for each product. For each assembly line, a manufacturing plant keeps a history of its products produced during a given time period. This information is used to calculate key performance measures for the line and plant.

PRINCIPLE 17
THE EVENT PRINCIPLE

Model the event of people interacting at a place with a thing as a `transaction` object. Model a point-in-time interaction as a `transaction` with a single timestamp; model a time-interval interaction as a `transaction` object with multiple timestamps.

PRINCIPLE 18
THE HISTORY PRINCIPLE

To record historical or time-sensitive information about a person, place, or thing, use a time-interval `transaction`.

Composite Events

Composite events involve people interacting at a place with one or more things. To distinguish and track each interaction with a single thing, a composite event contains smaller events, one for each thing.[9] The composite event is responsible for summary information and behaviors that work across all the interacting things.

---

9. Recall objects can play in many ways. People and places can act like things in a composite event. In those cases, they have their own smaller events within the composite event.

To model a composite event, use a `composite transaction`. Use a `line item` to record the interaction details for a single thing within a `composite transaction`. A `line item` is a dependent event in that it cannot exist by itself; it exists only as part of the `composite transaction`.

> EXAMPLE—An e-commerce order is a `composite transaction` with a `line item` for each product included in the order. The `line item` for a single product contains the quantity ordered, shipping information, and gift wrap and gift message options.

PRINCIPLE 19
THE COMPOSITE EVENT PRINCIPLE

> Model people interacting at a place with multiple things as a `composite transaction`; for each thing involved, include a `line item` to capture specific interaction details.

Follow-up Events

Often an interaction between a given set of people, places, and things is followed by another interaction with some of the same people, places, and things. In general, simple events are followed by simple events, and composite events are followed by composite events.

> EXAMPLE—Common follow-up events are a delivery following a shipment, an arrival at one place following a departure at another, and a return at one store branch following a sale at a different store branch.

To model an event following another event, use a `follow-up transaction` object. `Follow-up transactions` are not the same as `line items`. A `line item` records details about a thing inside a composite event. A `follow-up transaction` describes another event at a later time.

PRINCIPLE 20
THE FOLLOW-UP EVENT PRINCIPLE

> Model an event that follows and depends on a previous event with a `follow-up transaction`.

Next Step

With the object think principles and some familiarity with the core domain objects, you are now ready to learn the fundamental patterns for object modeling. Chapter 3 presents the 12 collaboration patterns that are the fundamental building blocks for building all object models. Not only do these shape the structure of the object model, they also help extract and organize the business rules, processes, and data.

Pattern Players

The 12 collaboration patterns are assembled from the vocabulary of objects discussed in the object selection principles. Since these objects play parts in one or more of the collaboration patterns, we call them pattern players. Table 2.1 lists the pattern players, loosely organized according to the people, place, thing, and event categories. These pattern players will be used throughout the remainder of this book.

TABLE 2.1
The Pattern Players

People	Actor
	Role
Places	Place
	Outer Place
Things	Item
	Specific Item
	Assembly
	Part
	Container
	Content
	Group
	Member
Events	Transaction
	Composite Transaction
	Line Item
	Follow-up Transaction

Collaboration Patterns

The central task of a natural science is to make the wonderful
commonplace: to show that complexity, correctly viewed, is only a
mask for simplicity; to find pattern hidden in apparent chaos.

Herb Simon

Complexity Made Simple

Patterns started when object modelers noticed certain groups of collaborating
objects occurring consistently in many object models, and generalized them.
As powerful as they were, these patterns did not always play well together
because they did not convey a consistent understanding of the real world and
its interactions. To get an integrated set of patterns, we set out to find the
optimal principles for modeling real-world entities and interactions, theoriz-
ing that these would lead us to the fundamental patterns. By scrutinizing past
object models involving people, places, things, and events, and considering
new hypothetical ones, we hoped to understand what our preferred objects
and collaborations represented about real-world entities. This inquiry into the
meaning of objects resulted in the object selection principles and pattern players discussed in the previous chapter.

Armed with the object selection principles and the pattern players, we re-evaluated our favorite object modeling patterns. We discovered that the majority obeyed the principles and could be expressed in terms of the pattern player objects; in fact, many patterns that appeared unrelated because they contained different objects were shown to contain objects that were several pattern players combined. These combination patterns were considered second-generation. In the end, only 12 patterns were irreducible; from these or combinations of these, we theorized that we could model nearly all real-world entities and their interactions.

As proof to ourselves, which became material for this book, we used the 12 patterns to build object models for commercial applications. In doing so, we determined that not only could object models be constructed from the patterns, but also that the patterns simplified the construction, organization, and coding of the object model. This chapter presents the 12 patterns; later chapters show how to organize behaviors, properties, and business rules around the 12 patterns, how to implement them in code, and how to use them to construct larger patterns.

Real-World Modeling

Any comprehensive methodology for modeling the real world requires a viewpoint, a vocabulary, and an organizational method. Our viewpoint is that the real world consists of entities having simple or complex structures, inter-acting with one another in space, time, and over a multitude of contexts. Our vocabulary consists of the people, place, thing, and event objects discussed in the previous chapter and known as pattern players. And our organizational method is to decompose all domains into collaborations between people, place, thing, and event objects, and to distribute all domain information and behaviors around these collaborations using object think principles.

Why Collaborations?

No object is an island.[1] An object isolated in an object model without any collaborators is an obvious mistake. Given that collaborations are so essential, any object modeling methodology lacking a theory of collaborations must be considered incomplete. At a minimum, a collaboration theory should specify the allowable collaborations between different types of objects. With all collab-orations limited to a known set, validation of the collaborations within any object model becomes feasible. A repository of collaborations also simplifies

---

1. However, an island is an object, a place typically.

finding objects, because the presence of a given type of object suggests the presences of its likely collaborators. Finally, as will be shown in later chapters, most domain business rules involve deciding which objects can collaborate, when they can collaborate, which collaborations can be dissolved, and when they can be dissolved. For all these reasons, we selected collaboration patterns as the natural foundation for building an object modeling methodology.

Collaboration Patterns

Collaboration patterns are the embodiments of the object selection principles presented in the pervious chapter. While the object selection principles describe the meaning and relevance of the objects, the collaboration patterns with their graphical formats concisely and unambiguously illustrate the interactions between the objects. By laying out the principles graphically, and revealing the common pattern players, collaboration patterns make clear how the principles work together to create object models.

Collaboration patterns are not design patterns. Design patterns focus on efficiency, reuse, and pluggability, and while these are important goals, they are concerned more with "how" to effect an interaction, not "what" is involved in it. Collaboration patterns describe the "what" of an interaction— the objects involved and the rules governing those interactions. This book focuses on specifying the "what" through object modeling and prototyping in code. It is not enforcing design principles, but it is expected that those will be applied at the appropriate time. These early chapters introduce collaboration patterns for object modeling, and later chapters introduce implementation patterns for translating collaboration patterns into program code.

Collaboration patterns are, by definition, patterns involving two pattern players. Each collaboration pattern involves two of the pattern players described by the object selection principles.[2] Larger patterns arise when two collaborations are "snapped together" by sharing a common pattern player, or when collaborations are merged by sharing an object that is acting as several different pattern players.[3]

The collaboration patterns are shown in Figure 3.1. The remainder of this chapter describes each collaboration pattern by indicating what its pattern players represent, and what their responsibilities are. This information is summarized in Appendix B. Equally important are the rules governing the

---

2. See Table 2.1, "The Pattern Players," p. 25.
3. Snapping and merging collaborations is discussed in-depth in Chapter 9.

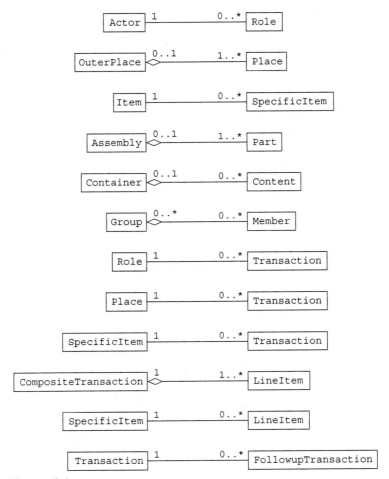

FIGURE 3.1

Collaboration patterns.

interactions between two pattern players, but these will not be described until the next chapter. Documentation formats for precisely specifying collaborations are discussed in Chapter 10.

Some of the collaboration patterns described below are the same as or were derived from patterns depicted in the *Object Models* book.[4] These patterns are indicated.

---

4. *Object Models: Strategies, Patterns, & Applications* (2nd ed.), Peter Coad, David North, and Mark Mayfield, 1997, Prentice Hall.

FIGURE 3.2
The actor - role pattern.

Actor – Role

The actor - role pattern models *entities* interacting in multiple contexts. It is most frequently applied to people, but can also be applied to places and things.[5] This pattern arises from the People, Context, and Role Principles (Principles 11, 12, and 13) that suggest two objects—one describing the person or organization (actor), and a second describing the person or organization within a context (role). For each context, a new role is created

Use the actor – role pattern shown in Figure 3.2 to model people, places, or things participating in one or more contexts.[6]

Actor Responsibilities

An actor can know about multiple roles, but can take on only one of each kind. The actor is responsible for knowing information—properties, services, and collaborations—that is relevant across all contexts.

> EXAMPLE—An e-commerce startup tracks people who are customers, employees, and brokers. A person (actor) can play multiple roles, but can only take on at most one customer role, one employee role, and one broker role (see Figure 3.3).

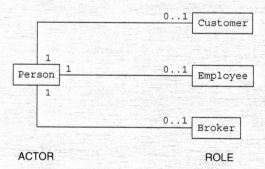

FIGURE 3.3
Multiple roles for an actor.

---

5. See discussion of places and things taking on roles, pp. 19–21.
6. Pattern #2 from *Object Models: Strategies, Patterns, & Applications* (2nd ed.), Peter Coad, David North, and Mark Mayfield.

Role Responsibilities

A role knows about exactly one actor, and without its actor, a role is not valid. Changes in the actor—new property values or new collaborations—may also impact the role. This dependency on an actor follows because a role is an individualized description of an actor, the guise of an actor within a context. If the collaboration is dissolved, then the role must be destroyed, because a different actor cannot reuse a role; for example, a customer profile cannot be transferred from one person to another. A role also knows the type of actors with which it can collaborate; some roles only work with organization actors.

> EXAMPLE—In a supply-chain application, a company can be both a supplier of goods and services and a distributor that buys from suppliers (see Figure 3.4).

Sometimes a role serves double duty as an actor for another role.

> EXAMPLE—A project team collaborates online. Within the team there are specialized roles: administrators and team chairs. Since these additional roles are on top of team membership, the team member role becomes the actor for them (see Figure 3.5).

Outer Place – Place

The outer place - place pattern models *locations* where interactions between people and things happen. This pattern arises from the Place Principle (Principle 14) that models a location for interactions with two types of objects—one describing the event location (place), and an optional second object (outer place) when the location is hierarchical.

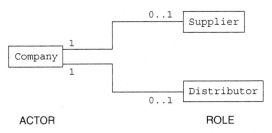

ACTOR   ROLE

FIGURE 3.4
An organizational actor with multiple roles.

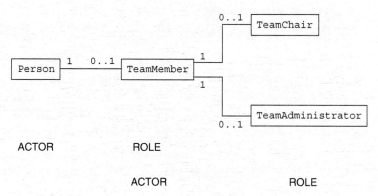

ACTOR   ROLE

FIGURE 3.5
TeamMember is a `role` for Person and an `actor` for TeamAdministrator and TeamChair.

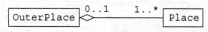

FIGURE 3.6
The `outer place` - `place` pattern.

Use the `outer place` - `place` pattern shown in Figure 3.6 to model locations for interactions between people and things.

Outer Place Responsibilities

An `outer place` knows at least one `place`, and serves as the container of its `places`.

> EXAMPLE—A manufacturing warehouse receives deliveries in its loading areas and dispenses shipments from its shipping areas (see Figure 3.7).

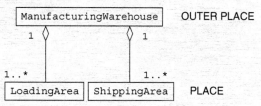

FIGURE 3.7
An `outer place` and two `places`.

Place Responsibilities

A place knows at most one outer place, which contains it. [7] Places are also responsible for knowing about events that happen at their locations. For a hierarchical place, its location depends on its own position and its outer place's position.

>EXAMPLE—An airplane flight arrives at and departs from a specific gate within a terminal (see Figure 3.8).

Sometimes a place serves double duty by acting as an outer place. Allowing the place to serve as an outer place enables modeling of hierarchical locations of arbitrary depths.

>EXAMPLE—Within a manufacturing warehouse, each loading area contains loading bins; deliveries happen at loading areas, and each delivery is subdivided into loads that are placed into loading bins (see Figure 3.9).

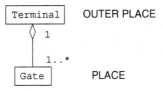

FIGURE 3.8

Flight events happen at a Gate located within a Terminal.

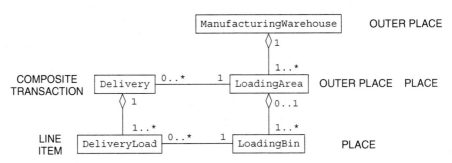

FIGURE 3.9

A LoadingArea is both a place and an outer place.

---

7. Recall that outer place - place represents a geophysical relationship, like an aisle within a store, a gate within a terminal, or an address on a street. When places are classified, such as being within voting districts, tax districts, or school districts, they are acting as members in groups.

Item – Specific Item

The item - specific item pattern models *things* that interact with people at given places, and that exist in multiple variations. Two objects are needed. The item describes the information that is common across all variations. The specific item describes the information that makes each variation distinctive. Also, the specific item participates in events. This pattern supports the Thing Principle (Principle 15).

Use the item - specific item pattern shown in Figure 3.10 to model things that come in varieties.[8]

Item Responsibilities

An item collaborates with zero or more specific items. The item has properties, collaborations, and behaviors that are shared by its specific items.

> EXAMPLE—Everyone's favorite example is the video store. A video title, for example, *Big Sinking Ship*, describes a set of videotapes available for renting. The video title has information about the movie and about how the movie is classified within the video store (see Figure 3.11).

Specific Item Responsibilities

A specific item collaborates with exactly one item, and is dependent on it, much like a role is dependent on its actor; a specific item cannot exist without its item, and is affected by changes in its item.[9] Because a

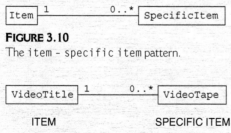

FIGURE 3.10
The item - specific item pattern.

ITEM   SPECIFIC ITEM

FIGURE 3.11
VideoTitle is the description for a set of VideoTapes.

---

8. Pattern #11 from *Object Models* (2nd ed.), Coad, North, and Mayfield.
9. A specific item differs from a role by existing in the same context of interaction as its item, and whereas a role represents a different view of one concrete thing, a specific item represents a particular instance of an abstract description.

specific item relies on its item for existence, the item is often designed as an object factory[10] for creating its specific items.[11] Each specific item knows properties that serve to distinguish it from other specific items of the same item, and knows about interactions with people at given places.

> EXAMPLE—In the video store example, each videotape has its own unique tracking number to distinguish it from other videotapes of the same title, and each videotape has its own history of rentals and returns.

Sometimes items perform double duty by acting as specific things.

> EXAMPLE—In a video store with both DVDs and videotapes for rent, different descriptions for the same movie are required because DVDs have additional options such as subtitles and dual formats not available on videotapes. DVDs are modeled with their own DVD titles, and videotapes with their own video titles. The DVD title and video title are described by a movie title description, which has the characteristics common to all media versions of it. See Figure 3.12.[12]

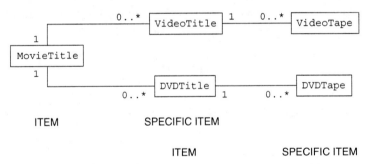

FIGURE 3.12
VideoTitle and DVDTitle acting like items and specific items.

---

10. See the Concrete Factory pattern, pg. 89, *Design Patterns*, Erich Gamma, Richard Helm, Ralph Johnson, and John Vlissides, 1995, Addison Wesley Longman, Inc.

11. The item - specific item pattern seems a lot like the class and object relationship because the item creates specific item objects and acts as a description for them. However, an item is an object with its own properties and collaborations. It would be silly to create a new class for every movie that came out on video. Better to create video title objects for each movie, and allow these to serve as descriptions for videotapes.

12. This example shows the difference between an analysis object model and a design model. The analysis object model is created to communicate to the client and assumes as little as possible about the implementation. The design object model would most likely involve a movie title collaborating with an abstract media title specialized by the video title and DVD title objects. Although the abstract class helps with code reuse, it does nothing to increase understandability, and so is not included in the analysis object model.

Assembly – Part

The assembly - part pattern is one of the patterns for modeling things with complex structures. It is used to model a thing that is constructed from other things. This pattern comes from the Aggregate Thing Principle (Principle 16), but an assembly differs from the other complex structures, container and group, because it cannot exist without at least one part.

Use the assembly - part pattern shown in Figure 3.13 to model a thing constructed from other things.[13]

Assembly Responsibilities

An assembly collaborates with one or more parts, and its parts determine many of its properties.

> EXAMPLE—A computer workstation is assembled from computer components. The price, weight, and availability of the workstation are partly determined from the characteristics of its parts[14] (see Figure 3.14).

Part Responsibilities

A part collaborates with at most one assembly; it may exist independently of its assembly, like a component in stock, but once a part is placed into an assembly, it cannot simultaneously be placed into another.[15]

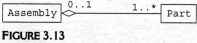

FIGURE 3.13
The assembly - part pattern.

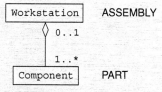

FIGURE 3.14
A Workstation assembled from Components.

---

13. Pattern #17 from *Object Models* (2nd ed.), Coad, North, and Mayfield.
14. Don't confuse the workstation with a "specification" of a workstation. The workstation is a physical assembly, and its components are physical parts with unique serial numbers.
15. In other words, the assembly - part pattern is not for categorizing objects; the group - member pattern does that (see p. 40).

EXAMPLE—In the workstation example, the computer components can be ordered and sold individually. Thus, for each part, the multiplicity constraints on its assembly are zero or one, implying that the part can be in zero or one assembly (see Figure 3.14).

As with places, assemblies can be nested into multiple layers. Allowing a part to serve double duty as an assembly supports modeling assemblies at different levels of granularity.

EXAMPLE—Some of the components in the computer workstation assembly are constructed out of smaller subcomponents; for example, the video card component is an assembly of a circuit board, graphics processors, memory, and so on[16] (see Figure 3.15).

Container – Content

The container - content pattern is the second of the patterns for modeling things with complex structures. It is used to model a thing that is a receptacle or storage place for other things. This pattern comes from the Aggregate Thing Principle (Principle 16).

Use the container - content pattern shown in Figure 3.16 when a thing is a receptacle or storage place for other things.[17]

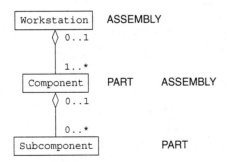

FIGURE 3.15
A Workstation with Components that are also assemblies.

---

16. Since not all components contain subcomponents the multiplicity is zero to many for the sub-components. Each component's specification would indicate whether it was an assembly or simple component, and that would lead to a business rule enforcing the multiplicity (see Chapter 4, "Collaboration Rules").

17. Pattern #14 from *Object Models* (2nd ed.), Coad, North, and Mayfield.

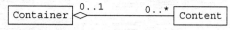

FIGURE 3.16
The container - content pattern.

Container Responsibilities

A container holds zero or more content objects. Notice that unlike an assembly, a container can be empty.

> EXAMPLE—In a distribution center for a manufacturing plant, cases of product are stored in pallets that are then loaded onto delivery trucks (see Figure 3.17).

Content Responsibilities

A content object collaborates with at most one container at a time. It can exist outside a container and can be moved between containers, but it cannot be in two containers at once.

> EXAMPLE—In the distribution center example, a case can be moved from one pallet to another, or stacked on the floor so that it is not in any pallet.

Containment can be hierarchical, meaning that a container can act as content in another container.

> EXAMPLE—A pallet of cases is placed within a truck (see Figure 3.18).

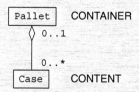

FIGURE 3.17
A Pallet is a container for some number of Cases.

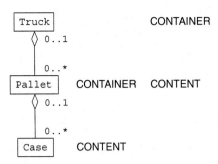

FIGURE 3.18
A Pallet is both a container of Cases and content within a Truck.

FIGURE 3.19
The group - member pattern.

Group – Member

The group – member pattern is the third and final pattern for modeling things with complex structures. This pattern also comes from the Aggregate Thing Principle (Principle 16). It is frequently used to model collections and classifications of things, and it can also be used for collections of people and places.

Use the group – member pattern shown in Figure 3.19 when classifying people, places, or things. [18]

Group Responsibilities

A group knows about zero or more members.

> EXAMPLE—A product catalog puts products into categories, such as sportswear, home and garden, etc. (see Figure 3.20).

Member Responsibilities

A member knows about zero or more groups. This means that unlike parts and content objects, members can belong to more than one group.

> EXAMPLE—In the product catalog example, products can belong to multiple catalog categories (see Figure 3.21).

---

18. Pattern #16 from *Object Models* (2nd ed.), Coad, North, and Mayfield.

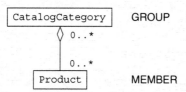

FIGURE 3.20
A Product can be in multiple CatalogCategories.

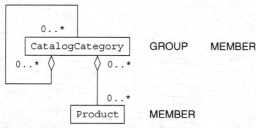

FIGURE 3.21
CatalogCategories can be contained within other CatalogCategories.

Sometimes a group serves double duty as a member. This occurs when groups are themselves classified within groups.

> EXAMPLE—Product catalog categories can be subdivided into smaller categories; for instance, the home and garden category may contain the kitchen and bathroom categories (see Figure 3.21).

Transaction – Role

The transaction - role pattern models an entity interacting with things at places. Usually the entity participating in the interaction is a person or organization, but occasionally, it is a thing or place. The point is that the entity is a real-world doer of the interaction. The role pattern player is used instead of actor because the role describes an entity's participation within a context, and an interaction always occurs within a context. This pattern comes from the Event Principle (Principle 17).

Use the transaction - role pattern shown in Figure 3.22 to describe an entity's interactions.[19]

---

19. Pattern #3 from *Object Models* (2nd ed.), Coad, North, and Mayfield.

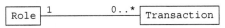

FIGURE 3.22
The transaction - role pattern.

Transaction Responsibilities

A transaction knows one role, which represents the real-world doer of the event modeled by the interaction. Occasionally, events coincide with two or more real-world doers engaged in a mutual interaction. If the event details for each doer are the same and simultaneous, then one transaction will work for both.[20] Using a single transaction to model simultaneous events is a common modeling shortcut, which results in combining two transaction - role collaborations (see Figure 3.23). Combining collaborations is discussed in Chapter 9.

In general, a transaction can know about multiple roles, but can take on only one of each kind.[21] Each role represents one of the real-world doers of the event modeled by the transaction. The transaction records details to pinpoint the event in time.

> EXAMPLE—In the office supplies example, a sales order placed over the telephone includes the participation of the sales rep taking the order (see Figure 3.24).

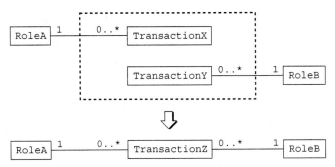

FIGURE 3.23
A transaction with two roles combines two simultaneous and related events.

---

20. Otherwise, two transactions collaborating as transaction - follow-up transaction are needed, with the first transaction representing the involvement of the initiator, and the follow-up transaction representing the involvement of the respondent.
21. A transaction that requires multiple objects of the same kind of role is really a composite transaction with line items detailing the involvements of the particular roles.

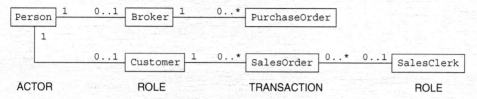

FIGURE 3.24
A SalesOrder can have two role objects.

Role Responsibilities

A role describes an entity within a context, including the information and behaviors necessary to participate in events within the context. A role is also responsible for remembering the events in which it participated. These events are recorded with transactions; and so a role knows about zero or more transactions.

> EXAMPLE—An office supplies system takes orders from people participating as customers and brokers. Brokers create purchase orders for businesses; their methods of payment and price lists differ from those of customers. Customers have customer identifiers and create sales orders. See Figure 3.25.

Transaction – Place

The transaction - place pattern models the fact that interactions between entities and things occur at a given location. This pattern comes from the Place Principle (Principle 14).

Use the transaction - place pattern shown in Figure 3.26 when describing the location where an event occurred.

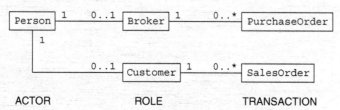

FIGURE 3.25
A Person participates in transactions through his roles.

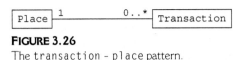

FIGURE 3.26
The transaction - place pattern.

Transaction Responsibilities

A transaction knows about one place. When a time-interval transaction occurs in more than one place, then it is best to model that event as a composite transaction containing multiple single transactions, each at a different location. In these cases, the single transactions are acting like line items within the composite transaction (see p. 46.) In some small domains where all transactions occur at the same location, the place may be eliminated as redundant, but then the system is unable to handle new locations being added.

> EXAMPLE—A delivery at a loading area is actually a composite transaction consisting of many delivery loads that are deposited into individual loading bins. The loading bins are constrained to be in the same loading area where the delivery is located. See Figure 3.27.

Place Responsibilities

A place knows about zero to many transactions; collectively, these transactions represent a history of interactions occurring at the place. A place also knows information sufficient to define a precise, unique location for events.

> EXAMPLE—In a manufacturing warehouse, deliveries arrive to one loading area. To track deliveries, loading areas must be uniquely identified (see Figure 3.28).

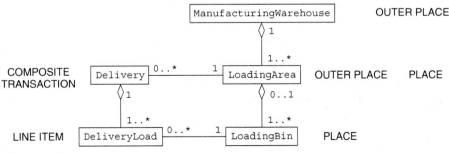

FIGURE 3.27
A Delivery contains smaller transactions that happen at different locations.

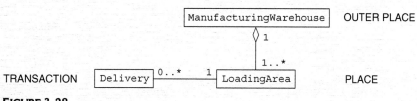

FIGURE 3.28
A Delivery occurs at a precise LoadingArea.

Transaction – Specific Item

The transaction - specific item pattern models the involvement of a thing in an interaction. Here the thing is involved as the subject of the interaction, not the doer of the interaction, and only one thing is involved. The specific item pattern player is used instead of the item pattern player because an event requires a thing with distinguishing details, whereas an item is a common description for a set of things.[22] This pattern comes from the Event Principle (Principle 20).

Use the transaction - specific item pattern shown in Figure 3.29 when describing a transaction involving a single thing.[23]

Transaction Responsibilities

A transaction knows one specific item. The transaction includes details about the specific item's involvement in the event.[24]

> EXAMPLE—In the online cattle breeding site, ranchers can browse the history of breeding events for a given bull and see individual event statistics as well as historical statistics about its success rates.

FIGURE 3.29
The transaction - specific item pattern.

---

22. One common exception is a reservation, which is a transaction against an item, but is followed by a purchase or rental with one of the specific items of the reserved item. In these situations, the item is acting like a specific item (see p. 35).
23. Pattern #6 from *Object Models* (2nd ed.), Coad, North, and Mayfield.
24. A transaction involving more than one specific item is better modeled as a composite transaction with line items to detail each specific item's involvement in the event.

Specific Item Responsibilities

A specific item knows about zero to many transactions. Collectively, these represent the history of the interactions in which the specific item has been involved.

> EXAMPLE—An online cattle breeding site allows ranchers to search for and reserve bulls for breeding services with their cows. A bull object belonging to a cattle breed that contains the general characteristics of the breed represents each bull on the site (see Figure 3.30).

Composite Transaction – Line Item _____

The composite transaction - line item pattern models the involvement of multiple things in an interaction. Each line item describes the details of involvement for one of the things involved. This pattern differs from the transaction - specific item pattern that includes all the interaction details in a single transaction and involves just one thing. This pattern comes from the Composite Event Principle (Principle 19).

Use the composite transaction - line item pattern shown in Figure 3.31 to describe an interaction of people with multiple things at a given location.[25]

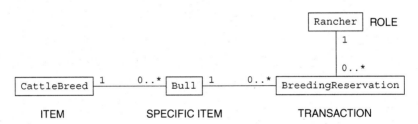

FIGURE 3.30
Examples of the transaction - specific item pattern.

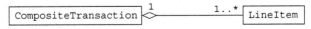

FIGURE 3.31
The transaction - line item pattern.

---

25. Also Pattern #6 from *Object Models* (2nd ed.), Coad, North, and Mayfield. As stated earlier, the patterns in this book are irreducible patterns, some of which were streamlined from the *Object Models* book.

Composite Transaction Responsibilities

A composite transaction must contain at least one line item. The composite transaction acts like a transaction in that it knows about the role and place of the event.

> EXAMPLE—An online entertainment site contracts with content (usually video) producers for the rights to show portions of the producer's content titles on the site. The license agreement[26] contains title terms for each content title covered. See Figure 3.32.

Line Item Responsibilities

A line item knows exactly one composite transaction, and it is entirely dependent on that composite transaction; the line item cannot be in a valid state without its composite transaction, and it cannot be transferred to another composite transaction. The line item contains details about one of the things involved in the event.

> EXAMPLE—In the online entertainment example, each title terms object includes the number of minutes of content that can be extracted from the content title for viewing on the site, the payment terms for viewing the title, and the commission rates for the title when the content showing results in any e-commerce revenues (see Figure 3.32).

Specific Item – Line Item

The specific item - line item pattern models the interaction of a single thing in a composite event. This pattern comes from the Composite Event Principle (Principle 19).

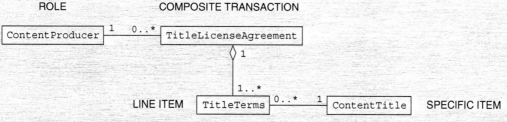

FIGURE 3.32
A TitleLicenseAgreement contains TitleTerms for each ContentTitle covered by it.

---

26. This is an example of a time-interval transaction (see p. 23, "Events").

FIGURE 3.33
The specific item - line item pattern.

Use the specific item - line item pattern shown in Figure 3.33 to describe one thing's interaction in an event involving many things.[27]

Specific Item Responsibilities

A specific item can be involved in zero to many line items. The collection of line items a specific item knows about is part of its history of interactions.

> EXAMPLE—In a video store customers can rent multiple videotapes in a single rental transaction (see Figure 3.34).

Line Item Responsibilities

A line item knows exactly one specific item. The line item captures details about the specific item's interaction with a composite transaction.

> EXAMPLE—In the video store example, when a videotape is rented, its due date and actual return date are recorded in a rental line item. The rental line item can also used to record the state of a videotape when it is returned.[28] See Figure 3.34.

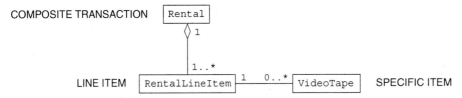

FIGURE 3.34
A RentalLineItem knows one VideoTape.

---

27. Pattern #10 from *Object Models* (2nd ed.), Coad, North, and Mayfield.
28. Alternatively, you could put the return date and state in a follow-up transaction (see next section).

Transaction – Follow-up Transaction _____

The transaction - follow-up transaction pattern models a subsequent interaction of some of the same people, places, and things involved in an original interaction. Typically, the things are the same but the people and/or places may be different. This pattern follows from the Follow-up Event Principle (Principle 20).

Use the transaction - follow-up transaction pattern shown in Figure 3.35 to model interactions that follow from earlier interactions.[29]

Transaction Responsibilities

A transaction knows about some number of follow-up transactions. These are often the next steps in processes.

> EXAMPLE—An e-commerce site allows a product (an SKU) to be ordered and shipped. Depending on the availabilities of the products ordered and if there are multiple ship-to addresses, multiple shipments may be required to deliver the entire order to the customer (see Figure 3.36).

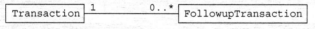

FIGURE 3.35
The transaction - follow-up transaction pattern.

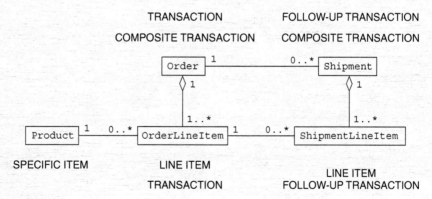

FIGURE 3.36
A Shipment is a follow-up transaction to an Order.

---

29. Pattern #7 from *Object Models* (2nd ed.), Coad, North, and Mayfield.

Follow-up Transaction Responsibilities

A follow-up transaction knows about one transaction; it cannot exist prior to this transaction or be in a valid state without it. Also, since the follow-up transaction is itself a transaction, it may know its own role and place, or it may be a composite transaction.

> EXAMPLE—For each line item of product ordered from the e-commerce site, there are some follow-up shipment line items to track how many of the product were sent in each follow-up shipment (see Figure 3.36).

To model a sequential chain of events, a follow-up transaction can act as a transaction for a subsequent follow-up transaction.

> EXAMPLE—All or part of a shipment can be returned (see Figure 3.37).

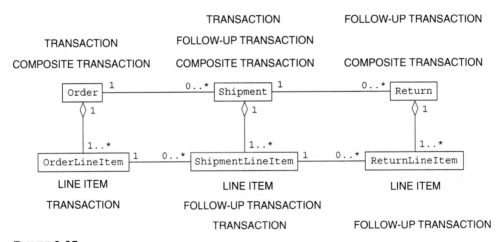

FIGURE 3.37
A Shipment serves as a transaction for a Return follow-up transaction.

Collaboration Rules

4

I am prepared to meet anyone, but whether anyone is prepared for the
great ordeal of meeting me is another matter.

Mark Twain

Object-Oriented Business Rules

The previous chapter discussed the 12 collaboration patterns and explained
their uses for modeling the people, places, things, and events in real-world
domains. Such domains are frequently called business domains, although
their realm may be non-business endeavors from government to entertain-
ment. This book will use the terms "business domain" and "real-world
domain" interchangeably, and will use the term "business rules" for constraints governing what actions and information are legal and valid within a
business domain. Business rules are the heart of any domain. Without their
constraining force, business processes may be initiated by the wrong people,
at the wrong times and places, and with things improperly selected or ille-
gally defined. Running business processes with illegal information not only
corrupts system integrity, but also induces egregious real-world effects.
Business rules prevent illegal product sales to under-age consumers and
overseas customers; business rules prevent movement by an elevator with
open doors; business rules define who can respond to a request-for-quota-

tion and enforce the deadline for quotes; and business rules determine which house of the U. S. Congress can initiate an appropriations bill or approve a treaty. Because business rules are so crucial to the success and goals of a business domain, it cannot be considered properly or completely modeled until its business rules are specified.

Capturing and specifying business rules is an analysis activity.[1] An ideal modeling methodology seamlessly integrates the business rules with the model, enabling them to be defined at the same time, and in the same vocabulary; integration simplifies and eases the process of keeping the rules and model in sync as one or the other evolves. Our modeling methodology achieves this integration by decomposing all business domains into pairs of collaborating objects, and transforming all business rules into tests between collaborating objects. These tests are called collaboration rules, and how to describe business rules as collaboration rules is the theme of this chapter.

Business Rules and Collaborations

Most business rules involve restrictions on which people can participate, what events can occur, where events can occur, what things can be involved, and how those things can be described, grouped, classified, and assembled. These relationships between people, places, things, and events are modeled by the 12 collaboration patterns; thus, a business domain modeled with collaboration patterns can easily express its business rules in terms of collaborating objects.

> EXAMPLE—Business rules determine whether a product (`specific item`) can be added to an order (`transaction`), whether an elevator (`specific item`) can accept a request (`transaction`) to go to another floor, whether a bidder (`role`) can bid (`follow-up transaction`) on a request-for-quotation (`transaction`), and whether a bill (`specific item`) can be submitted (`transaction`) for the calendar (`place`) of a particular house of the U. S. Congress.

Collaboration Rules

Collaboration rules test whether two objects can create a new collaboration or dissolve their existing one; in more technical terms, collaboration rules establish pre-conditions for setting or removing an object connection.

---

1. Some organizations might consider this a design activity. In the extreme case, some might consider it a programming activity. This chapter lends proof to the argument it is an analysis activity.

Because these rules often run in response to user actions, a common mistake is to give the human user interface responsibility for checking them. This is a bad move.[2] If business rules are not in the business objects, every redesign and enhancement of the user interface puts them in jeopardy. Business rules lost in a user interface are not easily extracted and ported to other platforms and other technologies. Business rules kept in the business objects live on, through all manner of user interfaces, platforms, and new technologies. Updating business rules is also considerably easier when they live in the objects they govern; it is easy to find them, and to keep them in sync with changes in the objects they affect. Objects are responsible for their own welfare and should not be governed by outside forces.

Collaboration rules do not run when an object and its collaborators are being restored from a database, or a non-finalized collaboration is being rolled back, which frequently happens with event collaborations.[3] In the first case, objects being restored from persistent storage are presumed to have already passed through the business rules. In the second case, an event involves collaborations between multiple objects—people, places, and things; if any one collaboration should fail, then the event is not valid, and any previous collaborations established with it must be dissolved—checking business rules would, therefore, simply be gratuitous.

Transforming Business Rules into Collaboration Rules __

Consistently transforming business rule constraints into collaboration rules requires: (1) deciding how to express the constraints, and (2) deciding how to distribute the rule checking between the two collaborating objects. Because collaboration rules involve two objects mutually deciding whether to make or dissolve a collaboration with the other, the first requirement boils down to deciding what information an object asks of itself and its potential collaborator. We believe that the following five categories handle all possible questions: type, property, state, collaborator multiplicity, and collaborator conflicts. These categories are discussed below.

The second requirement boils down to deciding which collaborator checks what rules, and herein lays the power of collaboration patterns. Because collaboration patterns represent real-world relationships, and each pattern player has a distinct meaning, knowing the pattern involved determines

---

2. Although putting these rules in the business objects requires making objects, trying them out, and then possibly throwing them away, that is a very small price to pay.
3. See p. 76, "Removing and Rolling Back Event Collaborations."

what rules are likely and how the work of checking them is to be distributed between the two pattern players. The remainder of this chapter describes the distribution of collaboration rules among the 12 collaboration patterns. The different types of collaboration rules are also summarized on page 336, "Five Kinds of Collaboration Rules."

Type Rules

Type rules limit the kinds of collaborators an object can have. Think of them as zoning laws: they keep away the wrong types of objects (for example, you can't put a business in a residential area). For simplicity, only one collaborator needs to enforce the type rule: "If it is the wrong type for me, then I am the wrong type for it." The simplest type rules can be depicted on the object model diagram by looking at the connected objects; however, some type rules are dynamic, relying on a derived type computed from the object's state, properties, or collaborations.

> EXAMPLE—A carton of perishable food can only be loaded into a refrigerated truck.

Type rules raise the possibility that a collaborator may need to be specialized into one or more subclasses. Indeed, if the collaborator has different types with clear differences in behaviors, properties, or collaborations, then the analyst can include multiple specializations in the object model.[4] Otherwise, the specialization of types is left to design because it affects efficiency, reuse, and optimization goals. Clearly written type rules assist and inform the designer.

Multiplicity Rules

Multiplicity rules regulate the number of collaborators of an object, and usually these rules are easily depicted on the object model diagram; however, an object can have more dynamic rules determined by its properties. Multiplicity rules come into play when an object tries to add or break a collaboration; an object may refuse to add or break a collaboration if doing so would put it above the maximum or below the minimum required for its existence.

> EXAMPLE—A system for delivering online interactive educational lectures limits the number of students that may enroll in each lecture. Different lectures may have different limits depending on the material and lecturer.

---

4. A specialization is a subtype that differs from its generalization in properties, behaviors, or collaborations. Often, specializations are implemented with subclasses, but they need not be.

Property Rules

Property rules come in two variations: validation and comparison. A validation rule verifies a property value against a standard that is not dependent on the properties of the other potential collaborator. The object with the clearest access to the standard is the owner of the collaboration rule. Alternatively, a comparison rule measures a property value of one object against one or more of the property values of the other potential collaborator. Comparison rules commonly occur in domains with age, residency, or security requirements. The object with the properties defining the acceptable values owns the collaboration rule. In both cases, property values evaluated can be either stored or calculated data.

> EXAMPLE—A customer cannot place an order if he lacks a valid name, billing address, or credit card. A perishable food product cannot collaborate with a shipping container whose average temperature is outside the product's minimum and maximum temperature range.

State Rules

State rules specify the proper states an object needs to be in to begin or end a collaboration. Basically, a state rule asks the question: Am I ready? State rules are often confused with property rules, but they differ in several ways. While validation property rules check for legal property values, state rules check for "proper" state; according to a state rule, an object in a legal state may still not be in the proper state to make or break the collaboration. Also, state rules are always internal and this distinguishes them from comparison property rules that examine property values in both objects.

> EXAMPLE—An order cannot be shipped if it has been cancelled. An auction cannot accept a new bid after the auction has expired.

Conflict Rules

Conflict rules define the conditions under which current collaborators protest gaining a new collaborator or losing an existing one. Conflict rules come in two varieties: collection and event rules. Collection conflict rules occur when an object with a group of similar collaborators polls the group for permission to add a new collaborator to the group or remove an existing one. Event conflict rules check for conflicts among the collaborators of an event; they run when assigning people, places, or things to the event. Conflict rules are themselves type, multiplicity, property, or state rules.

EXAMPLE—A flight arrival cannot be scheduled at a gate if it conflicts with the existing flight arrivals for the gate. A product cannot be added to an order if it conflicts with the order's customer, for example, the customer is under-age for the product.

Collaboration Rules Table

For each collaboration pattern we use a simple table (Table 4.1) to show the division of labor between the two pattern players for collaboration rule checking.

TABLE 4.1
Collaboration Rules Table

	Player 1	Player 2
Type		✓
Multiplicity	✓	✓
Property	✓	✓
State	✓	✓
Conflict		✓

Each column heading names a pattern player, and each row indicates a collaboration rule category. A checkmark indicates whether a pattern player can assume responsibility for that category of rules. Some rule categories can only be properly handled by one of the pattern players; other categories can be handled by both; and occasionally, neither pattern player handles a category of rules. The remainder of this chapter shows the collaboration rules table for each collaboration pattern. A unified table showing the collaboration rules for all 12 patterns is on page 337, "Pattern Player Collaboration Rules."

Rules for Entity Collaborations _____

Entity collaborations use two pattern players to model individual people, places, things, and aggregations of these. With entity collaborations, one of the pattern players is more particular—more specific (`role`, `specific item`), more local (`place`), or more detailed (`part`, `content`, `member`)—than the other. Good object think says put the behavior closest to the data and information, and for the entity patterns, that translates into putting the collaboration rules in the most specific, local, or detailed pattern player.

PRINCIPLE 21
MOST SPECIFIC, LOCAL, OR DETAILED OWNS THE RULE

For collaboration patterns involving people, places, and things, put the collaboration rules in the most specific, local, or detailed pattern player.

Rolling Back Entity Collaborations

If an entity plays in more than one collaboration pattern, then its existence may require multiple collaborations to be established simultaneously. When an entity requires multiple collaborators, the entity's failure to collaborate with one of them invalidates its collaborations to the others. The invalid collaborations are rolled back, and the entity ceases to exist. Rolling back a collaboration is not the same as dissolving it, which requires checking business rules. With a rollback, the failure of the entity to complete all the collaborations necessary for its existence prompted the roll back, and destroying the failed entity should not require business rule checking, as it does not alter persistent business data.

> EXAMPLE—A proposal generation system constructs proposals by selecting chapters from a proposal template. A chapter reference is created from the chapter and added as part of the proposal. The chapter reference acts as both a specific item to the chapter and a part of the proposal, and requires both objects to exist. The chapter reference's collaboration to its chapter is established first, followed by its proposal collaboration. If the proposal collaboration fails, then the chapter collaboration is rolled back, and the chapter reference ceases to exist.[5]

Actor – Role

Actor – Role Collaboration Rules

These collaboration rules test whether a `role` can be added or removed from an `actor`. Conceptually, the `role` is representing the `actor` in a specialized context, and as its representative, the `role` presents the `actor`'s properties, behaviors, and collaborations as its own. This familiarity with the details of the `actor` and the special requirements of each context are reasons why the `role` does all the rule checking in this collaboration, as shown in Table 4.2. In a nutshell, each context has different rules, so each context `role` checks the rules.

---

5. See page 246, "Item Assemblies," and Figure 9.15.

FIGURE 4.1
The actor - role pattern.

TABLE 4.2
Actor - Role Collaboration Rules

	Actor	Role
Type		✓
Multiplicity		✓
Property		✓
State		✓
Conflict		✓

Type Rules

RULE 1   A role knows the types of actors it can represent.

A role depends on its actor, so it has the burden of deciding if the actor is appropriate for it. Essentially, the role is checking that the actor has the correct interface to support its interactions in its context.

Multiplicity Rules

RULE 2   A role knows how many of its kind an actor can know.

RULE 3   A role knows exactly one actor, and it can never change its actor.

Occasionally, a domain allows an actor to support multiple roles for the same context, and hence the same type. As this rule is contextual, it belongs in the role. The personal and individual nature of a role prevents its transfer to another actor.

Property Rules

RULE 4   A role checks that the actor has valid property values.

Only the actor's properties necessary for the role's interactions are checked. There are several reasons why the role does the checking instead of the actor. Firstly, the role depends on these property values to carry out its interactions in the context. Secondly, what is "proper" and "legal" may depend on the context. Finally, the role may be specialized, and each specialization may require checking additional properties; having each role check the properties it needs is preferable to having the actor know a different set of rules for each variety of the role.

State Rules

RULE 5   A role checks that the actor is in the proper state.

RULE 6   A role checks its own state before breaking with its actor.

As with the property rules, the role does the checking since the proper state for an actor depends on the context. As it interacts in its context, the role gains its own state reflective of its ongoing business, so before breaking with its actor and becoming invalid, a role checks its state to ensure it has no outstanding business.

Conflict Rules

RULE 7   A role enforces rules that define conflicts with other roles.

Within some domains, certain roles are either/or with respect to the same actor. In other words, the actor can take on one or the other role, but not both. These scenarios happen when there are interdependencies among the contexts. Contexts know if they conflict, so this knowledge is more appropriate for the role than the actor.

Actor – Role Collaboration Rules Example

EXAMPLE—An online office supply store takes orders from home, business, and government customers, and allows individual service suppliers to advertise and take orders for services such as resume writing, document preparation, and logo design. See Figure 4.2.

Collaboration Rules

Type
R1. [Role]   A government customer or business customer requires an organization as its actor. A home customer or service supplier requires a person as its actor.

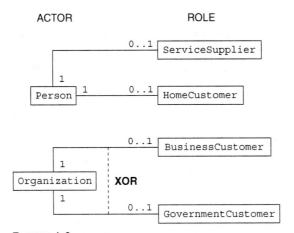

FIGURE 4.2

The actors and roles for an online office supply store.[6]

Multiplicity

R2. [Role]   A home customer cannot collaborate with a person that already has a home customer role. A service supplier cannot collaborate with a person that already has a service supplier role. A government customer cannot collaborate with an organization that already has a government customer role. A business customer cannot collaborate with an organization that already has a business customer role.

R3. [Role]   A home customer or service supplier cannot replace its person collaborator with another person. A government customer or business customer role cannot replace its organization collaborator with another organization.

Property

R4. [Role]   A government customer requires its organization to have a valid name, government ID number, and contact telephone number. A business customer requires its organization to have a valid name and contact telephone number. A home customer requires its person to be 18 or older, and to have a valid name and email address. A service supplier requires its person to be 21 or older, and to have a valid name, email address, and telephone number.

---

6. The "XOR" marking in Figure 4.2 indicates that an organization can collaborate with either the business customer or the government customer, but not both.

State

R5. [Role]   A business customer or government customer cannot collaborate with a closed or inactive organization.

R6. [Role]   A business, home, or government customer cannot be removed if it has unpaid or undelivered orders. A service supplier cannot be removed if it has pending service orders.

Conflict

R7. [Role]   A business customer cannot collaborate with an organization that is already a government customer, and vice versa.

Outer Place – Place

Outer Place – Place Collaboration Rules

With the `actor - role` pattern, all collaboration rules depend on a context of interaction, and consequently, are handled by the `role`. With the `outer place - place` pattern, both pattern players are in the same context, but one is more local than the other. As local objects tend to be more detailed and in greater varieties than global objects, the bulk of the work is pushed onto the local ones; accordingly, the `place` handles more of the collaboration rules in this pattern, as shown in Table 4.3.

TABLE 4.3
`Outer Place - Place` Collaboration Rules

	Outer Place	Place
Type		✓
Multiplicity	✓	✓
Property	✓	✓
State	✓	✓
Conflict		✓

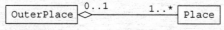

FIGURE 4.3
The outer `place - place` pattern.

Type Rules

RULE 8   A place knows the types of outer places that can house it.

Multiplicity Rules

RULE 9   An outer place may have an upper limit to the number of places it contains.

RULE 10   A place knows at most one outer place.

Instead of keeping a constant upper limit to the number of places, many outer places use property rules to keep within their limits. Not all places are in permanent locations. Some can move to new locations, and while in transition, exist without an outer place.[7]

Property Rules

RULE 11   A place uses property rules to avoid being located in an improper outer place.

RULE 12   An outer place uses property rules to constrain the places that go inside it.

Recall that with property rules, the object holding the standard or acceptable ranges owns the rule. With outer place and place, either one could have environmental constraints. An outer place may limit the maximum size of a place while a place may require its outer place to maintain an acceptable temperature.

State Rules

RULE 13   An outer place checks its own internal state before it allows a new place to be added or an old one to be removed.

RULE 14   A place checks its own internal state before it enters or leaves its outer place.[8]

Conflict Rules

RULE 15   A place enforces rules defining conflicts with other places.

Prior to adding a new place, an outer place asks its current place collaborators if any one of them conflicts with the proposed new place.

---

7. If y'all think like us, you may have imagined a mobile home almost immediately.
8. If your mobile home is still hooked to the main gas line, make sure it is unhooked before you pull away.

Outer Place – Place Collaboration Rules Example

EXAMPLE—Loading areas are locations within a warehouse where deliveries are deposited.[9] A loading area is either room temperature, refrigerated, or freezing, and contains smaller areas called loading bins that hold the goods and materials delivered to the loading area. A loading bin is capable of holding food, toxic materials, or non-toxic materials. Periodically, loading areas are reconfigured by removing old and adding new loading bins. Business rules define the legal partitions of a loading area into loading bins. See Figure 4.4.

Collaboration Rules

Type

R8. [Place]   A loading bin knows the types of loading areas—room temperature, refrigerated, or freezing—that can house it.

Multiplicity

R9. [Outer Place]   A loading area contains at least one loading bin.

R10. [Place]   A loading bin is always within one loading area, being moved between loading areas, or not in use.

Property

R11. [Outer Place]   A loading area cannot add a loading bin whose size is greater than its available space.

R12. [Place]   A loading bin cannot exist in a loading area whose average temperature is not within its acceptable temperature range.

State

R13. [Outer Place]   While it is receiving a delivery, a loading area cannot add or remove loading bins.

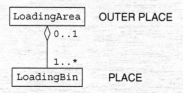

FIGURE 4.4
A LoadingArea is an outer place containing LoadingBins (places).

---

9. Loading areas and loading bins are places because they are locations where events occur (see p. 32, "Outer Place – Place," and p. 43, "Transaction – Place").

R14. [Place] While it contains goods, a loading bin cannot be removed from its loading area.

Conflict
R15. [Place]   A loading bin designated for food conflicts with a loading bin designated for toxic materials. One of these cannot be added to a loading area if one or more of the other is already part of the loading area.

Item – Specific Item

Item – Specific Item Collaboration Rules

The `item - specific item` pattern seems a lot like the `actor - role` pattern. Even though the two pattern players are in the same context, one represents a generic object, while the other represents something more specific. As usual, most of the rule checking falls to the more specific pattern player, as shown in Table 4.4.

TABLE 4.4
Item - Specific Item Collaboration Rules

	Item	Specific Item
Type		✓
Multiplicity	✓	✓
Property		✓
State	✓	✓
Conflict		✓

Type Rules

RULE 16   A `specific item` collaborates with only one type of `item`.

Multiplicity Rules

RULE 17   An `item` knows about zero or more `specific items`.

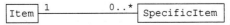

FIGURE 4.5
The `item - specific item` pattern.

RULE 18   A specific item knows exactly one item.

An item may have an upper limit to the number of its specific items. Often, an item acts as an object factory for its specific items, and the multiplicity check is executed prior to creating a new specific item. As with a role, a specific item is invalid without its item, and is not transferable to another.

Property Rules

RULE 19   A specific item must validate its properties before it can collaborate with an item.

A specific item does not check the properties of an item as a role checks the properties of an actor because the validities of its properties are not contextually dependent on the specific item, as an actor's are dependent on its role. On the other hand, while an item may act as the object factory for specific items and create each one from a given data set, the rules for validating the data set values belong in the specific item.[10]

State Rules

RULE 20   An item checks its state before adding a specific item.

RULE 21   A specific item checks its state prior to removing itself from its item.

A discontinued or obsolete item should not add new specific items, and a specific item involved in ongoing business should not let itself be removed from its item.

Conflict Rules

RULE 22   A specific item enforces rules defining conflicts with other specific items.

Typically, these are rules defining uniqueness conditions, ensuring that there are not two identical specific items for the same item.

---

10. Notice that both a role and a specific item must validate their properties before collaborating with the object on which they are dependent. This follows because the role and specific item do not exist prior to these collaborations, and so the validity of their properties has not yet been established. In the upcoming aggregation patterns the parts exist independently of the aggregate, requiring them to have valid properties even before they join it. Also, as the aggregate and part are in the same context, it does not make sense for one to validate the properties of the other.

Item – Specific Item Collaboration Rules Example

EXAMPLE—A video store puts tracking numbers on each videotape copy of a video title. Each video title has a unique identifier that is the root of the tracking numbers for its videotapes; thus, if the tracking number is unique to the video title, then it is unique to the store. A videotape has the following lifecycle states: uncirculated, in circulation, and out of circulation. A video title may be pulled from the shelf, taking all its videotapes out of circulation. See Figure 4.6.

Collaboration Rules

Type

R16. [Specific Item]   A videotape requires a video title to supply its description.

Multiplicity

R17. [Item]   A video title knows zero or more videotapes.

R18. [Specific Item]   A videotape knows exactly one video title, and cannot replace it with another. The video title describes the videotape's title, production date, cast, and rating.

Property

R19. [Specific Item]   A videotape must have a valid tracking number before it can collaborate with a video title, and hence belong to the video store.

State

R20. [Item] A discontinued video title cannot add a collaboration with a new videotape.

R21. [Specific Item]   A videotape cannot be removed from its video title unless the title's state is "uncirculated."

Conflict

R22. [Specific Item]   A videotape protests if its video title tries to add another videotape with the same tracking number.

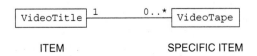

ITEM   SPECIFIC ITEM

FIGURE 4.6
A VideoTitle knows about some number of VideoTape copies.

Assembly – Part

Assembly – Part Collaboration Rules

The `assembly` - `part` collaboration is one of three patterns for modeling aggregations of things. All three of these patterns follow the same principle for distributing collaboration rules between the pattern players: Put the bulk of the rules in the more specific pattern player, which is the part. This same principle applies to `outer place` - `place`, where the more global `outer place` is treated as more generic than the local `place`. In `assembly` - `part`, the `assembly` is considered more generic because it derives many of its properties by rolling up the properties of its `parts`, thus smoothing and averaging their particular details. Accordingly, the more specific `part` carries more of the load in checking collaboration rules, as shown in Table 4.5.

TABLE 4.5
Assembly - Part Collaboration Rules

	Assembly	Part
Type		✓
Multiplicity	✓	✓
Property	✓	✓
State	✓	✓
Conflict		✓

Type Rules

RULE 23 A `part` knows which types of `assemblies` can contain it.

Multiplicity Rules

RULE 24 An `assembly` must know at least one `part`.

RULE 25 A `part` knows about at most one `assembly`.

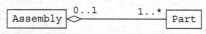

FIGURE 4.7
The `assembly` - `part` pattern.

Typically, things that contribute to an `assembly` can exist independently of it; however, once placed into an `assembly`, a `part` cannot be in another `assembly`.

Property Rules

RULE 26   An `assembly` uses property rules to keep out `parts` that do not meet its requirements.

RULE 27   A `part` uses property rules to avoid being placed inside an `assembly` that does not meet its requirements.

An `assembly` may require that a `part` conform to certain physical, logical, or business constraints, and a `part` may have its own physical, logical, or business constraints for selecting or rejecting an `assembly`.

State Rules

RULE 28   An `assembly` checks its state, allowing the addition or removal of a `part`.

RULE 29   A `part` checks its state before agreeing to join or leave an `assembly`.

Often an `assembly` has different lifecycle states; some states permit adding and removing `parts`, while other states lock the `assembly`, preventing the addition and removal of `parts`.

Conflict Rules

RULE 30   A `part` enforces rules defining conflicts between it and any other `parts`.

Before a `part` is added to an `assembly`, it must verify that it is compatible with the other `parts` in the `assembly`.

Assembly – Part Collaboration Rules Example

EXAMPLE—A made-to-order computer system is assembled from off-the-shelf components. Systems are either workstations or servers. As a component is added, a factory-floor tracking system records the serial numbers of the component added, reports any incompatibilities between the component and the system, and suggests a more compatible component. After a system is successfully completed according to its specification and approved by an inspector, the assembled components are decremented from inventory. See Figure 4.8.

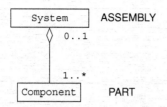

FIGURE 4.8
A made-to-order System and its core Components.

Collaboration Rules

Type
R23. [Part]   A component knows what type of system, a server or a workstation, it can join. Some components work in both types of systems.

Multiplicity
R24. [Assembly]   A system has at least one component.

R25. [Part]   A component can be part of at most one system; however, if removed from a system, it can be added to another system later, or it can be sold individually.

Property
R26. [Assembly]   A system cannot add a component whose price or weight would put the system over its maximums for those characteristics.

R27. [Part]   A component with domestic electrical requirements cannot go into a system intended for overseas use.

State
R28. [Assembly]   A system approved by an inspector cannot add or remove a component unless that approval is rescinded.

R29. [Part]   A component in a damaged or defective state cannot be added to a system.

Conflict
R30. [Part]   A component checks that it does not have incompatibilities with the other components in the system.

Container – Content

Container – Content Collaboration Rules

The `container - content` collaboration is another pattern for modeling aggregations of things. Many detailed and varied things can be placed in a plain brown box, and so like a box, a `container` is considered more generic than its `contents`. As with the other aggregate patterns, the more specific pattern player does more of the work of checking business rules, as shown in Table 4.6.

TABLE 4.6
Container - Content Collaboration Rules

	Container	Content
Type		✓
Multiplicity	✓	✓
Property	✓	✓
State	✓	✓
Conflict		✓

Type Rules

RULE 31   A `content` knows which types of `containers` can contain it.

Multiplicity Rules

RULE 32   A `container` may have an upper limit to the number of `contents`.

RULE 33   A `content` knows at most one `container`.

Instead of keeping a constant upper limit to the number of `contents`, many `containers` use property rules to keep within their limits. Contents, like `parts`, can exist outside of their `containers`.

FIGURE 4.9
The `container - content` pattern.

Property Rules

RULE 34 A `container` uses property rules to keep out `contents` that do not meet its requirements.

RULE 35 A `content` uses property rules to avoid being placed inside a `container` that does not meet its requirements.

These rules include physical, logical, and business requirements.

State Rules

RULE 36 A `container` checks its state before allowing the addition or removal of a `content`.

RULE 37 A `content` checks its state before agreeing to enter or leave a `container`.

Conflict Rules

RULE 38 A `content` enforces rules defining conflicts between it and any other `contents`.

Before a `content` enters a `container`, it verifies that it does not conflict with other `contents` already in the `container`.

Container – Content Collaboration Rules Example

EXAMPLE—In a distribution center for a manufacturing plant, cases of product are removed from inventory, placed onto pallets, and loaded onto trucks for delivery to one or more distributors. Pallets come in two types, those designed for refrigerated trucks, and those not. See Figure 4.10.

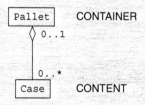

FIGURE 4.10
Cases are contained within Pallets.

Collaboration Rules

Type
R31. [Content] A case knows which type of pallet, refrigerated or non-refrigerated, can hold it.

Multiplicity
R32. [Container] The local trucking union, whose truck drivers are paid according to the number of pallets delivered, has negotiated that a pallet cannot contain more than 25 cases.

R33. [Content] A case can be placed on at most one pallet.

Property
R34. [Container] A pallet refuses any case whose weight puts it over its maximum limit.

R35. [Content] A case that is part of a rush order refuses to be placed on a pallet that is not scheduled to be loaded onto a truck within the next 24 hours.

State
R36. [Container] A pallet refuses to add or remove cases once it is loaded on a truck.

R37. [Content] An empty, damaged, defective, or expired case cannot be stored on a pallet.

Conflict
R38. [Content] A case of food cannot be stored on a pallet with a case of non-food product.

Group – Member

Group – Member Collaboration Rules

The group - member collaboration is the last on our list of patterns for modeling aggregations of things. Unlike the other two, a group does not have exclusive dominion over its constituent members; members can belong to multiple groups, which puts the burden on the group to check for conflicts with other groups, as shown in Table 4.7.

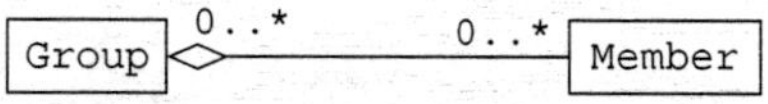

FIGURE 4.11
The group - member pattern.

TABLE 4.7
Group - Member Collaboration Rules

	Group	Member
Type		✓
Multiplicity	✓	✓
Property	✓	✓
State	✓	✓
Conflict	✓	✓

Type Rules

RULE 39 A member knows which types of group can contain it.

Multiplicity Rules

RULE 40 A group may have an upper limit to the number of members it can contain.

RULE 41 A member may have an upper limit to the number of groups it can join.

Property Rules

RULE 42 A group can require members to have properties within certain ranges or conform to certain standards.

RULE 43 A member can require groups to have properties within certain ranges or conform to certain standards.

State Rules

RULE 44 A group checks its own state before allowing a new member to be added or removed.

RULE 45 A member checks its own state before allowing itself to be added to or removed from a group.

Conflict Rules

RULE 46 A `group` enforces rules defining conflicts between it and any other `groups`.

RULE 47 A `member` enforces rules that define conflicts between it and any other `members`.

Group – Member Collaboration Rules Example

EXAMPLE—A luxury goods shopping site has a product catalog with shopping, promotional, and bargain categories. Shopping categories are ad hoc categories created to help the customer in browsing the site, and have names such as "sportswear," "pets," and "home and garden." Promotional categories are created to group and highlight unrelated products for seasonal events such as spring, school openings, and holidays. Bargain categories list products whose prices have been slashed appreciably. To protect the uniqueness of their products and brands, manufacturers can restrict the categories in which their products appear. See Figure 4.12.

Collaboration Rules

Type

R39. [Member]   A product knows the types of catalog categories—shopping, promotional, or bargain—that can contain it. Some products cannot be placed into promotional or bargain groups due to manufacturer prohibitions intended to protect their branding.

Multiplicity

R40. [Group]   A catalog category can limit the number of products it contains.

R41. [Member]   A product can limit the number of catalog categories in which it appears.

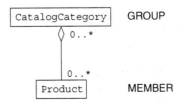

FIGURE 4.12
A Product can belong in multiple CatalogCategories.

Property

R42. [Group]   A catalog category can require that all its products exhibit one or more colors, or have prices within a given range.

R43. [Member]   To project uniqueness, a product can refuse to belong to any catalog category that is not limited in size, or that has an upper limit greater than is acceptable to the product.

State

R44. [Group].   A discontinued or expired catalog category cannot add or remove a product.

R45. [Member]   A discontinued product cannot be added to a catalog category.

Conflict

R46. [Group]   For branding purposes, some catalog categories are mutually exclusive so that product in one should not appear in the other, for example, a "his" category and a "hers" category. Before adding a product, a catalog category checks that it does not conflict with the product's existing categories.

R47. [Member]   A product can have manufacturer's restrictions that prohibit it from appearing in a catalog category with products from a competitor.[11]

Rules for Event Collaborations

Distributing Event Collaboration Rules

In entity collaborations, which use two objects to model a real-world entity, the collaborators are of the same kind—two people, two places, or two things. Having two collaborators of the same kind allows one to be designated as more particular than the other and responsible for more of the work. Finding the most particular does not work with event collaborations where one collaborator represents a real-world entity, but the other represents a real-world interaction. Instead, the choice boils down to putting the rules in the interaction or the entity undergoing the interaction. Since an entity participates in many interactions, the temptation is to build dumb entities with smart interactions knowing the rules. This is tempting, but it is bad object think as the entity is the one doing the interacting, has the proper-

---

11. When this happens, manufacturers must pay to have an exclusive category.

ties that shape the interaction, and is the one permanently affected by the interaction. The principle with event collaborations is to allow the entity involved to decide whether or not to interact.

PRINCIPLE 22
INTERACTING ENTITY OWNS THE RULE

> For collaboration patterns involving people, places, and things interacting with an event, each interacting pattern player that represents an entity owns its collaboration rules.

Removing and Rolling Back Event Collaborations

An entity's event collaborations reveal its history and are often a rich source for data mining. Therefore, in most business domains, removing a `transaction` from an entity is not permitted. Canceling an entity's real-world interaction is handled by changing the `transaction`'s state to cancelled or voided and not by removing its object-world `transaction`.

An interaction is not complete until all the entities involved agree to participate in the interaction. If one collaborator refuses to accept the interaction, then the event must roll back the collaborations it made with other entities. Recall that rolling back a collaboration is not the same as dissolving it, and does not require business rule checking.[12] The failure of the interaction to complete prompted the roll back, and destroying the failed interaction should not require business rule checking, as it does not alter persistent business data.

> EXAMPLE—A vehicle inspection (`transaction`) represents an interaction between a vehicle (`specific item`), inspection facility (`place`), and vehicle driver (`role`). If the collaboration between the vehicle inspection and vehicle driver should fail, then the collaborations between the inspection, the vehicle, and the facility are rolled back, and the vehicle inspection object is destroyed. The same behavior occurs if one of the other collaborations fails; the other two are rolled back. See Figure 4.13.

---

12. See p. 57, "Rolling Back Entity Collaborations."

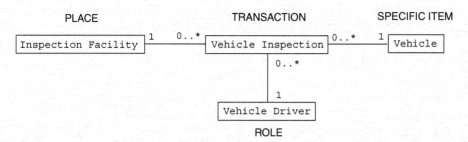

FIGURE 4.13

A VehicleInspection is not finalized if any of its collaborators reject it.

Transaction – Role

Transaction – Role Collaboration Rules

The transaction - role collaboration is the first of the event patterns, and its role represents the entity—the person, place, or thing—initiating an interaction in the real world represented by the transaction. Putting collaboration rules in the transaction looks tempting, as more transactions can easily be added for the same role; however, attaching many different kinds of transactions to a single type of role defeats the meaning of context.[13] Unrelated transactions that are not in the same context should not have the same type of role. Moreover, putting the rules in the transaction reduces a role to a mere data structure. Using a role to contain contextual data is good for data normalization, but without behavior, it is very bad object think. There are other ways of getting reuse while still keeping the rules with the role. Conclusion: The role does most of the work of checking its requirements for a transaction, as shown in Table 4.8.

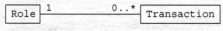

FIGURE 4.14

The transaction - role pattern.

---

13. "The set of circumstances or events in which a particular event occurs; situation." *The WordSmyth Educational Dictionary / Thesaurus (WEDT), http://www.wordsmyth.net.*

TABLE 4.8
Transaction - Role Collaboration Rules

	Transaction	Role
Type		✓
Multiplicity	✓	✓
Property		✓
State		✓
Conflict		✓

Type Rules

RULE 48   A role knows the kind of transactions in which it can participate.

Again, the role was created for the sole purpose of participating in these transactions; it darn well should know their types.

Multiplicity Rules

RULE 49   A transaction requires exactly one role; once set, the role cannot be removed without destroying the transaction.

RULE 50   A role knows zero to many transactions; typically, a role cannot remove a transaction.

The role is essential to the transaction because it is the real-world doer of the interaction represented by the transaction.[14] Allowing a role zero to many transactions gives it the option of interacting many times, or not at all. A role's transactions reveal its history; therefore, transactions are usually not removed.

Property Rules

RULE 51   A role can require that transactions have properties within certain ranges or conform to certain standards.

The role decides if the transaction is too big, too late, or in any other way beyond the limits within which the role can interact.

---

14. See p. 41, "Transaction – Role."

State Rules

RULE 52 A `role` checks its state before accepting a `transaction`.

Inactive, expired, or dead `roles` should not take on new `transactions`.

Conflict Rules

RULE 53 A `role` checks for conflicts between its existing `transactions` and a new `transaction`. A `role` also checks for conflicts between itself and the other collaborations of a `transaction`.

A `role` can refuse a new `transaction` if it overlaps with the `role`'s existing `transactions`; this happens when the `role` knows it cannot double-book itself by getting involved in coinciding events. Since the decision to permit or not permit double-booking lies in the `role`, it owns the conflict rule. A `role` can also refuse a `transaction` if its `specific item` is not suitable for the `role`; this occurs when the `role` has filters, for example, no green M&Ms, for screening out undesirable `specific items`. Since the filter is in the `role`, it owns the conflict rule. On the other hand, if the `specific item` has the standard, for instance, no one under 21, then it owns the rule.[15] The same principle applies for deciding conflict rules between the `role` and the `transaction`'s `place`.[16]

Transaction – Role Collaboration Rules Example

EXAMPLE—A public library allows patrons to place books and other resources on hold at its various library branches. Resources are either circulating or restricted, and can have retrieval or usage fees. A restricted resource can only be held for a researcher patron. A regular patron is limited to five holds per month, and a researcher patron is allowed an unlimited number of holds. An open-ended resource hold is active until the patron collects the resource at which time it is completed. A closed-ended resource hold that is not completed within a fixed duration after it was requested will expire. Only a researcher patron can request an open-ended resource hold. Any patron can set a preference, rejecting holds on resources with usage fees. Any patron with more than two overdue checkouts at a library branch cannot request a hold at that same library branch. See Figure 4.15.

---

15. See p. 85, Rule 65.
16. See p. 82, Rule 59.

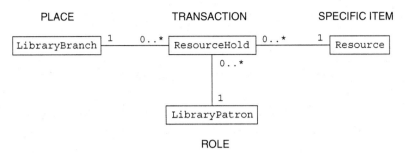

FIGURE 4.15
A LibraryPatron can request holds for library Resources at LibraryBranches.

Collaboration Rules

Type
R48. [Role] A regular library patron can only collaborate with closed-ended resource holds; a researcher patron can collaborate with open-ended or closed-ended resource holds.

Multiplicity
R49. [Transaction] A resource hold knows exactly one library patron, and cannot remove it.

R50. [Role] A library patron knows zero to many resource holds. If the patron is an educational researcher, he can collaborate with an unlimited number of resource holds; otherwise, the patron has an upper limit, currently five, to the number of resource holds per month.

Property
R51. [Role] To collaborate with a resource hold, a library patron must be an adult with a valid library registration number.

State
R52. [Role] A library patron whose registration has expired or has been inactivated cannot collaborate with a resource hold.

Conflict
R53. [Role] A library patron with a preference against resources with fees cannot collaborate with a resource hold for a resource with a fee, unless the patron has indicated that preferences should be ignored for this resource hold (here, the role conflicts with the specific item).

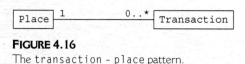

FIGURE 4.16
The transaction - place pattern.

Transaction – Place

Transaction – Place Collaboration Rules

The transaction - place collaboration is another pattern representing an entity participating in a transaction. These patterns use collaboration rules to define the entity's requirements for participating in the transaction. A place represents a location where interactions happen, and it knows its surroundings and their limitations. Therefore, a place is better qualified to judge whether an interaction should occur there. To personify the place, it has a strong vested interest in deciding what kind of people and things can show up at its location, and what they are permitted to do. Conclusion: A place does most of the work of checking its requirements for a transaction, as shown in Table 4.9.

TABLE 4.9
Transaction - Place Collaboration Rules

	Transaction	Place
Type		✓
Multiplicity	✓	✓
Property		✓
State		✓
Conflict		✓

Type Rules

RULE 54 A place knows what kinds of transactions it can accept.

Multiplicity Rules

RULE 55 A transaction knows about one place and cannot break with it.

RULE 56 A place knows zero to many transactions; typically, a place cannot remove a transaction.

A transaction generally happens at a place. If that information is recorded, it does not make real-world sense to forget where the transaction happened while the transaction remains in the system.

Property Rules

RULE 57 A place can require that transactions have properties within certain ranges or conform to certain standards.

The place decides if the transaction is in any other way beyond the limits of the place.

State Rules

RULE 58 A place checks its state before accepting a transaction.

Closed, under repair, or full places cannot accept new transactions.

Conflict Rules

RULE 59 A place checks for conflicts between its existing transactions and a new transaction. A place also checks for conflicts between itself and the other collaborations of a transaction.

A place has the responsibility of deciding if it can handle overlapping transactions, and so owns the conflict rule for coinciding transactions. A place can also refuse a transaction if its specific item or role is not suitable for the place; this occurs when the place has filters for screening out undesirable specific items or roles.

Transaction – Place Collaboration Rules Example

EXAMPLE—In the library resource example, some library branches do not allow open-ended resource holds, and some do not allow any resource holds except by researcher patrons. A library branch will not accept any resource holds while it is undergoing its yearly inventory review. A few library branches in religious communities have non-working hours during which resource holds cannot be requested. See Figure 4.15.

Collaboration Rules

Type

R54. [Place] A library branch knows the types of resource holds it allows—open-ended, closed-ended, or both.

Multiplicity

R55. [Transaction] A resource hold happens at exactly one place, where the resource is located.

R56. [Place] A library branch can collaborate with an unlimited number of resource holds.

Property

R57. [Place] A library branch with non-working hours cannot collaborate with a resource hold whose timestamp occurs during those hours.

State

R58. [Place] A library branch checks its state before accepting a resource hold; it cannot accept a hold while its inventory review is in progress.

Conflict

R59. [Place] A library branch that only allows resource holds by researcher patrons cannot accept a hold from a regular library patron (here, the place conflicts with the role).

Transaction – Specific Item

Transaction – Specific Item Collaboration Rules

The transaction - specific item collaboration also represents an entity participating in a transaction. A specific item represents a thing that can participate in interactions; it knows its properties and restrictions, and is qualified to judge if it belongs in an interaction. As with the other entities involved with transactions, the specific item does most of the work of checking its requirements for a transaction, as shown in Table 4.10.

FIGURE 4.17
The transaction - specific item pattern.

TABLE 4.10
Transaction - Specific Item Collaboration Rules

	Transaction	Specific Item
Type		✓
Multiplicity	✓	✓
Property		✓
State		✓
Conflict		✓

Type Rules

RULE 60   A specific item knows what types of transactions it can accept.

Multiplicity Rules

RULE 61   A transaction knows about one specific item and cannot break with it.

RULE 62   A specific item knows zero to many transactions; typically, a specific item cannot remove a transaction.

A transaction's sole purpose is to record a specific item's interaction. Specific items exist to a great extent for the purpose of taking part in a transaction.

Property Rules

RULE 63   A specific item can require that transactions have properties within certain ranges or conform to certain standards.

The specific item decides if the transaction does not fit within the specific item's limits.

State Rules

RULE 64   A specific item checks its state before accepting a transaction.

Out-of-stock, discontinued, or defective specific items cannot accept new transactions.

Conflict Rules

RULE 65 A specific item checks for conflicts between its existing transactions and a new transaction. A specific item also checks
for conflicts between itself and the other collaborations of a transaction.

A specific item has the responsibility of deciding if it can handle overlapping transactions, and so owns the conflict rule for coinciding transactions. A specific item can also refuse a transaction if its place or role
is not suitable for the specific item; this occurs when the specific item
has filters for screening out undesirable places or roles.

Transaction – Specific Item Collaboration Rules Example

EXAMPLE—In the library example, a resource can specify if it requires a
closed-end resource hold; typically, such a resource needs special storage or is very popular. A resource can include retrieval fees, which are
necessary to bring it to the library branch from special storage. These
fees are collected when the resource hold is requested. Resource usage
fees are charged during checkout, and cover the costs of viewing the
resource. See Figure 4.15.

Collaboration Rules

Type
R60. [Specific Item] A resource knows the type of resource holds it can
accept—open-ended, closed-ended, or both.

Multiplicity
R61. [Transaction] A resource hold knows exactly one resource; if the
resource hold removes its resource, the hold is no longer valid.

R62. [Specific Item] A resource knows zero to many resource holds.

Property
R63. [Specific Item] A resource with a retrieval fee cannot collaborate
with a resource hold that has not collected adequate payment to cover
the fee.

State
R64. [Specific Item] A damaged or defective resource cannot collaborate with a resource hold.

Conflict

R65. [Specific Item]   A restricted resource cannot collaborate with a resource hold by a regular library patron. A resource cannot collaborate with a resource hold if the resource already has an active resource hold.

Aggregate Event Collaboration Rules

Distributing Collaboration Rules

Unlike events that involve only one person, one place, and one thing, aggregate events involve multiple people, places, or things. To distinguish the separate interactions within it, an aggregate event is decomposed into smaller constituent events that record the details of a single entity's involvement in the interaction. Because these constituent events are the by-products of requesting a collaboration between an entity and the aggregate event, their fates rest not on their own collaboration rules, but on the collaboration rules between the aggregate event and the participating entity. If the entity cannot participate in the aggregate event, then the constituent event cannot either. Likewise, a constituent event can be removed only if the entity it represents can be removed.

Details vs. Collaboration Rules

Often when an entity seeks to participate in an aggregate event, it presents details about its interaction along with its request, for example, quantities involved, sales commissions, or time durations. Verifying these details is not the responsibility of the collaboration rules, which only determine if the entity is qualified to participate; instead, the constituent event created to represent the entity's involvement verifies the details, which are represented as its properties. Should one or more properties be invalid, then appropriate action can be taken.

> EXAMPLE—A customer uses an online system to order given quantities of products from a local office supply store. If a larger quantity of product is requested than is in stock, the product is still placed in the order. Store policies and customer preferences determine whether the order is held until more stock arrives, or if it is broken into multiple orders.

Composite Transaction – Line Item _____

Composite Transaction – Line Item Collaboration Rules

The `composite transaction - line item` collaboration represents the involvement of many entities in an aggregate event. As a constituent event within the `composite transaction`, a `line item` captures the interaction details of a single entity. Whether the `line item` collaborates with the `composite transaction` depends mostly on the collaboration rules between the `composite transaction` and the `line item`'s entity; however, there are a few collaboration rules between the two that are largely technical rules enforcing the meaning of the collaboration. The `line item` assumes most of the responsibility for these few rules because as the one adding further details to the aggregate event, it can be considered more particular or detailed than the `composite transaction`. This distribution of work is shown in Table 4.11.

TABLE 4.11
Composite Transaction - Line Item Collaboration Rules

	Composite Transaction	Line Item
Type		✓
Multiplicity	✓	✓
Property		
State		
Conflict		

Type Rules

RULE 66 A `line item` collaborates with only one type of `composite transaction`.

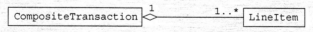

FIGURE 4.18
The `composite transaction - line item` pattern.

The composite transaction is the object factory for creating line items; as the most detailed, the line item has responsibility for ensuring it is not added to the wrong type of composite transaction.[17]

Multiplicity Rules

RULE 67   A composite transaction knows about at least one line item.

RULE 68   A line item knows exactly one composite transaction; a line item removed from its composite transaction is invalid.

A composite transaction without line items is an interaction without things interacting, which is not useful. Transferring line items to another composite transaction is not allowed.

Composite Transaction – Line Item Collaboration Rules Example

EXAMPLE—A customer uses an online system to order given quantities of products for delivery from, or pick-up at, a local office supply store. For each product ordered, a sales order line item captures its quantity ordered and allows it to be adjusted prior to submission of the order. See Figure 4.19.

Collaboration Rules

Type
R66. [Line Item]   A sales order line item can only collaborate with a sales order.

Multiplicity
R67. [Composite Transaction]   A sales order must include at least one sales order line item.

R68. [Line Item]   A sales order line item knows exactly one sales order; it cannot be transferred to another, and if removed, it becomes invalid.

---

17. This responsibility can be as simple as the parameter type in a setter method; for untyped languages, more work is required.

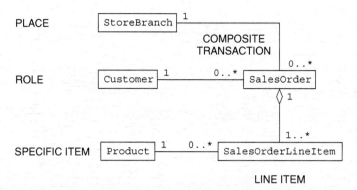

FIGURE 4.19
A SalesOrder creates SalesOrderLineItems for Products included in it.

Specific Item – Line Item

Specific Item – Line Item Collaboration Rules

The specific item - line item collaboration records the participation of a single entity in an aggregate event. While it is tempting to look at this like a transaction - specific item, that does not work because the specific item is not really aware of the line item, as it is with a transaction.[18] For an aggregate event, the specific item has collaboration rules for the composite transaction and conflict rules for its collaborators. Between the line item and specific item, collaboration rules are mere bookkeeping. In fact, there is not even a type rule. If the specific item is the right type for the composite transaction, then it is the right type for the line item. As shown in Table 4.12, multiplicity rules are the only collaboration rules checked in this pattern.

FIGURE 4.20
The specific item - line item pattern.

---

18. In Java implementations of this pattern, the line item implements an interface that gives it the appearance of a composite transaction, thus fooling the specific item into believing it is collaborating directly with the composite transaction.

TABLE 4.12
Specific Item - Line Item Collaboration Rules

	Line Item	Specific Item
Type		
Multiplicity	✓	✓
Property		
State		
Conflict		

Multiplicity Rules

RULE 69　A line item collaborates with exactly one specific item.

RULE 70　A specific item knows about zero to many line items.

The specific item relates to the line items as if it they were composite transactions. Because the line items represent the specific item's history of interactions, the specific item cannot remove them.

Specific Item – Line Item Collaboration Rules Example

EXAMPLE—A customer uses an online system to order given quantities of products for delivery from or pick-up at a local office supply store. Certain products are not available for delivery orders, and not all store branches carry all the products in the online catalog. Out-of-stock products are included in the order, but delivered or available for pick-up later. Specialty and promotional products are available only for preferred customers whose total yearly purchases have exceeded a minimum dollar amount. See Figure 4.19.

Collaboration Rules

Multiplicity
R69. [Line Item]　A sales order line item knows exactly one product; it cannot remove it.

R70. [Specific Item]　A product knows zero to many sales order line items; it may know them as sales orders. The product cannot remove any sales order line items.

Conflict Collaboration Rules

These event collaboration rules are run when a product is added to a sales order. Should any of them fail then the product is not added, and no sales order line item is created.

Type

R60. [Specific Item] A product knows the type of sales order it can accept—delivery or pick-up.

Conflict

R65. [Specific Item] A specialty or promotional product cannot collaborate with a sales order from a customer who is not preferred. A product cannot collaborate with a sales order from a store branch that does not stock it.

Transaction – Follow-up Transaction

Transaction - Follow-up Transaction Collaboration Rules

In the transaction - follow-up transaction collaboration, the transaction is acting more like a specific entity than an event. The transaction is now the participant in a new interaction represented by the follow-up transaction. As the one interacting, the transaction has ownership of the collaboration rules, as shown in Table 4.13.

Type Rules

RULE 71 A transaction knows what types of follow-up transactions can follow it.

Multiplicity Rules

RULE 72 A follow-up transaction knows about one transaction and cannot break with it.

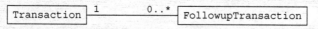

FIGURE 4.21

The transaction - follow-up transaction pattern.

TABLE 4.13
Transaction – Follow-up Transaction Collaboration Rules

	Transaction	Follow-up Transaction
Type	✓	
Multiplicity	✓	✓
Property	✓	
State	✓	
Conflict	✓	

RULE 73 A transaction knows zero to many follow-up transactions; a transaction cannot remove a follow-up transaction.

Property Rules

RULE 74 A transaction can require that follow-up transactions have properties within certain ranges or conform to certain standards.

The transaction decides if the follow-up transaction does not meet the transaction's requirements.

State Rules

RULE 75 A transaction checks its state before accepting a follow-up transaction.

Conflict Rules

RULE 76 A transaction checks for conflicts between its existing follow-up transactions and a new follow-up transaction. A transaction also checks for conflicts between itself and the other collaborations of a follow-up transaction.

Transaction – Follow-up Transaction Collaboration Rules Example

EXAMPLE—In the office supply example, a sales order is followed by some number of deliveries. A sales order that is cancelled or incom-

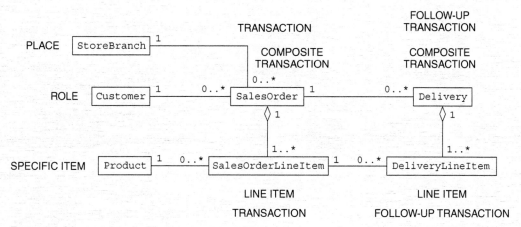

FIGURE 4.22
An online SalesOrder is followed by Deliveries.

plete cannot accept any deliveries. A sales order marked for hold until complete cannot be followed by a partial delivery. See Figure 4.22.

Collaboration Rules

Type
R71. [Transaction] A sales order knows the type of delivery that can follow it—partial or complete.

Multiplicity
R72. [Follow-up Transaction] A delivery knows exactly one sales order, and cannot break with it.

R73. [Transaction] A sales order knows zero to many deliveries, and cannot remove them, although a delivery can be cancelled.

Property
R74. [Transaction] A sales order rejects any delivery that does not have the same shipping address as itself.

State
R75. [Transaction] A sales order that is incomplete or cancelled cannot accept a delivery.

Conflict
R76. [Transaction] A sales order cannot accept a delivery involving sales order line items that have already been completely delivered.

Services and Properties

Do, or do not. There is no "try."

Yoda

Doing and Knowing

Streamlined object modeling boils object-oriented concepts down to the bare essentials necessary to fully model a complex domain: collaboration patterns, collaboration rules, and object services. Collaboration patterns simplify finding and representing objects, collaboration rules integrate business rules with objects, and object services carry out the work of business processes. This chapter deals with object services, including strategies for finding services, and strategies for distributing work among services. These strategies are expressed in terms of the collaboration patterns, so that the pattern players an object takes on in its collaborations significantly determine its services. Streamlined object modeling classifies all services into one of three categories: conduct business, determine mine, and analyze transactions services. These service categories follow from the types of interactions between collaborators, and later chapters organize behavior into these categories and show how to implement services in these categories for different collaboration patterns. Lastly, this chapter discusses object properties. Properties are the lowest priority in streamlined object modeling. Typically, only the business-related properties are captured, for these are the ones that facilitate communication of the model. An information or database architect will often work with the client to flesh out all the data properties necessary to complete the model. For completeness, this chapter presents some principles for finding and modeling the different types of properties typically found in object models.

Processing with Object Think _____

There's Something About Peanut Butter

Try this. Ask a few people how to make a peanut-butter-and-jelly sandwich. See how differently they answer. One person spreads the peanut butter first with a knife, then uses a spoon for the jelly. Another spreads the jelly first, always on the left slice of bread, which goes on top. A third puts the peanut butter slice on top, then slices it up into squares. Clearly, everyone has their own personal preferences—"how I like to do it"—for making peanut butter and jelly sandwiches. Build an object model of sandwich-making from these accounts and it will focus on knives, spoons, and handling bread slices.

Now consider another approach. Ask the same group to talk about a peanut-butter-and-jelly sandwich. Ask them to think about the parts of the sandwich. They will tell you that there are two slices of bread, peanut butter, and jelly. Ask them to list all the different varieties of bread, of peanut butter, and of jelly. They will tell you that there are wheat bread, white bread, bagels, and croissants; plain peanut butter and crunchy; grape jelly, apple jelly, strawberry jam, and so on. Ask if any varieties are taboo. Perhaps that orange marmalade with scotch is too over-powering for a peanutbutter-and-jelly sandwich, and that old-fashioned peanut butter with the oil floating on top is too messy.

Look for collaboration constraints: no chunky peanut butter on thin diet bread; never less than one ounce of jelly, nor more than three; a slice must have either jelly or peanut butter, but not both; a sandwich requires exactly two slices of the same type of bread; one slice must be spread with peanut butter and the other slice spread with jelly.

Think about personalizing the sandwich: slicing off the crusts, toasting the bread, cutting the sandwich, or flipping it to put either the jelly or peanut butter on top.

What a difference point of view makes! By asking people to think about a sandwich and not their personal experiences making a sandwich, you open up their minds to many more possibilities.

Objective vs. Subjective Descriptions

The peanut-butter-and-jelly sandwich example highlights the difference between asking people to describe a process and asking people to describe objects involved in a process. When asked to describe a process, people naturally describe it subjectively, in terms of "how I would do it," step-by-step. Some even detail imaginary interactions with a computer system, speaking in terms of "how I see the system," and focusing on "my favorite features." Right off the bat, you should notice that these user-centric process descriptions focus on "how" and not "what." Business requirements from "how" are only good as long as the "how" does not change, or until someone else wants a different "how." Business requirements from "what" can support all manners of "how" because the focus is on the people, places, things, and events that happen in the process, not a particular order in which they appear in the process.

Another thing you should notice about user-centric process descriptions is that each one reflects the speaker's unique experiences, biases, and point of view. Business requirements derived from individual experiences are difficult to verify as complete, since it is possible not all points of view were covered. Business requirements derived by discussing the people, places, things, and events are complete when all these types of objects are described and their involvements in the processes are modeled. It is neither a coincidence nor a pun to say that the trick to being objective is to talk about objects. Focusing on objects takes the inward-looking personal perspective out of the requirements gathering and replaces it with an outward-looking perspective; the requirements gathering session becomes more about reaching consensus than asserting will. User interactions are extremely useful, but only after the object model is built, when the vocabulary is established and "what" is clearly defined.

PRINCIPLE 23
BE OBJECTIVE WITH PROCESSES

Be objective when asking about processes. Talk instead about the objects—people, places, things, and events—involved in the process and the actions on these objects, rather than asking clients how they "want to do it."

Objects Doing

Peanut Butter, Again

Consider the peanut-butter-and-jelly sandwich example again. For simplicity, assume the process has two types of bread (thick or thin) and three kinds of ingredients: one jelly (grape) and two peanut butters (plain or chunky). Also, a sandwich is assembled from two bread slices and a given amount (light or heavy) of one ingredient is spread on each bread slice. The object model should not care whether the slices were added to the sandwich first, and then ingredients applied to them, or vice versa. However, regardless of the order, something in the object model should enforce the following business rules from our sandwich domain experts: (1) a sandwich requires two slices of the same type of bread; (2) a thin bread slice cannot support chunky peanut butter; (3) a thin bread slice cannot support a heavy application of an ingredient; and (4) one bread slice must contain peanut butter and the other must contain jelly.

The peanut-butter-and-jelly sandwich object model is shown in Figure 5.1. A peanut-butter-and-jelly sandwich is an assembly of two bread slices with ingredients applied on them according to the business rules. A transaction object, application, records how much of an ingredient was applied to each bread slice. Notice that a bread slice is both a part in an assembly, and a place for a transaction. Part conflict collaboration rules[1] keep a bread slice with an ingredient on it from being added to a sandwich that already has a bread slice with the same ingredient. Place conflict collaboration rules[2] prevent a bare bread slice from receiving an inappropriate ingredient.[3]

Now consider the peanut-butter-and-jelly sandwich business process. Creating the application transaction is the crucial step in the business process of building a peanut-butter-and-jelly sandwich because this step verifies the business rules as it tries to link the application object to its ingredient and bread slice collaborators. So, which object makes the application transaction? Is it (a) the sandwich, (b) the slice, (c) the ingredient, or (d) the ingredient manager-controller?

---

1. See Rule 30, p. 68, "Assembly – Part Collaboration Rules."
2. See Rule 59, p. 82, "Transaction – Place Collaboration Rules."
3. In this example, you may notice that the application is a transaction without a role. The role still exists—it is whatever is applying the ingredient—but the domain experts did not rate this important enough to record. Often, one or more of the event collaborators does not need to be recorded by the system.

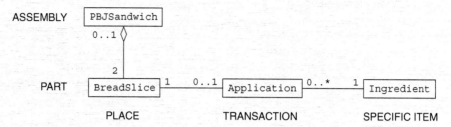

FIGURE 5.1
The peanut-butter-and-jelly sandwich object model.

If you answered (d), please go back to the beginning of this book and start over. And, (a) is not such a great answer, either, since all the information needed for the business rules lies in the bread slice and the ingredient. Clearly, the choice is between the bread slice and the ingredient; they are the collaborators of the application, and they have the relevant information and business rules. Use first-person object think to pick between the two. For the bread slice, object think says, "I am a bread slice. I have an ingredient applied on me in either a light or heavy amount." For the ingredient, object think says, "I am an ingredient. I apply myself to a bread slice in either a light or heavy amount." Notice that the action of applying ingredient is third-person for a bread slice, and first-person for an ingredient. Obviously, the correct answer is (c); an ingredient creates the application object when it applies itself on a bread slice.

Object Services

The peanut butter sandwich example reminds us that objects perform actions and make decisions; in fact, an object's ability to act is one of its three categories of responsibilities—"whom I know," "what I do," and "what I know." What an object *does* is known as its services.[4]

Technically, a service is simply a function, operation, method, routine, or procedure; but calling a service a function, while technically correct, flies against the object think perspective. Instead of viewing services as functions on objects, object thinkers see services as actions objects perform. The object think perspective says objects act rather than get acted on, and conduct their own business rather than hold data for functional processing.

---

4. *Object-Oriented Analysis* (2nd ed.), Peter Coad and Edward Yourdon, 1990, Prentice Hall.

Strategies for Finding Services

One clear lesson in the peanut-butter-and-jelly sandwich example is that actions people do to sandwich ingredients become in the object world actions the ingredients do themselves. For example, the ingredient applies itself to a bread slice. To state it more generally, actions *upon* a real-world entity become services provided *by* the object that represents the entity. The rationale here is simple: All the information needed to act on an object is inside the object, so let the object do the work. Putting actions with the data they act on follows the software engineering principle of encapsulation that says package related things because they tend to change together. Keeping related things together decreases the likelihood they will grow out of sync. Along these lines are our favorite principles for finding services, Strategies 86 and 87 in the *Object Models* book.[5] We paraphrased them below.

PRINCIPLE 24

DO IT MYSELF[*]

Objects that are acted upon by others in the real world do the work themselves in the object world.

* Strategy 86.

PRINCIPLE 25

DO IT WITH DATA[*]

Objects encapsulate data representing an entity together with the services that act on it.

* Strategy 87.

Real-World Service Examples

Real world: A person checks out books from a library.

Object world: A library book checks itself out.

Rationale: A library book knows any restrictions it has, plus its future reservations and its past checkout history, so let the book decide if a particular library patron can check it out.

---

5. *Object Models: Strategies, Patterns, and Applications* (2nd ed.), Coad, North, and Mayfield, 1997, Prentice Hall.

Real world:	A bank determines a loan applicant's line of credit.
Object world:	A loan applicant calculates his own credit limit.
Rationale:	A loan applicant knows his demographic, historical, and financial information, so let him determine his credit-worthiness.
Real world:	A missile aims at a target.
Object world:	A target says, "Strike me!"
Rationale:	A target knows its location and surrounding obstacles, so let the target calculate the best trajectory to destroy it.
Real world:	A person applies a sandwich ingredient to a bread slice.
Object world:	An ingredient applies itself to a bread slice in a given amount.
Rationale:	An ingredient knows how much of it remains in inventory, and knows how to create an application of itself on the bread slice.

Distributing Work

A subtle wrinkle in the "do it myself" principle is that real-world entities are modeled by the collaboration patterns as two or more objects, so an action performed on the entity maps to potentially many objects. One of these objects must be designated as the owner of the action; call this object the *director*. Although the director object has the service corresponding to the real-world action, it may delegate large chunks of the work to its collaborators.

PRINCIPLE 26
DIRECTOR PRINCIPLE

Real-world actions on entities map to one of the objects representing that entity. This object is called the director of the action because it directs itself and its collaborators in carrying out the action.

Entity Collaborations: Who Directs?

With entity collaboration patterns involving people, places, and things, two objects are representing one real-world entity, or an aggregation of entities. As noted in the previous chapter, one of the pattern players is more particular—more specific, more local, or more detailed—than the other.[6] These more particular pattern players direct the work of checking collaboration rules since they know more about the context, location, or details than their more general, more global, or more aggregate pattern players.

> EXAMPLE—A video store allows customers to reserve a video 48 hours in advance. To allow the reservation, the video title must have a videotape in stock or due back within 24 hours. This videotape is moved to the reservation shelf immediately, or when it is returned, to prevent its rental. Designate the video title as the director object, and add to it a "reserve" service. The video title reserve service proceeds by asking each videotape to reserve itself, and stops when one succeeds in doing so. The videotape has the responsibility of checking its availability and changing its status to prevent rental, so the videotape has the bulk of the work. The video title merely directs the walking through of the list of videotapes. See Figure 5.2.

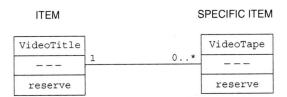

FIGURE 5.2

Most of the work in making a reservation lies in the VideoTape.[7]

PRINCIPLE 27
MOST SPECIFIC DIRECTS

> When a real-world action maps to two collaborators representing a single entity or an aggregation of entities, the director is the most specific, local, or detailed pattern player.

---

6. See p. 57, Principle 21.
7. To simplify the diagram, the properties in the objects were suppressed; this is indicated by the dashes in the center of the object symbols.

Event Collaborations: Who Directs?

With event collaborations, some actions require coordination between all the collaborators of the event. These actions are naturally directed by the event, as it is the only one with knowledge of all the others.

> EXAMPLE—A flight has a scheduled arrival at a gate in an airport. Airport scheduling software polls the scheduled arrival for its arrival gate status, which is either clear or gate-conflict. The scheduled arrival determines its arrival gate status by asking its gate for its availability for the flight. The gate uses its own schedule of arrivals and departures and the flight's current expected arrival time to answer whether it will be clear or have a conflict when the flight arrives. See Figure 5.3.

PRINCIPLE 28
EVENTS DIRECT THE WORK

When an action requires cooperation among the collaborating entities of an event, the event directs the action.

Types of Services

To sum up the previous sections, there are services an object does by itself, and there are services an object does with help from its collaborators. Collaboration patterns help distribute services among objects. To use the patterns to distribute services, we needed a better understanding of the different types of services. After spending some time reviewing code and models, we reduced services into three types: (1) conduct business, (2) determine mine, and (3) analyze transactions services. Using these types and the collaboration pattern players we developed strategies for distributing and implementing services according to the service type and the pattern players involved. The next few sections of this chapter discuss the different types of services.

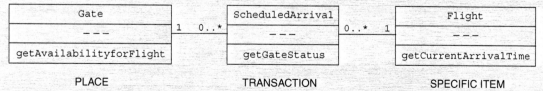

Gate			ScheduledArrival			Flight
---	1	0..*	---	0..*	1	---
getAvailabilityforFlight			getGateStatus			getCurrentArrivalTime
PLACE			TRANSACTION			SPECIFIC ITEM

FIGURE 5.3
An event directs actions that involve more than one of its collaborators.

Chapters 6, 7, and 8 discuss distribution and implementation strategies. "Three Kinds of Services," page 338, summarizes the different types of services.

Conduct Business Services

Actions Not Questions

Services that kick off processes are called conduct business services. A conduct business service accomplishes an action rather than answers a question.[8] By not returning results, conduct business services are distinguished from determine mine and analyze transactions services, which are covered in later sections.[9] Also, conduct business services are the only services that create new objects, or change objects' states. Typical conduct business services include creating new objects, establishing or dissolving collaborations, notifying collaborators, and setting property values. In languages that support multi-processing and multiple threads, conduct business services are the ones that kick off new processes or threads.

PRINCIPLE 29
LET THE DIRECTOR CONDUCT

Use the "specific directs" and "event directs" principles to find the director of a process. Assign the director a conduct business service to initiate the process.

Creating New Objects

Some conduct business services trigger the creation of new objects. This frequently occurs when a transaction is created to record an interaction initiated by a conduct business service. The director of the conduct business service does not necessarily create the transaction. Any of the objects (roles, places or specific items) involved in the transaction can create it. Good object think suggests allowing the object most knowledgeable about the interaction to create the transaction. Here, the most knowledgeable object is either the one supplying most of the details in the interaction or the object with the most constraints restricting its participation in the interaction. Choosing the most knowledgeable object is a judgment call. When no object

8. Conduct business services are analogous to procedures in Pascal, Ada, Modula-2, and Oberon.
9. By results, we mean the answer to a question such as "Are you checked out?" or "What is your total?" Some implementations of conduct business services return a success code such as "Yes, I finished" or a signal failure such as "Something blew up!"

leaps out, consider extensibility issues and then just pick one. What matters most is that you distribute the work and put the service near the information required to make the `transaction`. Some examples might help.

EXAMPLE—A team member nominates a document for publication on the team Web page. The document is not published to the Web page until the nomination is approved. Since the document is the entity being acted upon, it is the director of the nominate service. Also, since the document has the most restrictions on whether it can participate in the nomination, it creates the nomination object. To do this, the document nominate service requires a team member as a parameter. See Figure 5.4.

EXAMPLE—A missile targeting system creates planned strikes of missiles against targets. Since a target is the object being acted upon, it is the director of the strike service that creates the planned strike between the missile and the target. Also, since the target knows the obstacles and terrain around it, it is the most knowledgeable object, and best qualified to create the planned strike transaction. To do this, the target's strike service requires a missile as a parameter. See Figure 5.5.[10]

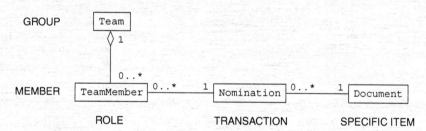

FIGURE 5.4
The Document (`specific item`) creates a Nomination.

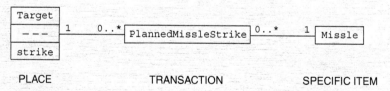

FIGURE 5.5
A Target (`place`) creates the PlannedMissileStrike.

EXAMPLE—An online money-lending site allows a loan applicant to apply to one or more financial institutions for a loan. The site has one

---

10. The target is saying, "Hit me with your best missile. Fire away."

standardized loan application form it sends to all its member financial institutions. Since there is only one loan application form, and most of information needed to complete it is within the loan applicant, the loan applicant creates the loan application `transaction`. To do this, the loan applicant has an apply service that takes the financial institution as a parameter. See Figure 5.6.

PRINCIPLE 30
MOST KNOWLEDGEABLE IS RESPONSIBLE

When a `role` acts on a `specific item` at a given `place` and the event is recorded, give the most knowledgeable or restrictive object a conduct business service that establishes the `transaction`.

Collaboration Accessor Services

Services for establishing and dissolving collaborations are also conduct business services. Known as accessor services, these services add or remove collaborations between two objects; they are noteworthy because they also enforce collaboration rules. Should a collaboration rule fail, a collaboration accessor signals failure and refuses to establish or dissolve the collaboration.

Services to establish collaborations always start with "add" instead of "set" for several reasons. Unlike properties, which are set and not removed, collaborations are added and removed. Prefixing collaboration accessors with "add" emphasizes the nature of collaborations and serves to differentiate them from property accessors. Even when there is only one collaborator, "add" is the best prefix for the accessor because it may evolve to be multiple collaborators. Because collaboration accessors play a crucial role in main-

ROLE   TRANSACTION   PLACE

FIGURE 5.6
A LoanApplicant (`role`) creates the LoanApplication.

taining the business model's integrity, they are discussed later in more detail, in the implementation chapters.[11]

EXAMPLE—A team member nominates a document for publication on the team Web page.[12]

The transaction has two collaboration accessors, addDocument and addTeamMember, which establish collaborations with document and team member, respectively.

The document has a collaboration accessor service, addNomination, which establishes the collaboration with a nomination and enforces the following collaboration rules for the nomination:

- A document must have a title to be nominated.
- A document cannot be nominated after it is published.
- A document cannot be nominated again while it is pending.

The team member has a collaboration accessor service, addNomination, which establishes the collaboration with a nomination and enforces the following collaboration rules for the nomination:

- A team member must have nomination privileges.
- A team member has an upper limit to the number of nominations in a month.

See Figure 5.7.

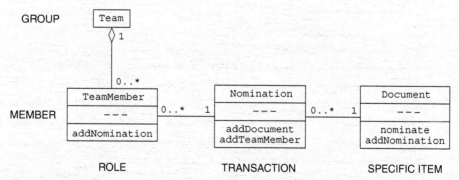

FIGURE 5.7

Document Nomination object model with collaboration accessors.

---

11. See p. 241, "Implementing Collaboration Rules."
12. To see how to implement this example, including the collaboration rules, see Chapters 7 and 8.

Notifying Collaborators

Publish-subscribe notification, which is popular in many object-oriented frameworks, is another type of conduct business service. Smalltalk's dependency mechanisms and Java's event listeners use publish-subscribe notification.

> EXAMPLE—When a new resource is posted to an online message board topic, the topic notifies its subscribers.

Write Accessors

A write accessor is a conduct business service that sets a property.[13] Similar to collaboration accessors, these services enforce property rules governing the validities of their property values. To simplify the object model, write accessors are not depicted on the diagram, but are assumed to exist for each property.[14]

> EXAMPLE—In the document nomination example, a nomination has the following properties: status, reviewer's comments, and date nominated. Accessors to set the values of these properties are not shown on the nomination object, but are assumed to exist. See Figure 5.8.

Determine Mine Services

Providing Answers

Determine mine services satisfy requests for current information. Unlike an analyze transactions service, which returns historical or future state infor-

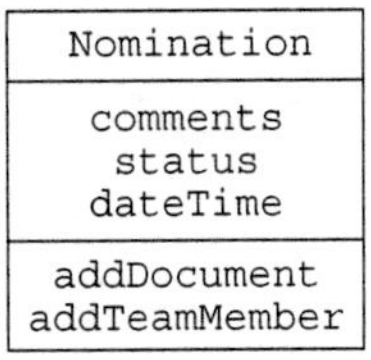

```
Nomination
-------------------
comments
status
dateTime
-------------------
addDocument
addTeamMember
```

FIGURE 5.8
The Nomination object.

---

13. Most object-oriented programming books recommend defining a service, setX, as the write accessor that sets the value for a property named X.
14. This may not be the case for read-only properties, which are specified in the business rules. Also, design models generally do show read and write accessors so that their accessibilities are included in the diagram.

mation about an object, and is discussed later, a determine mine service tells the state of the object, right now. Unlike a conduct business service, which starts a particular business process, a determine mine service can be part of many business processes. Like a conduct business service, a determine mine request might require the object to coordinate work among its collaborators. However, determine mine services should never alter the states of any objects.[15] Typical determine mine services include returning property values and collaborators, working with collaborators to determine an aggregate value, and performing a search.

PRINCIPLE 31
LET AN OBJECT DETERMINE MINE

Provide an object with determine mine services so it may answer requests for current information.

Read Accessors

Read accessors are special determine mine services that return the values of properties and collaborators.[16] As with write accessors for properties, read accessors are not depicted on the object model, but are assumed to exist for each property and collaboration.

EXAMPLE—In the document nomination example, a nomination has properties for status, reviewer's comments, and date nominated, and collaborations with a document and a team member. Read accessor services return the nomination's property values and collaborations, but are assumed and not shown on the nomination object. See Figure 5.9.

Not Always Simple

Determine mine services can be complex and involve many objects. Similar to a conduct business service, a determine mine service can have a director that coordinates work with its collaborators to establish a result, or a determine mine service can be state-dependent. A state-dependent determine mine signals an error if the object is not in the proper state to answer the request. An

---

15. This does not mean that determine mine services cannot cache intermediary or calculated results. Storing derived results are acceptable design-level decisions. Side-effects to be avoided are allowing an object to modify the properties or collaborations of one or more objects.

16. Most object-oriented programming books recommend defining a service, getX, as the read accessor that returns the value for a property or collaborator named X.

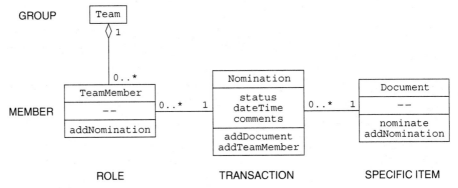

FIGURE 5.9
Read accessors are assumed and not shown in the model.

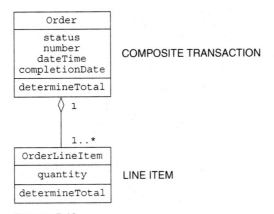

FIGURE 5.10
An Order directs its OrderLineItems to determine its total.

object can be in an improper state if properties are unset or collaborators are missing. For this reason, state-dependent accessors imply the need for other accessors to determine state.

EXAMPLE—An order recalculates its total when a product is added to it, and sets its completion date after all products have shipped. To determine its total, the order sums up the results of directing its order line items to determine their own totals. The order signals an error if asked for its completion date before it is set. See Figure 5.10.

Analyze Transactions Services

Time-Sensitive Information

Analyze transactions services assess information captured in associated events. As with a conduct business service, an analyze transactions service starts with a director object. The director in the analyze transactions service directs its `transaction` collaborators to determine a result. Because they return results and do not generate side-effects in the system, analyze transactions services resemble determine mine services; however, unlike a determine mine service, an analyze transactions service relies on historical or future events to reach its results. This distinction, which matters more during the system design phase, means that determine mine services can be answered by an object and its immediate collaborators, whereas analyze transactions services require doing work across the object's event collaborators from possibly a long time back. A common mistake to avoid when specifying an analyze transactions service is putting too much work in the director object; instead, the analyze transactions service should request one determine mine service of each `transaction` collaborator involved.

Business Objects Direct

Another mistake is to ignore analyze transactions services entirely. Some do this because they think analyze transactions services can be implemented much more efficiently in the database. That may well be true, but where the implementations of analyze transactions services reside should be worked out during the design or implementation activities. Regardless of where the implementations reside, all analyze transactions services should start in the affected business objects. These objects have the business rules and security privileges for deciding if the analyze transactions services can run and under what constraints. Once a business object verifies that it can run an analyze transactions service, the work can be delegated to a data manager object to invoke the appropriate database routines. Putting analyze transactions services in the object model ensures business rules govern their uses and the object model is sufficiently detailed to handle most analyze transactions queries.

PRINCIPLE 32
LET AN OBJECT ASSESS EVENTS

Provide an object with analyze transactions services so it may assess its
historical information, past events, and future scheduled events.

Historical Information

Some analyze transactions services summarize and survey an object's historical information, which is data recorded periodically about the object, such
as monthly performance measurements or price changes. These analyze
transactions services assess the historical information by computing sums,
averages, and other statistical results and invoking information queries.

> EXAMPLE—Every month, a bottling plant records the production log for
> each of its bottling lines. A production log knows the number of liters
> produced by the bottling line, the total production time spent, and the
> stoppage time lost; the production log uses this information to deter-
> mine the line's efficiency. A bottling line has an analyze transactions
> service that works across its production logs to determine its average
> line efficiency for a given range of time periods. See Figure 5.11.

Summarizing Events

Another category of analyze transactions services examines events to
deduce summary behavior and statistics. These are similar to services that
assess historical data; however, unlike historical information, events include
collaborations with people, places, and things, so services assessing events
may summarize information about their collaborators as well.

> EXAMPLE—A retail clothing store tracks the point-of-sale orders of
> customers buying with a proprietary credit card. Proprietary card owners

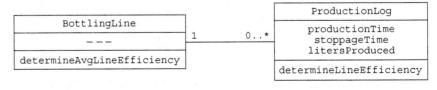

SPECIFIC ITEM   TRANSACTION

FIGURE 5.11
A BottlingLine analyzes its ProductionLog to determine average line efficiency.

earn discounts according to the number of different items purchased with the card during given date ranges. A determine mine service provided by the order returns its number of distinct items during a date range, or zero if the order did not occur during the date range. An analyze transactions service of the proprietary card owner gets the total number of distinct items purchased during the date range. See Figure 5.12.

Future Scheduling

Yet another type of analyze transactions service assesses future scheduled events. Common forms of these services include looking to see if an event has been scheduled, and searching for conflicting events.[17] Services that locate conflicting events are often used in verifying conflict collaboration rules.[18]

> EXAMPLE—A meeting room can be reserved on a given date in blocks of 30 minutes. Analyze transactions services on the meeting room check if it is available at a given date/time by asking each room reservation if it conflicts with the given date/time. See Figure 5.13.

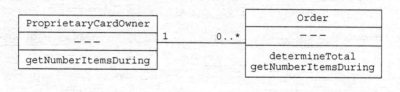

ROLE   COMPOSITE TRANSACTION

FIGURE 5.12
A ProprietaryCardOwner analyzes its Orders to get the number of items purchased.

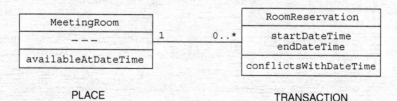

PLACE   TRANSACTION

FIGURE 5.13
A MeetingRoom checks its availability by analyzing its RoomReservations.

---

17. Never assume the human interface will prevent a user from scheduling conflicting events. The business object being scheduled has the business rules for deciding what is a conflict; let that object do it.

18. See p. 75, "Distributing Event Collaboration Rules," p. 77, "Transaction – Role Collaboration Rules," p. 81, "Transaction – Place Collaboration Rules," and p. 83, " Transaction – Specific Item Collaboration Rules."

Objects Knowing

In object modeling, properties are lowest priority. Getting objects, collaborations, and behaviors properly modeled are far more pressing concerns and take more object thinking skills. This is an important part of streamlined object modeling. You end up with streamlined objects containing only those properties necessary for effective communication. Once the skeleton of the object model is built, filling in the properties is the finishing touch. In object think, properties are "what I know," and they reflect the characteristics of the real-world entity. This section covers the following categories of properties often encountered in object modeling:

- Descriptive   –Domain and tracking properties
- Time   –Date or time properties
- Lifecycle state –One-way state transitions (e.g., nomination status: pending, in review, approved, rejected)
- Operating state –Two-way state transitions (e.g., sensor state: off, on)
- Role   –Classifies people (e.g., team member role: chair, admin, member)
- Type   –Classifies places, things, and events (e.g., store type: physical, online, phone)

This table also appears in "Six Kinds of Properties," page 339.

Descriptive Properties

Descriptive properties are the most obvious because they come from real-world characteristics of the object. Real-world objects have loads of characteristics, so the challenge is to separate the relevant ones from the irrelevant ones. Good object modelers identify properties by talking to domain experts and examining legacy databases and information architectures when they are available. During design, some of the complex descriptive properties, like address, may be fleshed out into reusable objects.[19]

> EXAMPLE—Interesting characteristics of a person include weight, height, hair color(s), piercings, and tattoos; however, an online banking system is only interested in the person's name, address, Social Security Number, and date of birth.[20] See Figure 5.14.

---

19. See p. 120, "Complex Properties."
20. In some systems, such as police and insurance databases, the date of death is also of interest, and thus included in the object model.

FIGURE 5.14
Relevant properties of a Person for an online banking system.

Tracking Properties

Tracking properties are special descriptive properties used to distinguish objects and give them unique identities. During the object modeling sessions, ask domain experts how they track and distinguish between customers, orders, students, employees, shipments, parts, etc. Analysis object models should not include non-descriptive keys or object IDs in the object diagram. These may be added later during design.

> EXAMPLE—An online e-commerce site tracks its registered customers by their email addresses. A college tracks its students by their Social Security Numbers. A fulfillment center tracks its shipments by carrier tracking numbers.

Assumed Property Accessors

Unless explicitly stated otherwise, assume that each property shown in the object diagram has a read and a write accessor, which return and change the property value, respectively. Accessors are usually not shown on the model because they clutter the diagram, and clutter defeats communication. Properties help communicate the domain by showing what an object knows, but accessors don't add any new information.

Properties Can Be Derived

It is tempting to imagine an object property as simply a field holding a data value, and many properties are implemented that way, but some properties are derived or calculated. Ultimately, whether a property is stored or derived is an implementation decision, but even during object modeling, some of what an object needs to know is obviously derived from other information. Derived properties are listed in the service section as services, usually with a prefix of "get" or "determine."

EXAMPLE—A person's age is a derived property. Storing a person's age is highly impractical since it would require continual updating. The simpler approach is to model the person's date of birth as a stored property and the person's age as a derived property. See Figure 5.14.

Time-Dependent Properties

Time and date properties are necessary for `transaction` objects that record time-based events. A non-`transaction` object can also have time and date properties when it needs to remember a non-repeatable occurrence or repeatable occurrences where history is not required; otherwise, the object should use historical properties. To reduce object model clutter, smash the time and date properties together into one "dateTime" property.

EXAMPLE—A nomination is a moment-in-time `transaction` with a property indicating the date and time of the nomination. A timeshare condo reservation is a time-interval `transaction` with properties indicating its start and end dates and times. A document is a `specific item` with a creation date-time property, which is a non-repeatable occurrence. A user is a `role` with a last login date-time, which is a repeatable occurrence and its previous values are not important.

Historical Properties

Most properties can change values, but for some properties, the history of past values is important to the business processing. When an object has an historical property, the property is promoted to a history object collaborator,[21] the default read accessor retrieves the value in the most current history object, a special read accessor retrieves the value on a given date, and the write accessor creates a new history object.

EXAMPLE—An e-commerce site needs to remember price changes for its products. Each product has one or more price history objects, which include a price and its effective dates. See Figure 5.15.

PRINCIPLE 34
TRACK BUT DON'T KEY

Keep keys and object IDs off the diagram. Include identifying properties only if they come from the domain.

---

21. That being said, if you have a lot of these—that is, lots of properties needing history—then you might keep them as properties and make it a design pattern that all properties need history.

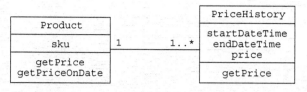

SPECIFIC ITEM   TRANSACTION

FIGURE 5.15
A Product's price as a derived property with history.

PRINCIPLE 35
HIDE REDUNDANT ACCESSORS

Assume each property listed in the object definition has a read and write accessor, but don't put them in the diagram.

PRINCIPLE 36
SHOW DERIVED ACCESSORS

Represent a derived property with a read accessor in the service section.

PRINCIPLE 33
MAKE IT REAL AND RELEVANT

Descriptive properties come from an object's relevant real-world characteristics. Use domain experts, legacy databases, and information architectures to locate relevant descriptive properties.

PRINCIPLE 37
ALWAYS DATE EVENTS

Transaction objects always include date and/or time properties.

PRINCIPLE 38
DATE OBJECTS WITH SPECIAL OCCURRENCES

Put date and/or time properties in non-transaction objects to record a non-repeatable occurrence or a repeatable occurrence that does not require history.

PRINCIPLE 39
HISTORICAL PROPERTIES NEED OBJECTS

Use history event objects to keep an audit trail of values for a property. Treat the property like a derived one; include a special accessor to read the property value for a given date.

State Properties

Lifecycle State Properties

Some objects go through a one-way lifecycle, from an initial state to a final state. With people, places, and things, lifecycle states depend on their interactions and so are derived properties determined by analyze transactions services.[22] Events actually record state, usually in read-only properties that are changed during conduct business services.[23]

> EXAMPLE—In the document nomination example, a document progresses through lifecycle states of un-nominated, pending, approved, and rejected. Which state a document is in depends on its nomination collaborators. See Figure 5.16.

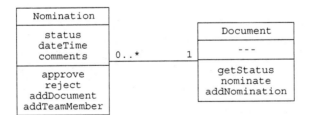

```
  Nomination
 ┌──────────────┐
 │   status     │                    Document
 │  dateTime    │              ┌──────────────────┐
 │  comments    │ 0..*      1  │      - - -        │
 ├──────────────┤              ├──────────────────┤
 │  approve     │              │    getStatus     │
 │  reject      │              │    nominate      │
 │  addDocument │              │  addNomination   │
 │ addTeamMember│              └──────────────────┘
 └──────────────┘
```

TRANSACTION   SPECIFIC ITEM

FIGURE 5.16

A Nomination has a state property, status.[24]

---

22. With people, places, and things steps in their lifecycles are recorded by `transactions` marking when the step was reached.
23. `Transactions` with `follow-up transactions` can have a derived lifecycle state.
24. To highlight them, status properties are listed at the top of the object diagram, followed by the tracking, time, and descriptive properties.

Caching Properties

Objects with derived properties and a lifecycle state may reach a final state when the derived properties cannot change.[25] The conduct business service that puts the object into its final state can then determine the derived properties and cache their values.[26] Future requests for the derived property would return the cached value. Whether to include the final property in the object symbol is optional. Do whatever helps the client best understand the model.

> EXAMPLE—An order, when committed, can cache its final total. The get total accessor in the order checks the order's state. If the state is submitted, the final total property is returned; otherwise, the determine total service is invoked and its result is returned.[27] See Figure 5.17.

Operational States

Lifecycle states are one-way, but often objects flip back and forth between different states, and which state an object is in influences how it behaves. These are called the object's operational states. As with lifecycle states, operational states can only be set during conduct business services.

> EXAMPLE—A team member can be in either an active or inactive state. A store can be open or closed. A sensor can be off, initialized, on, or failed. A product can be available or unavailable.

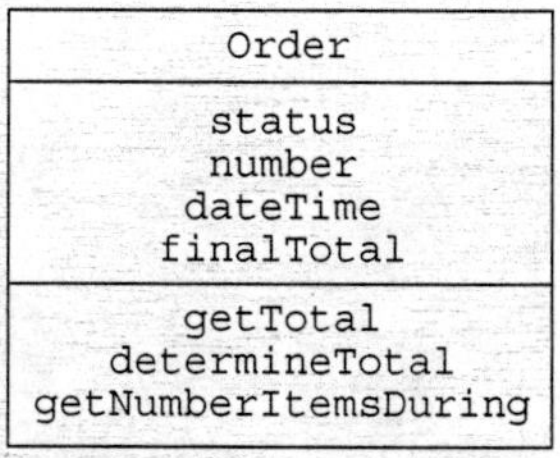

```
        Order
       status
       number
       dateTime
       finalTotal
       getTotal
     determineTotal
  getNumberItemsDuring
```

FIGURE 5.17
An Order caches its total when it reaches a final state.

---

25. For instance, in the person example, age may be cached when the date of death is set.
26. In some cases, cached values exist for legal reasons. Caching the final price paid for a product in an order is especially important in systems where prices change frequently.
27. Actually, e-commerce and point-of-sale systems have separate tax, subtotal, and shipping totals that contribute to the final total, and these would have their own determine mine methods and be cached in separate final properties.

PRINCIPLE 40
KNOWING WHERE IN THE LIFECYCLE

In a person, place, or thing object, make the lifecycle state a property derived from event collaborators. In an event, make the lifecycle state a property, unless it is derived from follow-up events.

PRINCIPLE 41
KNOWING WHICH OPERATIONAL STATE

Put an operating state property in any person, place, or thing object that switches between different operational modes.

PRINCIPLE 42
CACHE WHEN FINAL

When an object reaches one of its final lifecycle states, consider caching its derived properties.

PRINCIPLE 43
ONLY CHANGE STATE WHEN CONDUCTING BUSINESS

Allow only conduct business services to change an object's lifecycle or operational state properties.

Complex Properties

Clutter Objects

Clutter defeats communication. A sure way of reducing clutter is to depict complex information as properties. Defer until design fleshing these properties out as full-blown objects. To find clutter objects, look for object connections that are one-to-one and do not fit into any of the 12 collaboration patterns. This is another important part of streamlined object modeling: you end up with a streamlined diagram containing only those objects necessary for effective communication.

> EXAMPLE—A person's name, Social Security number, and address are collapsible objects that can be depicted as properties but are implemented as individual objects. See Figure 5.18.

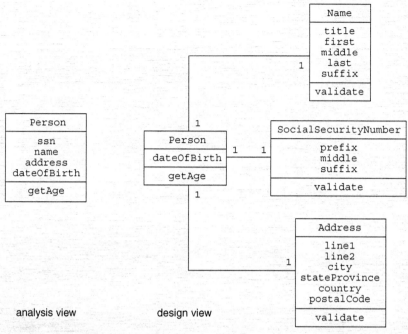

FIGURE 5.18
During design, properties may be fleshed out into objects.

Role Classifications

While participation in a context is modeled with a `role` object, often there are different levels or classifications of participation. Depending on their complexities, different levels can be modeled as separate objects or as properties. If the classifications are solely for bookkeeping reasons, do not require history, and have no special behaviors, then add a role classification property to the `role` object to indicate the different classifications. Otherwise, use a subsequent `role` to follow up the original role.[28]

> EXAMPLE—In the document nomination example, team members are classified as members, admins, or chairs. Histories of past chairs and admins are not retained for the team or for individual team members. The business process for nominating a document is the same for all team members, regardless of their classification, but the collaboration rules allow chairs to nominate more documents. Because there are no

---

28. See p. 284, "Actor – Fundamental Role – Subsequent Role."

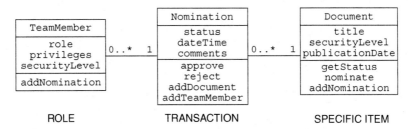

FIGURE 5.19
TeamMember with role property.

history requirements, and the behavior is the same, a role property is added to the team member object to classify a team member as a chair, admin, or member. See Figure 5.19.

Role Classification Accessors

A role classification property is typically designed and implemented as an enumerated type, meaning that it can take on one of a few symbolic values. Such properties lack the usual read and write accessors; instead, the object has services that check if the property is a particular value or command the object to set the property to a particular value. These services are assumed unless the role is a derived property. An example with these services is implemented in a later chapter.[29]

> EXAMPLE—The team member in the document nomination system has read accessor services, isRoleChair, isRoleAdmin, and isRoleMember, which return true or false, depending on the role property; team member also has write accessor services, setRoleChair, setRoleAdmin, and setRoleMember, which set the role property accordingly.

Role History

If a role classification does not have special behaviors, but needs history, then expand it into a role history object, much like the price property was expanded to a price history.[30]

> EXAMPLE—If a team member is required to know his current and past team roles, then expand the role classification property into a role history object. See Figure 5.20.

---

29. See p. 175, "Accessing: Properties."
30. See pp. 116–118.

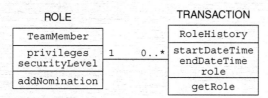

FIGURE 5.20
A TeamMember with a history of his role classifications.

Subsequent Roles

If a role classification has properties and services not present in others, then expand it into a further role object.[31]

> EXAMPLE—A team member keeps history of his role classifications. If the team member becomes a chair, he can use the online system to call meetings, and must supply a secondary contact to handle meeting inquiries. See Figure 5.21.

Type Properties

Just as `roles` can be classified, places, things, and events can be typed. The same rules apply. If the type classifications are solely for bookkeeping reasons, do not require history, and have no special behaviors, then just add a

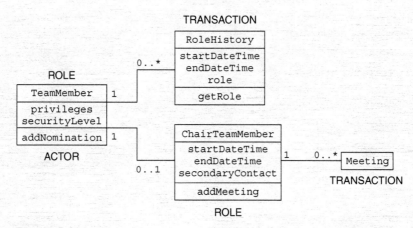

FIGURE 5.21
The ChairTeamMember has additional services, properties, and collaborations.

---

31. See p. 284, "Actor – Fundamental Role – Subsequent Role."

type classification property to the object. Otherwise, consider defining type history and subsequent type objects.

EXAMPLE—A hotel reservation system keeps a description of each hotel room that includes whether the room is smoking or non-smoking.

PRINCIPLE 44
COLLAPSE CLUTTER OBJECTS

Collapse objects whose only purpose is to represent complex information into properties.

PRINCIPLE 45
CLASSIFY ROLES

Use a role classification property to distinguish different levels of participation only if the participation level requires no history and no additional properties, behaviors, or collaborations.

PRINCIPLE 46
CLASSIFY TYPES

Use a type classification property to distinguish different object types only if the type requires no history and has no additional properties, behaviors, or collaborations.

Object Inheritance Strategies

---

6

*Our children will be as wise as we are and will establish in the fullness
of time those things not yet ripe for establishment.*

Thomas Jefferson

Organization is Key

Good organization brings clarity. Streamlined object modeling is a technique
that uses 12 collaboration patterns to organize domain objects, business rules,
and business services into recognizable structures that repeat throughout the
model. This repetition helps communicate meaning to the client. Streamlined
object modeling also consistently organizes business rules and services within
objects, highlighting regularities in how collaborators distribute work. With
these regularities in objects, rules, and services, streamlined object models
support all manners of programming templates for defining objects, creating
collaborations, checking collaboration rules, and running business services.
This book discusses programming techniques and templates intended primarily for prototyping. These prototyping templates show how to quickly transform collaboration patterns into code for testing business rules and services,
but they do not promote the level of code reuse and pluggability necessary for
a professional release. However, because the programming templates were
carefully designed according to good object-oriented programming standards,

transforming them into templates for pluggable, reusable frameworks is not that difficult. In fact, the authors are currently engaged in doing just that for commercial endeavors, so expect to hear more from us about that, but not in this book.

This chapter focuses on object inheritance, which is a mechanism for concisely specifying dependencies in behaviors and properties within several collaboration patterns. Object inheritance simplifies the object model by reducing the visible amount of detail, but requires some additional care during implementation. This chapter describes what services and properties are involved in object inheritance. The following chapter shows how to implement object inheritance and a prototyping template for coding object collaborations.

Our Prototyping Focus

We are big believers in prototyping object models early in the development process. Not big fans of waterfall development, we prefer a more iterative development cycle that encourages jumping between analysis and design, design and implementation,[1] and analysis and implementation. The path between analysis and implementation is important as a means for verifying and refining analysis results. Prototyping streamlined object models primarily involves implementing collaboration patterns, collaboration rules, and higher level business services. This book focuses on implementing collaboration patterns and collaboration rules. Teaching the gritty details of writing business services is beyond the scope of this book; however, this book does provide ample principles for distributing services between collaborators that can be applied to organize the implementation of most business services. Also included in this book are detailed Java[2] and Squeak samples that illustrate our prototyping templates for defining objects, creating collaborations, and checking collaboration rules. Our templates and strategies, though illustrated in Java and Squeak, are language-independent and assume no preexisting packages or code bases. Four concepts underlie our prototyping templates and strategies: (1) certain collaboration patterns use object inheritance, (2) three prototyping templates cover all 12 collaboration patterns, (3) one object definition template works for defining all objects, and (4) one template works for defining services that check collaboration rules.

---

1. See baseball model, pp. 11–13, *Object-Oriented Programming*, Peter Coad and Jill Nicola, 1993, Prentice Hall.
2. The syntax of Java and C++ are sufficiently close that the Java examples should be readable to the C++ programmer.

The first concept, object inheritance, is a useful mechanism for specifying behaviors within certain collaboration patterns. These patterns involve a parent – child object relationship in which one object "inherits" information and behaviors from the other through a selective form of delegation. Object inheritance is described in detail in this chapter, and illustrated in code in the next chapter.

The second of our prototyping concepts is that each of the 12 collaboration patterns can be classified into three categories: generic - specific, whole - part, or transaction - specific. The same prototyping template can implement all collaborations within a given category; thus, only three templates are required to implement all 12 collaboration patterns. The three categories are introduced in this chapter, and the three templates are presented in Chapters 7 and 8.

Our third concept comes from the fact that almost every business object has a similar infrastructure. Having one template that organizes an object's definition makes creating collaborations and checking collaboration rules between objects significantly simpler. Chapter 7 presents our object definition template.

The fourth prototyping concept is that regardless of the collaboration pattern involved, the same processes are followed when two objects check their collaboration rules prior to making or dissolving their collaborations. Standardizing the services involved in checking collaboration rules takes the guesswork out of coding business rules, and makes them easy to find and change. These services can then be extracted into policy objects or rules databases to transform the prototype code into production release code. Chapter 8 introduces our collaboration rules template.

Object Inheritance in Collaboration Patterns _____

Object inheritance pops up when two collaborating objects are needed to represent one real-world object. For example, the actor - role pattern requires two pattern players to enable an entity to participate in and switch between different contexts. One pattern player represents the entity, and the other pattern player represents its participation within a particular context. Also, the item - specific item pattern uses two pattern players to describe a thing that comes in many variations. One pattern player represents the general description, shared by all the variations, and the second pattern player represents the particular details, which distinguish each variation from the other.

Finally, the `composite transaction - line item` pattern uses two pattern players to describe an event involving many entities of the same kind. The first pattern player records the event details common to all the entities, and the second pattern player records the interaction details of an individual entity.

In each of these collaboration patterns, one pattern player represents what is constant and shared while the other pattern player represents what is specialized, varied, or particular. The pattern player representing constancy is designated as the parent, and the pattern player representing specificity is designated as the child. Object inheritance enables information within the parent object to be "reused" by its child objects. In other words, the child knows some of its parent's properties, and can be asked for their values. The child also knows some of its parent's collaborations and behaviors, but not all of them. A later section in this chapter describes techniques for deciding which collaborations and behaviors are inheritable and which are not. The information and behaviors in the parent that are object inheritable by the child are known as the parent's profile. The notation for specifying a parent – child object inheritance is a collaboration line labeled with the word "parent" next to the parent object[3] (see Figure 6.1).

Object inheritance allows two objects representing a single entity to be treated as one object by the rest of the system. Questions and requests answerable by the parent object can be addressed to the child object because it exhibits the same outward appearance, or profile, as the parent. The child answers these requests by retrieving the information from its parent, typically by delegating the requests to it. In this way, the child stands as a representative for its parent within specialized contexts, variation, and interactions.

For a parent to keep its constancy across contexts, variations, and interactions, it must remain unaffected by what its child objects do. Accordingly, object inheritance is read-only; a child object may request its parent's properties and collaborations, but it can do nothing to change them. The requests it can make of its parent are limited to those that read information. In fact, as is shown later in this chapter, there are rules specifying exactly what information and services a child can request of its parents. These rules make

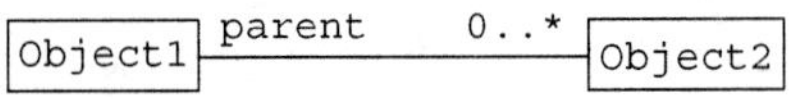

```
Object1 ──── parent     0..*  ──── Object2
```

FIGURE 6.1
Parent – child notation. Object1 is the parent of Object2.

---

3. A more "proper" use of the UML would be to stereotype the relationship. You are welcome to use that format, but we find this clearer and easier to scribble on a whiteboard.

object inheritance a powerful modeling mechanism that communicates many capabilities with a very concise notation.

Actor – Role Object Inheritance

The `actor - role` pattern uses object inheritance to describe an entity participating in multiple contexts. The `actor` is the parent object describing how the entity looks, acts, and collaborates across all contexts. The `role` is the child object describing the entity's participation within a particular context, and projecting the entity's profile into that context.

> EXAMPLE—An airline uses one system to track its employees and frequent flyers. It also allows its employees to enroll as frequent flyers. An `actor` object, person, describes information and behavior about the individual that is the same across all contexts. The `role` objects, frequent flyer and employee, contain the information and behaviors necessary to participate in that context, and exhibit the information and behaviors of a person. See Figure 6.2.

> COUNTER-EXAMPLE—If the airline example were modeled without using `actor - role` and object inheritance, then frequent flyer and employee objects would replicate personal information and behaviors. Reconciliation routines would be required to synchronize employees and frequent flyers with the same personal information. See Figure 6.3.[4]

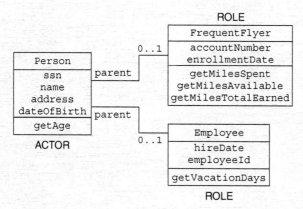

FIGURE 6.2
FrequentFlyer and Employee objects inherit from Person.

---

4. The result would be the same if we used a common superclass for both frequent flyer and subscriber. Using a common superclass allows some code reuse, but there are significant downsides. These will be discussed more when class inheritance and object inheritance are contrasted.

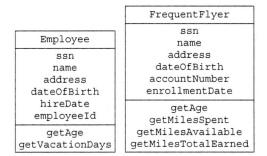

FIGURE 6.3
Employee and FrequentFlyer without `actor - role` and object inheritance.

Item – Specific Item Object Inheritance

The `item - specific item` pattern uses object inheritance to separate a common description from the particular things that share the description. The `item` is the parent object describing information and behaviors shared by all its variations. The `specific item` is the child object describing information necessary to distinguish one variation from another and assuming the profile of the common description.

> EXAMPLE—A videotape for rent is described by a video title that includes the movie title, rating, cast, production date, and release level, which determines how long the videotape can be rented. A videotape for a newly released video title can only be rented for one day. Other levels have longer durations. An individual videotape has a status and a tracking number. The checkout procedure requires that a videotape determine its due back date. This service is object inherited from its video title. See Figure 6.4.

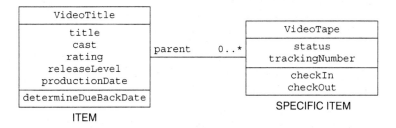

FIGURE 6.4
A VideoTape object inherits from a VideoTitle.

Composite Transaction – Line Item Object Inheritance

The composite `transaction - line item` pattern uses object inheritance to describe the interactions of many entities within a common event. The `composite transaction` is the parent object describing information and behaviors of the overall event. The `line item` is the child object describing an interaction of a single entity and projecting the overall event's profile to the interacting entity.

> EXAMPLE—A commission for a sale involves one or more sales agents, and each sales agent earns a percentage of the sale. A commission split describes an agent's involvement in a commission. The date of the sale and the total sale amount are properties in the overall commission event that are object inherited by the commission split. See Figure 6.5.

PRINCIPLE 47
OBJECT INHERITANCE

Use object inheritance between two objects representing a single entity or event when the entity participates in multiple contexts, when the entity comes in many variations, or when the event involves multiple interactions.

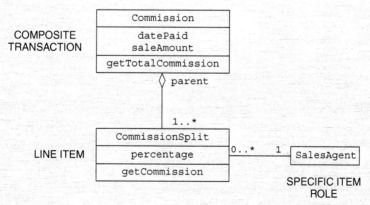

FIGURE 6.5
A CommissionSplit presents details of the Commission to the SalesAgent.

PRINCIPLE 48
PARENT RESPONSIBILITIES

In object inheritance, the parent object contains information and behaviors that are valid across multiple contexts, multiple interactions, and multiple variations of an object.

PRINCIPLE 49
CHILD RESPONSIBILITIES

In object inheritance, the child object represents the parent in a specialized context, in a particular interaction, or as a distinct variation.

PRINCIPLE 50
CHILD ASSUMES THE PARENT'S PROFILE

In object inheritance, the child object assumes its parent's profile, enabling it to answer read-only requests for information about properties and collaborators of the parent.

Comparing Object Inheritance to Class Inheritance ___

Object inheritance differs from class inheritance because it is a relationship between objects, not classes. While typical object-oriented programming languages include support for class inheritance, support for object inheritance is not yet widely available; however, techniques for implementing it are presented in Chapters 7 and 8. Object inheritance adds conciseness and precision to the object model, so we encourage its use because the organization and rigor it brings to the code more than compensates for the additional work. This section compares class inheritance to object inheritance. The sections following it explain the rules for object inheritance of properties, collaborations, and services.

Object inheritance is a relationship between objects that allows you to create a new view on an existing object. The new object, the child, represents another view of the existing object, the parent, and the parent can support many such views. Both objects represent the same entity. While the parent object represents the fundamental qualities of the entity, the child object represents the additional qualities the entity takes on within a given context, in an interaction, or as a distinct variation. Class inheritance is a relationship between classes; it allows you to create a new class from an existing one. The new class, the specialization, extends the structure of the old class, the generalization, by defining new properties, collaborations, and behaviors.[5] Instances of the specialization cannot represent instances of the generalization without using some form of object inheritance. In short, class inheritance is specialization without representation.

One reason specializations cannot represent their generalizations is that class inheritance determines the structure of objects in specialization classes, but not their values. When a property or collaboration is inherited through class inheritance, objects in the specialization class have their own storage space for that property or collaboration reference and can store their own values there, subject to the business rule constraints. When a property or collaboration is inherited through object inheritance, child objects retrieve the value from the parent object, where it is stored. Object inheritance requires additional services of the child, to retrieve values, but no additional storage space.[6]

> EXAMPLE—If the airline example were modeled with class inheritance, then only two objects would be required, but there is duplication of information as both frequent flyer and employee inherit SSN, name, address, and date of birth properties from their mutual generalization class, person[7] (see Figure 6.6). And because each object has its own set of property values, these must be kept in sync for objects belonging to the same person. Modeling with object inheritance requires three objects, but frequent flyer and employee objects share the property values in person (see Figure 6.2). Sharing the values means no duplication or syncing of data is necessary.

Class inheritance is static. It occurs between classes that define objects. This means that an object's class inheritance is specified before the object exists. Few applications allow an object to change its class, or allow the class inheritance to be modified on-the-fly. So for most applications, once an object is created, its class inheritance is permanently established. Early binding of typed languages also discourages most applications from generating new specialization classes on-the-fly. So it is difficult or impossible to extend class inheritance dynamically.

Object inheritance is dynamic. Even in typed languages, child objects can be added to and removed from a parent object during the parent's lifetime.

---

5. Most object-oriented programming languages refer to a generalization class as a base class or superclass, and refer to its specialization classes as subclasses.
6. Exceptions happen when a child customizes default values in the parent (see pp. 147–151).
7. This example models roles with class inheritance. We strongly recommend against this approach.

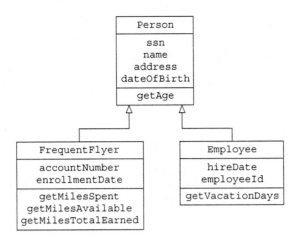

FIGURE 6.6
FrequentFlyer and Employee modeled with class inheritance.

Only business rules prevent a child from being added to a parent, and the business rules accept or reject child objects based on their states and values, aspects determined dynamically. Under object inheritance, a child could switch to a new parent during its lifetime, but semantically, such a switch corrupts the purpose of the parent – child collaboration, which is to represent a single entity. Switching the child to another parent implies transferring a specialized view of an entity to another entity. So, while this is rarely done, it is very powerful, when necessary.

Both object inheritance and class inheritance are useful object modeling and coding concepts. It is, however, important to remember the key differences when deciding which to use. The principles below highlight these differences.

PRINCIPLE 51
OBJECTS NOT CLASSES

Object inheritance relates two objects, each representing different views of the same entity or event. Class inheritance relates two classes, one extending the structure defined in the other.

PRINCIPLE 52
REPRESENTATION VS. SPECIALIZATION

Use object inheritance to represent multiple views of an entity. Use class inheritance to specialize an existing class of objects.

PRINCIPLE 53
VALUES VS. STRUCTURE

Object inheritance is the sharing of actual property values from a parent object. Class inheritance is the sharing of the structure for holding property values from an existing class definition.

PRINCIPLE 54
DYNAMIC VS. STATIC

Object inheritance is dynamic since shared property values often change their state during the course of a parent object's lifetime. Class inheritance is static because the structure for holding property values rarely changes during a class definition's lifetime.

Object Inheritance and Properties

Not all property values of the parent should be object inherited by its child objects. The first criteria for object inheritance is that the property must have at least one read accessor.[8] In other words, if the property value cannot be requested from the parent, then it cannot be requested from the child, either. The set of readable properties includes those that are *read-only*. If a property has a read accessor, then it is readable. If a property has a read accessor without a complementary write accessor, then it is read-only but still readable. Since children cannot be allowed to modify their parents, the write accessors for properties are never object inherited regardless of whether corresponding read accessors are. This means that when looking at the child, all object inherited properties appear to be read-only.

Recall that read accessors are not depicted on the object model.[9] Part of the information implied by the parent – child notation, is that the child object has read accessors that duplicate the read accessors in its parent object. This makes the notation that much more concise.

> EXAMPLE—An employee object inherits all the readable property values in its parent object, a person. For each readable property in the person, including the derived properties, add to the subscriber a read accessor that retrieves the requested value from the person parent. Figure 6.7 shows both the expanded version of the person – employee collabora-

---

8. Recall that accessor services read and write the value of a property.
9. See pp. 109–110, "Read Accessors."

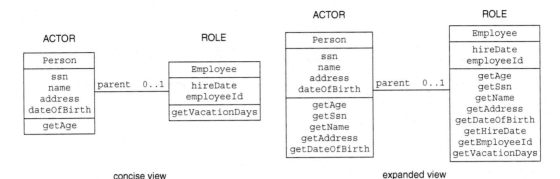

FIGURE 6.7
Concise and expanded version of the Person – Employee collaboration.

tion with all the read accessors depicted, and the concise version that is used throughout this book.

Properties Not to Inherit

Object inheritance does not mean that every variable implemented in the parent's class is object inherited by the child object. Certain variables might be added during implementation to improve efficiency or support a programming package. Some of these might even have public accessor services. Since these variables are not business properties, they are not usually object inherited.

> EXAMPLE—Certain data persistence schemes require every object to have an object ID field that can be read by the data management layer. Although the object ID field has a public read accessor in the parent, its value cannot be object inherited in the child objects, since the child should have its own unique ID.

Even sticking just to the business properties identified during object modeling, there are still some property values that should not be object inherited. The values of state, role, and type properties should never be object inherited. Although these are important for business scenarios, the child does not need the values directly, and should instead inherit the services that query for particular values of these properties.

> EXAMPLE—A store reorders a product SKU when the inventory of SKU falls below a minimum, unless the SKU belongs to a product that has been discontinued. The product description has a state variable that indicates whether it is planned, current, or discontinued as an item for

sale by the store. A product description is a parent to the product objects that represent the different variations of it. The child objects do not object inherit the state property, but do object inherit the state accessors, isPlanned, isCurrent, and isDiscontinued. See Figure 6.8.

PRINCIPLE 55
VALUES THROUGH SERVICES

Use object inheritance to allow a child to share property values with its parent. Add a read accessor in the child for each property value it object inherits from its parent.

PRINCIPLE 56
READ BUT NO WRITE

Never allow a child object to change property values in its parent.

PRINCIPLE 57
ONLY PUBLIC PROPERTIES

Properties of the parent that are not publicly accessible cannot be object inherited by a child object.

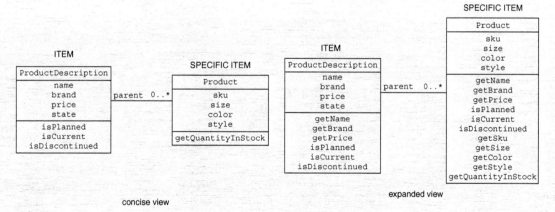

FIGURE 6.8
The Product does not object inherit its parent's state variable.

PRINCIPLE 58
NO DESIGN, JUST BUSINESS

Don't allow a child to object inherit design properties that were added to the parent to improve efficiency, support persistence storage, allow interactive display, or satisfy programming practices.

PRINCIPLE 59
QUERIES NOT STATES

Don't allow a child to object inherit read accessors for state, type, or role properties. Do allow the child to object inherit related property value services, such as "isPublished," "isCancelled," "isAdmin," etc.

Object Inheritance and Collaborations

A child object inherits most of the collaborations of its parent. As with properties, for every collaborator a child object inherits from its parent, the child has a read accessor that retrieves the collaborator from the parent. To the outside world, which requests the collaborator from the child, the fact that the collaborator actually belongs to the parent is hidden. As with property accessors, collaboration accessors, which establish or dissolve collaborations, are not depicted in the object model but assumed.

> EXAMPLE—An e-commerce clothing store categorizes each of its products into one or more categories. All products of the same product description belong to the same categories, so their parent object is the one categorized. When a product is asked for its containing categories, it delegates the request to its parent, product description. And when a product is asked if it is in a particular category, it delegates the request to its parent. These services belong in the product description and are assumed to exist in the product through object inheritance. See Figure 6.9.

A parent object contains information valid across many contexts, variations, and interactions. It cannot allow one child to change its properties or collaborations because that change might make another child invalid. For these reasons, a child cannot establish new collaborators or dissolve old ones for its parent. This is similar to the read-only restriction on properties.

> EXAMPLE—A product cannot add or remove its product description from a product category.

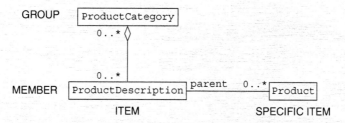

FIGURE 6.9
A specific Product object inherits its categories from its parent.

Groups, Assemblies, and Containers

Object inheritance involves two objects representing one entity or event. If the parent is part of any groups, assemblies, or within any containers, the entity or event being represented is assumed to be part of them. Since the parent and child both represent the entity, the child object inherits the knowledge of the groups, assemblies, and containers.

> EXAMPLE—In the e-commerce clothing store example, a product object inherits the categories (groups) of its parent product description (see Figure 6.9).

Role Collaborations

Object inheritance in events happens when many entities of the same kind are interacting. Separate child events record the details of each interaction, while the parent records details that are common for all the entities interacting. When the parent event involves a role, that role is involved in the overall interaction, and therefore is object inherited by the child events.

> EXAMPLE—An order line item object inherits the customer (role) from its parent (see Figure 6.10).

Place Collaborations

Events occur at a place. When a parent event occurs at a given place, it is usually the case that all of its child events happen at the same one. Therefore, this collaboration is object inherited by the child events.

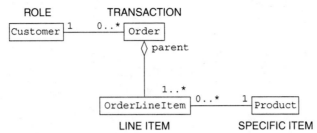

FIGURE 6.10
An OrderLineItem object inherits Customer from its parent, Order.

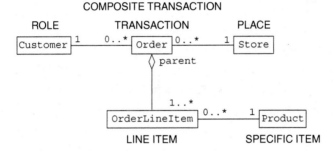

FIGURE 6.11
An OrderLineItem object inherits Store from its parent.

> EXAMPLE—An order line item object inherits the store (`place`) from its parent order (see Figure 6.11).[10]

Event Transactions

If a parent is involved in events that pertain to all of its children, then those event collaborations are object inherited. Events that are not relevant for some or all of the parent's children are not object inherited.

> EXAMPLE—A distributor signs an agreement to distribute products from a manufacturer. The agreement gives the distributor rights to all variations of the product. Rights include co-branding, distributor fees, and renewal rates and are established product by product. An agreement line item captures the distributor rights for a single product description.

10. In e-commerce systems involving multiple stores, an order is partitioned into separate store orders, which have a store collaborator and a collection of order line items for product purchased at that store.

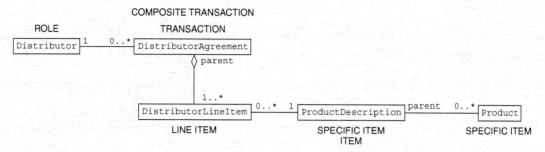

FIGURE 6.12
A Product object inherits involvement in DistributionAgreements.

All the products that are variations of the product description object inherit the agreement line item from the product. See Figure 6.12.

Followed Transactions

If the parent is involved in events that imply follow-up events involving only one or some of the child objects, then those collaborations are *not* object inherited. This happens most often with line items. Composite transactions often have follow-up transactions that are also composite transactions. When this happens, the follow-up transactions only involve some of the line items in the original composite transaction. An object should only object inherit information that pertains to it, so line items should not object inherit follow-up transactions that do not involve them.

> EXAMPLE—An order is followed by some number of shipments. A shipment has shipment line items that relate back to the order line items. Each shipment line item takes some or all of the quantity of product designated by the order line item. An order line item does not object inherit shipments from its parent order because an order line item may not be involved in all the shipments. Instead, the order line item knows its own shipments because shipments involving it have shipment line items collaborating with it. See Figure 6.13.

Historical Transactions

A parent's history affects its children. In other words, the entity that both the parent and child are representing is the real-world object whose history is being tracked. Therefore, if the parent has historical events, then those collaborations are object inherited.

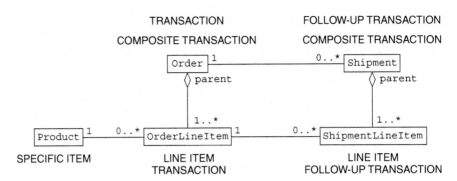

FIGURE 6.13
An OrderLineItem does not object inherit Shipments from its parent, Order.

EXAMPLE—An employee object inherits change of address events from its person. A product object inherits price changes from its parent.

Parent Collaborations

If the parent is also a child with its own parent collaboration, then the grand-child object inherits the grandparent's profile. All three objects are still representing one real-world object in more and more specific contexts or variations.

EXAMPLE—Example. An airline allows its frequent flyers to become subscribers to its online service center, which allows them to enroll in forums and receive email updates about forum news. Since only frequent flyers can join, the online subscriber is a further `role` and child object of the frequent flyer. The online subscriber object inherits the parent collaboration from the frequent flyer so that object inheritable information in the person can be asked of the online subscriber. See Figure 6.14.

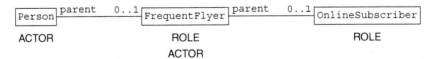

FIGURE 6.14
An OnlineSubscriber object inherits the parent link to Person.

Child Object Collaborations

When parent objects have multiple child objects, a child does not object inherit the other child objects. The reason for this is that each child represents a more specific version of the parent. If each child inherited all of the other children's specific details, there would be no way to tell them apart, and their usefulness would be limited at best. In the case of the actor - role pattern, each role object would have more information than would be useful in its context. That makes things more complicated and is contrary to the reason object inheritance is used.

> EXAMPLE—An e-commerce system includes people who are customers, employees, and brokers. A person can take on multiple roles; however, a role does not know about the other roles. For example, a customer object does not object inherit knowledge of the person's employee or broker roles, if they exist. See Figure 6.15

PRINCIPLE 60
IN MY PARENT'S GROUPS

Always allow a child to object inherit its parent's group, assembly, and container collaborations.

PRINCIPLE 61
REMEMBERING MY PARENT'S EVENTS

Always allow a child to object inherit its parent's historical and event transactions.

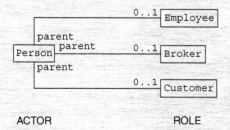

ACTOR   ROLE

FIGURE 6.15
A role does not object inherit the other roles of its parent.

PRINCIPLE 62
FAMILY TIES

Always allow a child to object inherit its parent's parent, but do not allow a child to object inherit other child objects belonging to its parent.

PRINCIPLE 63
SHARE AND SHARE ALIKE

Allow a child to object inherit `follow-up transactions` for its parent's events if and only if the `follow-up transactions` are valid for all the parent's children.

PRINCIPLE 64
MY PARENT THE EVENT

Allow a `line item` child to object inherit the `role` and `place` collaborations of its `composite transaction` parent.

Object Inheritance and Services

A child object inherits only some of its parent's services. The following sections describe the rules governing when services can and cannot be object inherited. These rules are also summarized in "Object Inheritance Interfaces," p. 342.

Determine Mine Services

Almost all determine mine services are object inherited because these are the services that satisfy requests for information and return readable properties and collaborations. The exceptions are those determine mine services that do not make sense for the child because they return aggregate information summarized from all the child objects, or they return information about only a few of the child objects. To decide if a determine mine is object inheritable, ask if every child object could be asked the question it answers. A service that aggregates information from all the child objects cannot be asked of a single child object, so it is not object inheritable. A service that involves filtering or ranking the child objects, such as finding the highest or lowest ranking child object, is not object inheritable either.

EXAMPLE—In the store example, a product object inherits all the read accessors for properties and collaborators from its parent product description. The product description service "get best-selling SKU," which returns the best-selling specific product, is not object inherited.[11] This service is not object inherited by the product objects because it is information about only one of the child objects. The service "is in category" is valid for all the child-specific products so it is object inherited. See Figure 6.16.

Analyze Transactions Services

A child object inherits an analyze transactions service if the child object inherits the `transaction` collaborators analyzed by the service. In other words, a child cannot object inherit information about `transactions` it cannot object inherit. `Transaction` collaborators are not object inheritable if the `transactions` do not apply to all the child objects. This happens with certain `follow-up transactions`.[12]

EXAMPLE—A product manufacturer sets wholesale prices and distributor prices at the product description level. Wholesale prices are remembered through price history objects, while distributor prices are remembered as line items within distributor agreements. A product description calculates its average wholesale price and finds its current

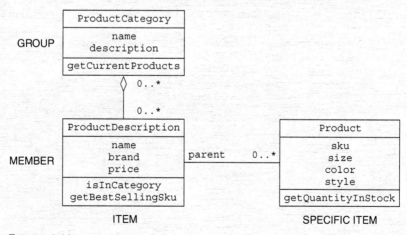

FIGURE 6.16
The service for locating the best-selling SKU is not object inherited.

---

11. Notice that this is a determine mine service on product that asks its specific products to analyze their `transactions`, and then selects the specific product with the best result.
12. See pp. 141–142.

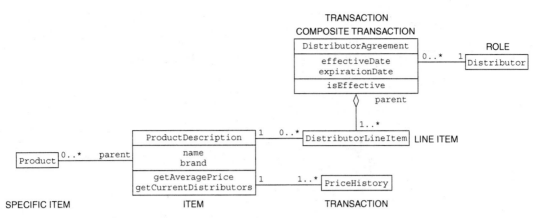

FIGURE 6.17
Services analyzing PriceHistories and DistributorAgreements are object inherited.

distributors.[13] A product object inherits these services from its product description. See Figure 6.17.

EXAMPLE—A hotel reservation system allows customers to reserve a type of hotel room (smoking, double beds). A reservation may be followed by a room rental for a hotel room of the type reserved. A hotel room type analyzes its reservations to count the number of completed room reservations. Since this service counts reservations for all hotel rooms defined by the hotel room type, it cannot be object inherited. Instead, a hotel room has its own service that counts completed reservations by looking at its own room rentals. See Figure 6.18.

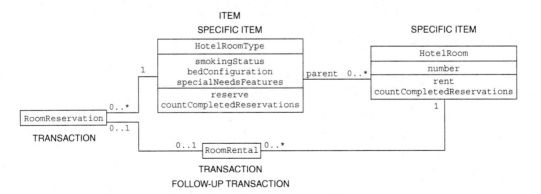

FIGURE 6.18
Services analyzing RoomReservations are not object inherited.

---

13. Notice that distributor line items object inherit the "is effective" service and the distributor collaborator from their parent distributor agreements.

Conduct Business Services

Child objects do not object inherit conduct business services because child objects cannot do work that alters the state of the system beyond their own context, interaction, or variation. This eliminates all parent services that create new objects, alter properties, or change collaborations.

> EXAMPLE—A hotel room type knows how to reserve itself. The reserve service creates a reservation for a customer and is not object inherited by the child hotel rooms. Write accessors for setting the smoking status, bed configuration, and special needs features of a hotel room type are not object inherited by the child hotel rooms. Collaboration services for adding and removing hotel rooms from the hotel room definition are not object inherited by the child hotel rooms. See Figure 6.18.

PRINCIPLE 65
DETERMINE MINE, TOO

A determine mine service of a parent is object inheritable if every child object could be asked the question the determine mine service answers.

PRINCIPLE 66
ANALYZE ONLY WHAT YOU KNOW

An analyze transactions service of a parent is object inheritable if the child object can object inherit the transactions being analyzed.

PRINCIPLE 67
CHILDREN CANNOT CONDUCT BUSINESS

A conduct business service of a parent is never object inheritable because the child cannot alter the parent or the context of the parent.

Overriding Object Inheritance

Properties and collaborations in the parent object frequently serve as defaults child objects can override. This section discusses techniques for selectively overriding object inherited information.

Overriding Properties

To depict a property overridden by a child, duplicate the property in the child. The read accessor for the property checks first for the property value in the child, and returns that value if it is set. Otherwise, the read accessor retrieves the property value from the parent.

> EXAMPLE—An e-commerce site marks down product SKUs that are not selling well because they have unpopular styles or colors out of season. A marked down product has its own price, while a product not marked down uses the price in its parent product description. See Figure 6.19.

Overriding Collaborations

To depict a collaboration overridden by a child object, provide a collaboration line between the child and the collaborator.[14] Business rules decide what it means for an object to override its parent's aggregate collaborators. The child may use its own collaborators instead of its parent's, or the child may use the union of its collaborators and those of its parent's.

Overriding Aggregate Collaborations

Group collaborators classify objects, and many domains allow child objects to classify themselves in different groups than their parent's, business rules permitting. This permits more finely grained classification. In these domains, a child belongs to all groups obtained by the union of its parent's and its own group collaborators. Parts construct their assembly collaborators, and some domains allow both a child and its parent to be parts of different

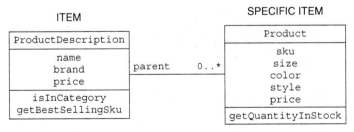

FIGURE 6.19
A Product can override its parent's price.

---

14. When collaboration lines go to both the parent and child, additional notation is required to show that the collaboration is with either the parent or the child, but not both. Our diagrams include the "XOR" notation to indicate a mutually exclusive collaboration, which is to one or the other but not both. See Figure 6.19.

assemblies. Since no object can be in more than one assembly, the child uses its parent's assembly, unless it has its own assembly collaborator. A child cannot use the union of its own and its parent's assembly. Containers are similar to assemblies. A child object that overrides its parent's container uses its own container, not the union of the two.

> EXAMPLE—An e-commerce site has broad product categories for classifying product descriptions describing many product SKUs. Special, narrow categories classify product SKUs based on colors, sizes, styles, etc. A product SKU has two services, one of which is the normal collaboration accessor that returns its product category collaborators and defaults to its parent's. The second service returns all its product categories: the union of its own and its parent's. The product SKU also has a service to check if it is in a particular category. This service also uses the union of the category collaborators. See Figure 6.20.[15]

Transaction Collaborations

With history transactions, the child's collaborations override the parent's. Business rules decide if a union of transactions is appropriate, but typically mixing the child's history with the parent's is not a good idea, especially when

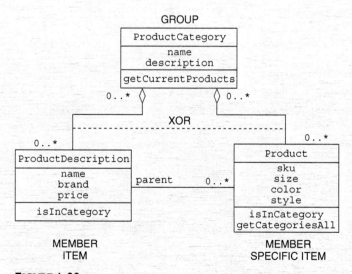

FIGURE 6.20
A ProductCategory contains either ProductDescriptions or Products.

---

15. This is one set of business rules for product categorization. Some businesses mix products and product descriptions into the same product categories. That requires a slightly different model.

the history records property changes. With event `transactions`, business rules more often permit the child to know the union of its parent's and its own event `transactions`. Usually, there are different services to return just the child's event `transactions` or the union's.

EXAMPLE—A product SKU can have its own price history (see Figure 6.21).

EXAMPLE—Some distributors wish to distribute only some product SKUs of a product. A product SKU knows its own distributor agreements, plus the ones object inherited through its parent. See Figure 6.22.

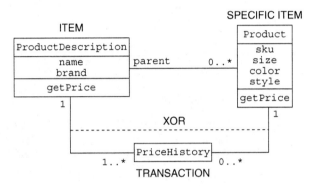

FIGURE 6.21
A Product's PriceHistory overrides its parent's.

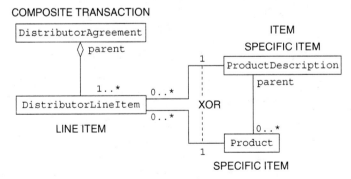

FIGURE 6.22
A Product can belong to its own DistributionAgreements.

Overriding Role and Place Collaborations

Occasionally, a line item has its own role or place collaborators, and uses these instead of the role and place collaborators of its composite transaction. This is often the case when the parent transaction is fulfilled over time.

> EXAMPLE—A delivery at a loading area deposits delivery loads into individual loading bins. Each delivery load knows its loading bin as its place instead of its parent's place. See Figure 6.23.

Switching Contexts vs. Delegating Behavior _____

Object inheritance smells a bit like a design pattern. In fact, in their book, *Design Patterns*, Gamma and his co-authors specify design patterns where one object delegates complex behaviors to an associated object. The design pattern often confused with object inheritance is the "Strategy" pattern, which also involves delegation. Strategy objects receive delegated requests from Context objects[16] (see Figure 6.24). By delegating the work to its Strategy object, a Context object can change how it responds to these requests by swapping in a new Strategy object. This makes the Strategy pattern extremely useful for designing pluggable implementations of a behavior. Typically, a Strategy class is implemented as an abstract class that establishes the interface of the behavior being delegated, and is extended by subclasses that define concrete implementations of that behavior.

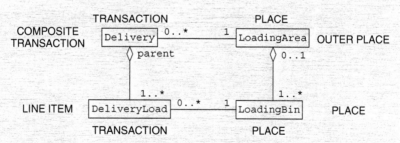

FIGURE 6.23
A DeliveryLoad occurs at its own place.

---

16. See Strategy pattern, pp. 315–323, *Design Patterns*, Erich Gamma, Richard Helm, Ralph Johnson, and John Vlissides, 1995, Addison Wesley Longman, Inc.

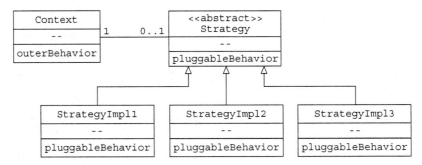

FIGURE 6.24
The Strategy design pattern.

Internal and Functional

Strategy objects are internal and functional. Their sole purpose is to encapsulate behavior for reuse and maintenance; they are stateless objects. A Strategy object comes into play when a service is requested of its "Context object." The Context object then delegates all or part of the request to its internal Strategy object. Since all requests come from its Context object, the interface of the Strategy object derives from the implementation of the Context object.

External with State

Child objects are external and contain state. Their purpose is to represent another view of the parent object; they have their own state appropriate to the realm in which they represent the parent. Once a child object is instantiated, then it is on its own. Since it can receive requests from the outside world, the interface of the child includes many of the parent's behaviors plus additional behaviors specific to its own context.

PRINCIPLE 68
IT'S A CHILD NOT A FUNCTION

> Use internal, stateless Strategy objects to encapsulate pluggable functionality for Context objects. Use external, stateful child objects to model another view of parent objects.

Fundamental Patterns

Patterns About Patterns

This chapter has highlighted deep similarities in three of the collaboration patterns: `actor - role`, `item - specific item`, and `composite transaction - line item`. The objects in these patterns communicate through object inheritance, an interaction mechanism that significantly determines their implementations. Accordingly, strategies for implementing these three collaboration patterns are identical. In fact, all 12 collaboration patterns can be collapsed into three fundamental patterns, and each fundamental pattern has its own implementation strategies. This categorization of the 12 collaboration patterns into the fundamental patterns is shown in "12 Collaboration Patterns," pp. 333-335.

The `generic - specific` pattern depicted in Figure 6.25 summarizes all collaborations that involve multiple views of an object, detailed interactions with an object, or multiple variations in an object. `Generic - specific` patterns are always implemented with object inheritance.

Collaboration patterns described by the `generic - specific` pattern are:

- `actor - role`
- `item - specific item`
- `composite transaction - line item`

The `whole - part` pattern shown in Figure 6.26 summarizes all aggregate collaborations involving entities. It does not cover `composite transaction - line item` because `line items` are not `parts`. `Parts` are independent things with existences and identities distinct from the `whole`. `Line items` cannot exist without the `composite transaction` because they represent a portion of the same event described by the `composite transaction`.

Collaboration patterns described by the `whole - part` pattern are:

- `container - content`
- `assembly - part`
- `group - member`
- `outer place - place`

FIGURE 6.25
The `generic - specific` fundamental pattern.

FIGURE 6.26
The whole - part fundamental pattern.

FIGURE 6.27
The transaction - specific fundamental pattern.

The transaction - specific pattern shown in Figure 6.27 summarizes all collaborations between an object and an event.

Collaboration patterns described by the transaction - specific pattern are:

- transaction - role
- transaction - specific item
- transaction - place
- follow-up transaction - transaction
- line item - specific item

The Big Picture

Expressed in terms of people, places, things, and events, the three fundamental patterns become even more obvious.

Generic - Specific collaborations:

- People, places, or things involved in multiple contexts
- Things existing in many varieties
- Events with multiple interactions involving people, places, or things

Whole - Part collaborations:

- People, places, things, or events put into classifications, assemblies, containers, or geographic locations

Transaction - Specific collaborations:

- People, places, things, or events involved in interactions that need to be remembered

As we will see starting in the next chapter, using the implementation strategies of the three fundamental patterns, we can implement all 12 collaborations with just three coding templates. Pretty cool.

Implementing Collaboration Pairs

7

Don't learn the tricks of the trade. Learn the trade.

Anonymous

Nuts and Bolts

This chapter shows how to translate the collaboration patterns into programming code in the Java and Squeak Smalltalk languages. The next chapter shows how to build on this code to implement business rules. While there are many ways to implement an object model, and many styles for coding objects, this chapter shows the advantages of using a consistent approach. By consistently using collaboration patterns and consistently organizing business rules into property and collaboration rules, it is rather straightforward to construct a coding process for implementing the patterns and rules.

The benefits of using a consistent collaboration-based coding process are:

- Faster code development
- Efficient code reviews
- Sound business rule management

There is no magic bullet for faster code development. In general, coding is difficult and requires much thought and organization; however, occasionally we uncover coding tasks that are repetitive and mechanical, and these lend themselves to a repeatable process. Two such tasks are coding an object definition and setting up collaboration rules. These tasks can be systematized into repetitive processes, thus enabling a developer to quickly lay the infrastructure needed to build the real guts of the system—the business services.

Code reviews are something lots of people will tell you are needed, but few of those people actually do them. If everyone is following a consistent approach for defining objects and setting up collaboration rules, then the code produced can be reviewed methodically and thoroughly by peers familiar with the standard. By having something concrete to compare against the code, the reviews can be more straightforward and less uncomfortable.

Business rules change as markets change and e-businesses evolve. Having a consistent methodology for coding collaboration rules allows us to quickly scan the code to find rules that need updating and locate where new rules should be added. We can then make changes without upsetting the rest of the code base. Additionally, since the rules are organized in a consistent manner, the rules can be extracted into a more flexible, pluggable architecture.

Object Definitions

An "object definition" is the code needed to define the properties, services, and collaborations for a single kind of object in the object model. Object definitions are implemented in non-object-oriented programming languages by mapping the object paradigm onto the languages' constructs. Regardless of how a language supports objects, the "parts" of the object definition are remarkably the same. This consistency means that a standard checklist for defining objects will work within multiple languages.

Defining Objects: DIAPER

The "DIAPER" process is a six-step process for creating an object definition with the minimum infrastructure to support collaboration rules and business services. We devised the mnemonic while teaching Smalltalk to COBOL programmers. The name helped them grasp the object-oriented programming paradigm. We have translated the DIAPER process to C++ and Java and have used it to great effect in our own development efforts. The DIAPER steps are described in Table 7.1, and a summary version is included in Appendix B.

1. DEFINE	*Define the structure of the objects created by this definition:*
Name	Give the class a name
Heritage	Indicate superclass
Protocol	Indicate interfaces exhibited
Properties	Define variables for object model and design properties
Collaborations	Define variables for single and collective collaborations
2. INITIALIZE	*Write code to initialize each newly created object:*
Properties	Set to default or initial values
Collaborations	Create collections for collective collaborations
3. ACCESS	*Write code to access each object's properties:*
Properties	Write get and set accessors
Collaborations	Write get, add, and remove accessors
4. PRINT	*Write code to return a textual description of each object:*
Properties	Describe values of select properties
Collaborations	Ask select collaborators to describe themselves[*]
5. EQUALS	*Write code to test for equality:*
Properties	Compare values from select properties
Collaborations	Compare select collaborators[†]
6. RUN	*Write code to create objects with good values for testing:*
Properties	Generate good values for testing
Collaborations	Use test objects from select collaborator classes

TABLE 7.1
DIAPER Steps for Creating Object Definitions

[*] Principles for selecting which collaborators to print are described later.
[†] Principles for selecting which collaborators to compare are described later.

As discussed earlier, all 12 collaboration patterns can be summarized by three fundamental patterns: (1) generic - specific, (2) whole - part, and (3) transaction - specific. Using the three fundamental patterns along with the DIAPER steps gives us three coding templates capable of imple-

menting all 12 collaboration patterns. The remainder of this chapter presents
the three coding templates.

Generic – Specific Object Definitions _____

This section discusses guidelines for implementing `generic - specific` collaborations. Some of these apply to other fundamental patterns, and some
only apply to `generic - specific` collaboration. Subsequent sections apply
the guidelines to Java and Squeak implementations.

Collaboration patterns described by the `generic - specific` pattern are:

- `actor - role`
- `item - specific item`
- `composite transaction - line item`

Specifying Object Inheritance

Any coding template for the `generic - specific` pattern must accommodate the object inheritance mechanism, which specifies the properties and
services in the `generic` that are accessible from the `specific` object. What
object inheritance really means is that certain determine mine and analyze
transactions services available in the `generic` are also available in the
`specific`.[1] Restating this in implementation terms, object inheritance
requires the `specific`'s object definition to include some of the same services in the `generic`'s object definition. The code is not the same in each
object definition, but services with the same names have the same inputs
and outputs in each object definition. This description of a service in terms
of its name, inputs, and outputs is called a "service signature." A service
that is object inherited has the same service signature in the child object definition as it does in the parent object definition.

> EXAMPLE—A person can play different roles—chair, admin, or member—
> on many different teams, and each person has a name, title, and email.
> Using the collaboration patterns, a person object (`actor`) serves as the par-
> ent to some number of team member objects (`roles`). See Figure 7.1.

> Object inheritance requires that the object definitions for a Person and
> for a TeamMember both contain methods with the following signatures:

---

1. See p. 144, "Object Inheritance and Services."

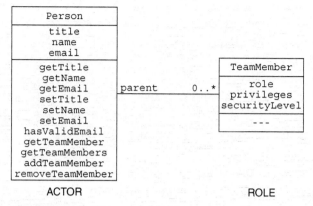

ACTOR   ROLE

FIGURE 7.1

Person – TeamMember object model with Person accessor services showing.

Service Output	Service name	Service Inputs
String	getTitle	—
String	getName	—
String	getEmail	—
boolean	hasValidEmail	—

In the Person object definition, the getTitle service is described in pseudo-code to return a Person object's title property:

```
String getTitle { return my title }
```

In the TeamMember object definition, the getTitle service is described in pseudo-code to return the result of the TeamMember object asking its Person object to get its title.

```
String getTitle { ask my person to return its title }
```

Define: The Parent Profile Interface

While the previous chapter presented strategies for determining which services are object inherited, the Person – TeamMember example highlights the need for a mechanism capable of specifying method signatures for those object inherited services. In object-speak, the construct for specifying expected behavior is an "interface."[2] Technically, an interface is nothing more than a collection of method signatures. Some people understand interfaces, and some people don't so be careful when using them in your analysis object models. When an object definition is associated with an interface, the object

---

2. Also known as "protocols" in some programming circles.

definition must implement a matching method for each method signature in the interface. In object-speak, the object definition *implements* the interface, and its objects *exhibit* the interface.

Object inheritance uses an interface to specify parent behaviors object inherited by its child objects. This interface is called a profile interface because any child exhibiting the interface takes on the appearance of its parent. Both parent and child object definitions implement the profile interface.

> EXAMPLE—In the Person – TeamMember collaboration, the IPersonProfile interface contains all the object inheritable services of Person. The Person and TeamMember object definitions show that they implement the IPersonProfile interface by including it in their service sections.[3] This shorthand implies that all the services in the interface are also included in the Person and TeamMember object definitions. See Figure 7.2.

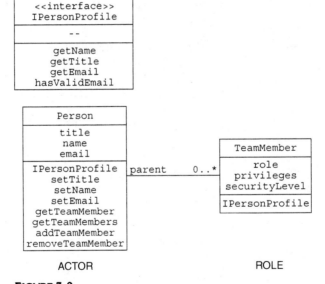

FIGURE 7.2
Both Person and TeamMember implement the IPersonProfile interface.

---

3. We prefer this shorthand notation because it is easy to understand and reduces the number of lines crisscrossing in the model. This shorthand notation was first used in the book *Java Design: Building Better Apps and Applets* (2nd ed.), Peter Coad, Mark Mayfield, 1999, Prentice Hall.

Define: The Conduct Business Interface

Interfaces help achieve object pluggability, which means that different objects can be plugged into the same system component. The profile interface helps object pluggability by allowing a child object to pass itself off as its parent in read-only scenarios. Either a parent or a child object can be plugged into a system component designed to request the services described in the profile interface. In other words, the component is not hardwired to work with only one type of object. Instead, the system component is built to use an interface and can work with any object exhibiting the interface. A system component built to use a profile interface has read-only pluggability.

Read-only pluggability is not enough for frameworks and systems expected to grow over time. These require pluggability in handling collaborations and performing conduct business services. To achieve full object pluggability, all the services of the objects must be described with interfaces.[4] Interfaces that include conduct business services are called conduct business interfaces. Any object exhibiting a conduct business interface can be plugged into a system component built to use that interface. Business rules permitting, such a component can edit the object, change its collaborations, and kick off conduct business services. In object inheritance, the parent's conduct business interface extends its profile interface. For a reference table highlighting the different responsibilities of the profile and conduct business interfaces, see Appendix B.

> EXAMPLE—Define an interface, IPerson, that contains all the conduct business services and the non-profile determine mine and analyze transactions services. The arrow indicates that the IPerson interface extends the IPersonProfile interface and that IPerson enforces all the method signatures enforced by IPersonProfile. See Figure 7.3.

Define: The Child Profile Interface

In many parent – child collaborations, the child object may later become a parent to another kind of object. This is especially common with systems involving many types of `roles` where a `role` serves as the parent to a more specialized `role`. To prepare for this, frameworks and evolving systems make child objects parent-ready by defining two interfaces for them, a profile interface and a conduct business interface. With a profile interface of its

---

4. Do not confuse services with methods. Not all the methods in an object definition are visible in the object model. Services in the object model correspond to the public methods involving business logic.

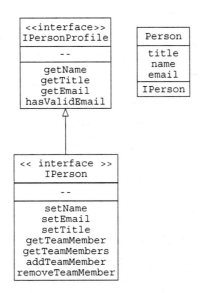

FIGURE 7.3
The Person conduct business interface extends the Person profile interface.

own, the child object definition can support object inheritance of its own properties and services.

EXAMPLE—Define profile and conduct business interfaces for Team-Member (see Figure 7.4). The TeamMember profile interface extends the Person profile interface. If TeamMember ever becomes a parent, the new child profile interface will extend the TeamMember profile interface.

PRINCIPLE 69
SHOWING YOUR PROFILE EVERYWHERE

To implement object inheritance, describe the parent's object inheritable services with a profile interface, and require all child objects to exhibit the profile interface.

PRINCIPLE 70
CONDUCT BUSINESS INTERFACES

A conduct business interface includes all the business services of an object, either directly or by extending the object's profile interface.

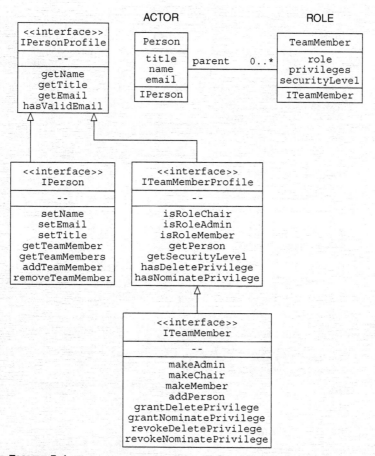

FIGURE 7.4
Profile and conduct business interfaces for TeamMember.

PRINCIPLE 71
HOW I SEE YOU

Collaborators refer to one another using their conduct business interfaces.

PRINCIPLE 72
MAKE THE CHILDREN PARENT-READY

To allow future system growth, define profile interfaces for child objects so they can later become parents.

Initialize: Initialization Rules

Often, a type of object cannot exist without certain data or a certain collaborator. Rules specifying information an object needs to exist are called initialization rules. A `specific` always has an initialization rule requiring a `generic`, because a `specific` cannot be created without a `generic` parent. A `generic` may have an initialization rule for properties it needs to exist.

> EXAMPLE—A person cannot exist without a valid name. A videotape cannot exist without its video title, which is also its parent object.

Initialize: Object Construction

Object construction is the process by which objects are created and initialized. Initialization sets the newly created object's properties to default values or to given values supplied when the object is created. Because objects frequently have many properties, it is impractical to allow given values to be supplied for all the properties when creating a new object. We use object initialization rules to select which properties can be supplied given values during object creation. With this approach, an object construction method can only accept given values for the properties and collaborators mentioned in the initialization rules. This approach cuts down on "constructor explosion," where an object definition has lots of construction methods based on many permutations of the object's properties and collaborators.

PRINCIPLE 73
MINIMUM PARAMETER RULE

Only properties and collaborations necessary for an object to exist should be passed into the object's construction method.

Access: Object Definition Variables

Objects require storage to hold their properties and collaborations, and they get their storage allocations from the variables specified within their object definitions. The decision about whether a property is stored or derived is made either during the design or during the implementation of the object definition. Derived properties will be determined by a method; stored properties will be held in a variable specified in the object definition.

An object definition usually includes references to its collaborators.[5] In the `generic` - `specific` collaboration, how many `specific` collaborators a

---

5. In some implementations, collaborations can be derived from other collaborations.

generic knows can vary, so there are three approaches for referencing specific collaborators of a generic. First, if a generic knows only one specific of a particular type, then it includes a variable to store a reference to
that specific. Second, if a generic knows multiple specifics of the same
type, it can store a homogeneous collection of those. Third, if a generic
knows multiple specifics of different types, it can store a non-homoge-
neous collection of specifics. This book uses the first and second
approaches. While the third approach has merit in its flexibility and extensibility, it requires too much searching to locate an appropriate specific. In
general, the object definition of a generic includes a collection of specifics only if its specifics are all the same type. Otherwise, a generic should
have a distinct variable for each distinct specific type. Define a specific
with a variable to contain its generic.

> EXAMPLE: actor - role—A domain allows a person to take on
> employee, customer, and broker roles. A person can have at most one
> employee role, one active customer role, and any number of broker
> roles. The person object definition includes separate collaboration vari-
> ables for each role type. The employee variable, if set, references a sin-
> gle employee object. The customer variable references a collection of
> customer objects, but only one can be active. The broker variable refer-
> ences a collection of broker objects. Each role includes a collaboration
> variable that references its person object.

> EXAMPLE: item - specific item—A video store with both DVDs and
> videotapes for rent describes each movie with a movie title description.
> A movie title may have several video versions: wide-screen, standard
> format, Spanish subtitles, etc. Each video version is described with its
> own video title, which is a child of the movie title. DVD titles describe
> different DVD versions (see Figure 7.5). The movie title object definition
> has two collaboration variables: one references its collection of video title
> child objects, and the other references a collection of DVD titles. Each
> video title and DVD title includes a collaboration variable that references
> its movie title.

> EXAMPLE: composite transaction - line item—A point-of-sale
> transaction for a retail clothing store includes both sale and return line
> items. The point-of-sale transaction object definition has two collabo-
> ration variables: one references its collection of sale line items objects,
> and the other references a collection of return line items. Each line
> item includes a collaboration variable that references its point-of-sale
> transaction.

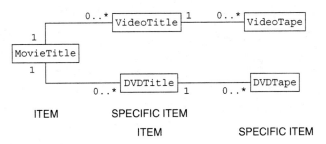

FIGURE 7.5
A MovieTitle with two kinds of child objects.

Access: Collaborator Accessors

Collaborator accessors add, remove, and get collaborators.[6] All `generics` add and remove `specifics` with the following accessors:

add (aSpecific)	Adds designated `specific` to `generic` if collaboration rules allow.
remove (aSpecific)	Removes designated `specific` if collaboration rules allow.

A `generic` with a single `specific` has the following accessor:

get ( )	Returns `specific`, if it exists.

A `generic` with multiple `specifics` has the following accessors: The second one is optional, and used as needed by the domain.

get ( )	Returns collection of `specifics`.
get (criteria)	Returns particular `specific` that satisfies the criteria, if it exists.

A `specific` has the following accessor methods:

add (aGeneric)	Adds designated `generic` to `specific` if collaboration rules allow.
remove (aGeneric)	Removes designated `generic` from `specific` if collaboration rules allow.
get ( )	Returns `generic`.

---

6. See p, 106, "Collaboration Accessor Services."

Print: Describing Objects

Don't confuse printing an object with displaying an object. Print methods are used primarily for debugging and testing. A useful print method returns a description of an object in terms of its properties and collaborators.

The smart technique for printing an object's collaborators is to ask each collaborator to print itself; however, with two-way collaborations, print methods calling other print methods leads to infinite loops. Yikes! Clearly, only one collaborator should be using the print service of the other collaborator, but which one?

Here is a good rule of thumb: Put work in the most specific collaborator. The `specific` has the most knowledge and so putting the work there places it closer to the data. Also, a `generic` may have many kinds of `specifics` and each may require a different implementation of the work.

A `generic` should print its own properties, but should not ask its `specific` to print itself. On the other hand, a `specific` should print its own properties, and ask its `generic` to print itself.

PRINCIPLE 74
MOST SPECIFIC CARRIES THE LOAD

When work requires cooperation between two collaborators, encapsulate the majority of the effort within the most specific collaborator.

Equals: Detecting Duplicate Objects

Frequently, object models have collaboration rules that prohibit duplicate objects. Most systems don't want to add an object to a collection twice, or at least want smart processing to handle it when it happens. The trick is having a way to compare the object being added against the ones already there.

What makes two objects equal depends on collaboration rules and design considerations. Two persons with the same Social Security Number may be considered equal, but two with the same date of birth are not. Business rules and design considerations determine which properties and collaborations come into play when comparing objects for equality.

Good object think dictates that an object can determine for itself if it is equal to another object. Within the equals method, the object doing the work compares its properties and collaborators against those of the other object. Much like the print method, infinite loops in the equals method are a possibility with two-way collaborations. Again, let the `specific` do the work.

When a generic compares itself to another generic, their specifics don't enter into it. However for a specific, the generic holds a significant portion of its state. So when a specific compares itself to another specific, the generics must also be compared.

Run: Test Objects

Test objects are objects populated with realistic property values, and are, when possible, associated with collaborators with realistic data. Test objects do not replace full-fledged test cases and testing harnesses, but they do provide the following:

- Quick tests of the object infrastructure
- Building blocks for growing the system incrementally
- Instructive examples for understanding the object

Test objects live with the code, so they can be used by a developer to test code as it is written and when it is modified. Think unit testing. The point of test objects is to avoid the big-bang-test-at-the-end syndrome, and to allow testing even when test databases are not available.

After unit testing, another value of test objects is that they can be linked together according to the collaboration patterns in the object model. Connecting collaborators together allows testing of the collaboration rules and non-trivial business services.

New people coming on-board an expanding project need to ramp up quickly. Sometimes that means reading other people's code. If that code contains test objects, then they can see examples as they read the code, and can, with little additional effort, write test cases to exercise the code.

Create test objects to illustrate interesting scenarios, to test state changes and border conditions on property values, and to create stereotypical objects for collaborations. Use the "Most Specific Carries the Load" principle (74) to code the test objects. Define a generic test object with realistic property values but without a specific collaborator; define a specific test object with realistic property values and a generic test object collaborator.

Generic – Specific Template

Putting all this together gives a concise coding template for generic – specific collaborations. What follows is an example of that template applied to an actor – role collaboration.

A quick note on terminology: From here on, we will refer to object definitions as *classes*, call the class inheritance generalization class the *superclass*, call the specialization class a *subclass*, and refer to coded services as *methods*.

Generic – Specific Example

For our generic - specific example, we implement the Person – Team-Member object model shown in Figure 7.4. This model is an example of a generic (Person) with many specifics (TeamMembers) of the same type.

Business Rule Violations

Objects resist accepting an illegal property value, violating a collaboration rule, or performing a service while in an invalid state. These actions would violate business rules. How objects handle business rule violations is an important design consideration when translating object models into code. Objects in object models do not have presentation logic, so they cannot beep, flash, or present a dialog box. Rather, if asked to break a business rule, the appropriate response for one of these objects would be to stop processing and raise an exception describing the violation. Other objects within the system can decide how to handle the business exception, by notifying a user, logging it in a report, or notifying some external system.

Java Business Exception Class

This example defines a simple subclass of the Java Exception class to throw messages when illegal values are encountered or business rules are violated (see Listing 7.1).

```
public class BusinessRuleException extends Exception
{
    public BusinessRuleException() { super(); }
    public BusinessRuleException(String message) { super(message);
                     }
}
```

LISTING 7.1
Java class for BusinessRuleException.

Squeak Business Exception Class

In Squeak, business exception classes are subclasses of the Error class hierarchy. No extra methods are necessary as the inherited ones will do everything we need (see Listing 7.2).

```
Error subclass: #BusinessRuleException
    instanceVariableNames: ''
    classVariableNames: ''
    poolDictionaries: ''
    category: 'Nomination-Example'
```

LISTING 7.2
Squeak class for BusinessRuleException.

Person: Java DIAPER

This section uses Java to apply our coding template for implementing a `generic` object definition. The class implemented is the Person modeled in Figure 7.4. Immediately after this section, the same example is presented in Squeak.

Person Initialization Rules

A person has the following initialization rule: A person must have a name to exist.

Define: Person Profile Interface

The `IPersonProfile` interface is implemented by any class that has objects that assume a person profile. In Listing 7.3, both person objects and team member objects exhibit this interface.

```java
public interface IPersonProfile
{
  // ACCESSORS -- get properties
  public String getName();
  public String getTitle();
  public String getEmail();

  // DETERMINE MINE
  public boolean hasValidEmail();
}
```

LISTING 7.3
Java profile interface for Person.

Define: Person Conduct Business Interface

Only the `Person` class implements the `IPerson` interface. It consists of: (1) the methods that change the state of the object by setting properties or adding collaborators, and (2) the collaboration accessors that are not object inherited (see Listing 7.4). The accessors to get the team members are included in the conduct business interface because child objects do not object inherit their parent's other children.[7] Since these methods change the object, they throw business rule exceptions, except the collaboration get accessor.[8] Also, according to the "How I See You" principle (71), collaborators refer to each other through their conduct business interfaces, so the collaboration accessors expect the team member conduct business interface as a parameter.

```
public interface IPerson extends IPersonProfile
{
    // ACCESSORS -- set properties
    public void setName(String newName) throws BusinessRuleException;
    public void setEmail(String newEmail) throws BusinessRuleException;
    public void setTitle(String newTitle) throws BusinessRuleException;

    // ACCESSORS - collaborations
    public List getTeamMembers();
    public void addTeamMember(ITeamMember aTeamMember)
                    throws BusinessRuleException;
    public void removeTeamMember(ITeamMember aTeamMember)
                    throws BusinessRuleException;
}
```

LISTING 7.4
Java conduct business interface for Person.

Define: Person Class

To define the `Person` class, specify the superclass and interfaces implemented, and define the property and collaboration variables (see Listing 7.5). A Java collection object, `ArrayList`, is used to contain the person's team members. To represent the person's email address, we defined our own utility class, `EmailAddress`, with rules for validating email addresses.[9]

---

7. See p. 143, "Child Object Collaborations."
8. It is a matter of preference whether "get" collaborator accessors should also throw business rule exceptions. Since a person can exist without team members, one can argue it is not a business rule exception not to have any. Others argue an exceptional condition arises when a person is asked for team members but does not have any.
9. The `EmailAddress` class is listed on the CD.

```
public class Person extends Object implements IPerson
{
  // DEFINE
  private String name;
  private String title;
  private EmailAddress email;
  private ArrayList teamMembers;
}
```

LISTING 7.5
Java class specification for Person.

Initialize: Person Constructor

Initialization occurs when an object is created and sets the object's properties to default or given values.[10] Following the "Minimum Parameter Rule" principle (73), we use the person initialization rules to determine the information necessary to create a person object. Because these rules state that a person object cannot exist without a name, two facts become clear: (1) all constructors require a name parameter, and (2) every constructor must validate the name. Consequently, there is no default constructor for the class, and every constructor must be capable of throwing a business rule exception.

The Person class has one constructor that takes a name value and throws a business rule exception if the name is invalid (see Listing 7.6). The accessor method for setting the name is used to check the validity of the name, and this method throws the business rule exception if the name is bad. Business rule checking is not necessary for the other properties since the object is setting the property values itself. The email property is set to an "empty" email address.

```
public Person(String newName) throws BusinessRuleException
{
  this.setName(newName);
  this.title = new String();
  this.email = new EmailAddress();
  this.teamMembers = new ArrayList();
}
```

LISTING 7.6
Java constructor for Person.

---

10. Because our constructors invoke methods that check business rules and modify state, we prefer to localize all the property and collaboration initializations in the constructors.

Accessing: Properties

Property accessors are public methods that get and set property values. The set accessors validate the new values and throw business rule exceptions when an illegal value is supplied. A person has accessors for its name, title, and email properties (see Listing 7.7). To the outside world, the email address is a string, thus the get accessor returns a string and the set accessor takes a string. Internally, the string is placed within an email address object that raises an exception if the string is not a valid email address. A special "remove" accessor sets the email address back to its "empty" value.

```java
// ACCESSORS - get properties

public String getName()
{
  return this.name;
}

public String getTitle()
{
  return this.title;
}

public String getEmail()
{
  return this.email.getAddress();
}

// ACCESSORS - set properties

public void setName(String newName) throws BusinessRuleException
{
  if ((newName == null) || (newName.length() == 0))
    throw new BusinessRuleException("Name cannot be null or empty.");
  this.name = newName;
}

public void setTitle(String newTitle) throws BusinessRuleException
{
  if (newTitle == null)
    throw new BusinessRuleException("Title cannot be null.");
  this.title = newTitle;
}
```

(continued)

LISTING 7.7
Java property accessors for Person.

```
public void setEmail(String newEmail) throws BusinessRuleException
{
  this.email.setAddress(newEmail);
}

public void removeEmail( ) throws BusinessRuleException
{
  this.email.setAddressEmpty();
}
```

LISTING 7.7
Jave property accessors for Person. (continued)

Accessing: Collaborations

Collaboration accessors add, remove, and get collaborators. A person has collaboration accessors for its team member collaborators (see Listing 7.8). Collaboration rules are not being checked here; those checks will be added in the next chapter. However, this code does check the logic validation rules. For example, the add accessor throws an exception if there is an attempt to add a null team member object because that is a sneaky way of getting around the remove method. Objects don't like sneaky code.

Similarly, the `getTeamMembers` method returns the team member objects in a list that cannot be modified.[11] Returning an "unmodifiable" list prevents attempts to add or remove team members without using the accessor methods and checking the collaboration rules. For subclasses that may legitimately need the ability to add and remove from the list, a protected accessor returns a list iterator on the array list. Using a list iterator gives subclasses edit abilities, but not the ability to reset the variable.

Finally, for maximum flexibility, the parameters and return values are typed using interfaces rather than hardwiring them to be a particular class.

Print

Following normal Java coding standards, an object prints its properties and collaborations in its `toString` method. Under the "Most Specific Carries the Load" principle (74), the person object, which is a `generic`, does not print its team member collaborator, which is a `specific` (see Listing 7.9).

---

11. The method for returning an "unmodifiable" list belongs to the `Collections` class, which is part of the new collections framework added in JDK2.

```
// ACCESSORS - collaborations

public List getTeamMembers()
{
  return Collections.unmodifiableList(this.teamMembers);
}

protected ListIterator getTeamMemberList()
{
  return this.teamMembers.listIterator();
}

public void addTeamMember(ITeamMember aTeamMember)
throws BusinessRuleException
{
  if (aTeamMember == null)
    throw new BusinessRuleException("Cannot add null team member.");
  this.teamMembers.add(aTeamMember);
}

public void removeTeamMember(ITeamMember aTeamMember)
throws BusinessRuleException
{
  if (aTeamMember == null)
    throw new BusinessRuleException("Cannot remove null team member.");
  this.teamMembers.remove(aTeamMember);
}
```

LISTING 7.8
Java collaboration accessors for Person.

```
// PRINT

public String toString()
{
  StringBuffer buffy = new StringBuffer(60);
  buffy.append("Person: ");
  buffy.append("\nName: " + this.name);
  buffy.append("\nTitle: " + this.title);
  buffy.append("\nEmail: " + this.email);
  return buffy.toString();
}
```

LISTING 7.9
Java method for printing Person.

Equals

Again, following normal Java coding standards, an object checks if it is equal to another object in its `equals` method, which takes a parameter of type `Object`. Under the "Most Specific Carries the Load" principle (74), the person, as a `generic`, does not compare its team member collaborator to that of the other person. See Listing 7.10.

```
// EQUALS

public boolean equals(Object anObject)
{
  if (anObject instanceof Person)
  {
    Person other = (Person)anObject;
    if (!this.name.equals(other.name)) return false;
    if (!this.email.equals(other.email)) return false;
    if (!this.title.equals(other.title)) return false;
    return true;
  }
  return false; // not instance of Person
}
```

LISTING 7.10
Java method for checking for equal Persons.

Run: Test Objects

Run services create objects in the class, pre-loaded with data for testing business services and collaboration rules. We implement services that create objects in the class as static methods (see Listing 7.11).

```
// RUN

public static Person testPerson() throws BusinessRuleException
{
  Person aPerson = new Person("Alfred E. Neuman");
  aPerson.setEmail("al@neuman.com");
  aPerson.setTitle("President");
  return aPerson;
}
```

LISTING 7.11
Java test object for Person.

Run: Test Case

Once the DIAPER process is complete, a simple test case (see Listing 7.12) ensures the test object works, and exercises some of the accessors with business rules.[12] Code that asks an object to perform a service that can potentially throw an exception must be wrapped in try - catch blocks to handle the exceptions.

```
class TestCase
{
  public static void main(String args[])
  {
    Person aPerson = null;

    /** Try to create Person test object.
      * If fail print business rule exception message.
      * If pass print person test object.
    */
    try { aPerson = Person.testPerson(); }
    catch (BusinessRuleException ex)
    {
      System.out.println("BOOM: " + ex.getMessage());
    }
    System.out.println("\n" + aPerson);

    System.out.println("\nPress ENTER to exit");
    try { System.in.read(); }
    catch (java.io.IOException e) { return; }
  } // end main
} // end class TestCase
```

LISTING 7.12
Java code to run test object.

---

12. Although outside the scope of this book, JUnit may ease the writing of unit tests. See
    www.junit.org.

Person: Squeak DIAPER

This example was implemented in Squeak 3.0.

Define: Person Class

To define the Person class, specify the superclass and the property and collaboration variables. Using the Model dependency mechanism, all our problem domain classes are subclasses of Model (see Listing 7.13).

```
Model subclass: #Person
    instanceVariableNames: 'name title email teamMembers '
    classVariableNames: ''
    poolDictionaries: ''
    category: 'Collaboration-Examples'
```

LISTING 7.13
Squeak class definition for Person.

Initialize: Person New Methods

Similar to Java constructors, Squeak has class methods for creating objects. These methods must be made to respect the business rule that a person object cannot exist without a name; here is how: (1) override the default object creation method, new, to throw an exception and prevent a person from being created without a valid name; and (2) write a newWith: method for creating a person with a name (see Listing 7.14). In the newWith: method, the inherited new method is invoked to create an uninitialized person object, and the newly created object is asked to initialize itself. As with the Java constructors, the set accessor for the name property throws a business rule exception if the proposed name is bad.

Here is a quick note on our parameter naming conventions: Since Squeak does type checking only at run-time, method arguments should be named to

```
Person class methodsFor: 'instance creation'

new
    BusinessRuleException signal: 'Cannot create person without a name.'

newWith: aNameString
    | aPerson |
    aPerson ← super new initialize.
    aPerson name: aNameString.
    ↑aPerson
```

LISTING 7.14
Squeak methods for creating Persons.

indicate the kind of object expected.[13] When an argument is to be used for a particular purpose, such as representing a person's name or address, then include the purpose in the argument name, too.

Following this convention, property accessors have two-part arguments:

- The first part indicates what the argument represents ("aName").
- The second part indicates the object type ("String").

Initialize: Initialize Method

The initialize method sets a person's properties to default values, which in this case, are empty strings, and sets the collaboration variable to an empty ordered collection (see Listing 7.15). Usually an object only initializes itself once, when it is created.

Person methodsFor: 'initialize-release'

initialize
    name ← String new.
    title ← String new.
    email ← String new.
    teamMembers ← OrderedCollection new

LISTING 7.15
Squeak method for initializing a Person.

Accessing: Properties

Using the Model dependency mechanism, each set accessor sends a change notification when the property value changes. For validating email addresses, the email set accessor uses the Squeak library class, MailAddress-Parser (see Listing 7.16).

Accessing: Collaborations

Collaboration accessors are placed into their own message category to distinguish them from property accessors. As with the Java implementation, these accessors are not yet checking the collaboration rules. See Listing 7.17.

Collaboration accessors follow the same argument naming conventions as property accessors; however, with collaboration accessors, the argument's type is usually the same as what it represents. For example, a person's team member collaborator is an object of type TeamMember. So, the argument for a collaboration accessor is named after the type of the collaborator ("aTeamMember").

---

13. Java does type checking at both compile-time and run-time.

Person methodsFor: 'accessing'

email
 ↑email

email: anEmailAddressString
 | aTrimmedEmailAddressString |
 [MailAddressParser addressesIn:
   (aTrimmedEmailAddressString ← anEmailAddressString withBlanksTrimmed)]
   on: Error do: [:ex | BusinessRuleException signal: 'Bad email address.'].
 email ← aTrimmedEmailAddressString.
 self changed: #email

name
 ↑name

name: aNameString
 | aTrimmedNameString |
 (aNameString isNil or:
   [(aTrimmedNameString ← aNameString withBlanksTrimmed) isEmpty])
  ifTrue: [BusinessRuleException signal: 'Person name cannot be nil or empty.'].
 name ← aTrimmedNameString.
 self changed: #name

title
 ↑title

title: aTitleString
 aTitleString ifNil: [BusinessRuleException signal: 'Person cannot have nil title.'].
 title ← aTitleString withBlanksTrimmed.
 self changed: #title

LISTING 7.16
Squeak property accessors for Person.

Person methodsFor: 'collaboration-accessing'

teamMembers
 ↑teamMembers

addTeamMember: aTeamMember
 aTeamMember
  ifNil: [BusinessRuleException signal: 'Tried to add nil team member.'].
 self teamMembers add: aTeamMember.
 self changed: #teamMembers

removeTeamMember: aTeamMember
 aTeamMember
  ifNil: [BusinessRuleException signal: 'Tried to remove nil team member.'].
 self teamMembers remove: aTeamMember ifAbsent: [ ].
 self changed: #teamMembers

LISTING 7.17
Squeak collaboration accessors for Person.

Print

Following normal Squeak coding standards, an object prints its properties and collaborations in its printOn: method. Under the "Most Specific Carries the Load" principle (74), the person object, which is a generic, does not print its team member collaborator, which is a specific. See Listing 7.18.

Person methodsFor: 'printing'

```
printOn: aStream
    aStream nextPutAll: 'Person:'.
    aStream cr; nextPutAll: self name.
    aStream cr; nextPutAll: self title.
    aStream cr; nextPutAll: self email
```

LISTING 7.18
Squeak method for printing Person.

Equals

Squeak allows the = operator to be overridden in any class (see Listing 7.19). This operator enables an object to check if it is equal to another. Under the "Most Specific Carries the Load" principle (74), the person, as a generic, does not compare its team member collaborator to that of the other person.

Person methodsFor: 'comparing'

```
= anObject
    self species = anObject species ifFalse: [↑false].
    self name = anObject name ifFalse: [↑false].
    self title = anObject title ifFalse: [↑false].
    self email = anObject email ifFalse: [↑false].
    ↑true
```

LISTING 7.19
Squeak method for checking for equal Persons.

Run: Test Objects

Many Squeak library classes have examples that create sample objects to assist with learning about the class. In a similar vein, the examples message category contains one or more class methods for building person objects preloaded with data. See Listing 7.20.

Run: Inspect It

Squeak has such an interactive environment, programmers often unit test by inspecting the test object and sending it messages from the inspector.

Person class methodsFor: 'examples'

testPerson
    "Person testPerson"
    | aPerson |
    aPerson ← Person newWith: 'Alfred E. Neuman'.
    aPerson email: 'al@neuman.com'.
    aPerson title: 'President'.
    ↑aPerson

LISTING 7.20
Squeak test object for Person.

Team Member: Java & Squeak DIAPER _____

This section applies our coding template for implementing a `specific` object definition. The class implemented is `TeamMember`, which is modeled in Figure 7.4, and both the Java and Squeak code are shown in this section.

Team Member Initialization Rules

A team member has the following initialization rules:

- A team member must have a person to exist.
- A team member has its initial security level set to "low."
- A team member has its initial role set to "member."

Define: Profile Interface

To specify object inheritance between a team member and its person, the team member profile interface extends the person profile interface. The team member profile interface also describes the get accessors and determine mine services of team members. The implementation of this interface in Java is shown in Listing 7.21.

In part, because Squeak is a late-binding language that does not do compile-time type checking, there is no Squeak equivalent to the Java interface. A Squeak object exhibits its interface at run-time; it either understands a message or it doesn't.

Define: Conduct Business Interface

The team member conduct business interface extends the team member profile interface and includes the set accessors and conduct business services particular to team members. Because a team member's privileges are cou-

```java
public interface ITeamMemberProfile extends IPersonProfile
{
  // ACCESSORS -- get properties
  public SecurityLevel getSecurityLevel();

  // ACCESSORS - get property values
  public boolean isRoleAdmin();
  public boolean isRoleChair();
  public boolean isRoleMember();

  // ACCESSORS -- get collaborators
  public IPerson getPerson();

  // DETERMINE MINE
  public boolean hasNominatePrivilege();
  public boolean hasDeletePrivilege();
}
```

LISTING 7.21
Java profile interface for TeamMember.

pled to the value of its role property, special conduct business services—makeAdmin, makeMember, and makeChair—set both properties together. Set accessors for the role property exist, but are not included in the conduct business interface because using them alone could put a team member in an invalid state. The Java code for this interface follows in Listing 7.22.

Again, there is no Squeak equivalent. From this point forward, we will assume the reader knows that interfaces are not used in Squeak, and therefore only the Java code for them will be presented.

Define: TeamMember Class

The TeamMember class has instance variables for its properties and its person collaborator. Both the Java and Squeak code implement a utility class, SecurityLevel, to represent the security levels for team members. Later, we will see that a document also has a security level, and it plays a part in the collaboration rules that govern the document's nomination process. Since SecurityLevel must be reused among several different domain classes, it is a standalone class and not implemented as an inner class. The complete code for this class is on the CD available with this book.

In Java, the TeamMember class implements the team member conduct business interface (see Listing 7.23). The role property is implemented using an inner class, TeamRole, whose objects have an integer code to efficiently represent, compare, and store the different role values and a string to cleanly

```java
public interface ITeamMember extends ITeamMemberProfile
{
  // ACCESSORS -- add collaborators
  public void addPerson(IPerson aPerson) throws
                  BusinessRuleException;

  // CONDUCT BUSINESS
  public void makeAdmin() throws BusinessRuleException;
  public void makeChair() throws BusinessRuleException;
  public void makeMember() throws BusinessRuleException;
  public void grantNominatePrivilege() throws BusinessRuleException;
  public void grantDeletePrivilege() throws BusinessRuleException;
  public void revokeNominatePrivilege() throws BusinessRuleException;
  public void revokeDeletePrivilege() throws BusinessRuleException;
}
```

LISTING 7.22

Java conduct business interface for TeamMember.

```java
public class TeamMember extends Object implements ITeamMember
{
  // DEFINE
  private IPerson person;
  private byte privileges;
  private TeamRole role;
  private SecurityLevel securityLevel;
}
```

LISTING 7.23

Java class specification for TeamMember.

print and display the role value[14] (see Listing 7.24). Three team role objects, representing the admin, chair, and member role values, are created and stored in static variables within the TeamMember class.[15] These are used in the property value accessors defined later.[16]

In Squeak, TeamMember goes into the same class category as Person (see Listing 7.25). The role property is implemented using Squeak association objects. Each association has a symbol key to efficiently represent, compare, and store the different role values and a string to cleanly print and display the role value. Values for the role property are returned by methods in the constants message category (see Listing 7.26).

---

14. This is an implementation pattern for creating enumerated types. For more on this pattern, see p. 231, "Descriptive and Time Property Business Rules."
15. See the code listing on the CD.
16. See Listing 7.31.

```
private static class TeamRole
{
  private int code;
  private String role;

  TeamRole(int roleCode, String roleString)
  {
    this.code = roleCode;
    this.role = roleString;
  }
  public int getCode() { return this.code; }
  public String toString(){ return this.role; }
  public boolean equals(Object anObject)
  {
    if (anObject instanceof TeamRole)
    return (this.code == ((TeamRole)anObject).getCode());
    else return false;
  }
}
```

LISTING 7.24
Java inner class definition for TeamRole.

```
Model subclass: #TeamMember
   instanceVariableNames: 'person team privileges role securityLevel '
   classVariableNames: ''
   poolDictionaries: ''
   category: 'Collaboration-Examples'
```

LISTING 7.25
Squeak class definition for TeamMember.

TeamMember methodsFor: 'constants'

roleAdmin
   ↑Association key: #admin value: 'Admin'

roleChair
   ↑Association key: #chair value: 'Chair'

roleMember
   ↑Association key: #member value: 'Member'

LISTING 7.26
Squeak constants for TeamMember role.

Initialize: TeamMember

Applying the initialization rules and the "Minimum Parameter" principle (73), `TeamMember` requires one constructor in Java and one class new method in Squeak; each takes only a single parameter. The following Java and Squeak methods initialize the new object's properties before making the collaboration. Often, collaboration rules check property values, and if the properties are not yet initialized, then errors can occur.

PRINCIPLE 75
PROPERTIES BEFORE COLLABORATORS

Object construction methods initialize properties before establishing collaborations because collaboration rules may check property values.

The default constructor is not implemented in the Java version because the person collaboration is required for the parent – child relationship. The collaboration accessor for adding a person can throw a business rule exception; therefore, the constructor is declared to throw an exception. See Listing 7.27.

```
public TeamMember(IPerson aPerson) throws BusinessRuleException
{
   this.makeMember();
   this.securityLevel = new SecurityLevel();
   this.addPerson(aPerson);
}
```

LISTING 7.27
Java constructor for TeamMember.

The Squeak version's default new method is overridden to throw an exception, and a newWith: method requiring a person object provides the only means for creating team member objects (see Listing 7.28).

Accessing: Properties

To support object inheritance `TeamMember` has get accessors for three of its person's properties: name, title, and email. Notice there are no set accessors for these properties. Also, the security level cannot be set. Instead, the security level has its own accessors for changing its level.

In Java, the accessors for object inherited properties return the same types as similarly named accessors in the `Person` class. See Listing 7.29.

TeamMember class methodsFor: 'instance creation'

new
    BusinessRuleException signal: 'Cannot create team member without a person.'

newWith: aPerson
    | aTeamMember |
    aTeamMember ← super new initialize.
    aTeamMember addPerson: aPerson.
    ↑aTeamMember

TeamMember methodsFor: 'initialize-release'

initialize
    person ← nil.
    self makeMember.
    securityLevel ← SecurityLevel new

LISTING 7.28
Squeak methods for creating and initializing TeamMembers.

```java
// ACCESSORS -- get properties


public SecurityLevel getSecurityLevel()
{
  return this.securityLevel;
}


// ACCESSORS -- get inherited properties

public String getName()
{
  return this.person.getName();
}


public String getTitle()
{
  return this.person.getTitle();
}


public String getEmail()
{
  return this.person.getEmail();
}
```

LISTING 7.29
Java property accessors for TeamMember.

The Squeak implementations of the accessors for the inherited properties go in the same message category as the team member accessors to emphasis the transparency of these properties (see Listing 7.30).

TeamMember methodsFor: 'accessing'

securityLevel
   ↑securityLevel

privileges
   ↑privileges

role
   ↑role

title
   ↑self person title

email
   ↑self person email

name
   ↑self person name

LISTING 7.30
Squeak property accessors for TeamMember.

Accessing: Property Values

Instead of simple accessors for the role and privileges properties, `TeamMember` has special get and set accessor services to protect values of these properties and encapsulate their implementations. The special get accessors check the properties for particular values, and the special set accessors assign the properties particular values. In both cases, the name of the particular value is encoded in the accessor name.

The naming convention supports the evolution of these properties into full-blown role history objects.[17] If that should happen, then all the methods with "role" in their name would be delegated to services in the role history object.[18]

Also shown here are the conduct business services that ensure that the proper privileges are assigned when the role property is set. Putting that code in the role set property value accessor would be doing too much work. For example, having the `setRoleAdmin` accessor also changing privileges would be creating a side-effect in addition to setting a property, and pro-

---

17. See p. 122, "Role History."
18. This naming convention is known as the "Jarzombek Princple" in honor of its author, Chris Jarzombek, a literary man with exceptional object-think skills.

gramming by side-effects has bad karma. To discourage use of the role property value set accessors, such as `setRoleAdmin`, we prefix them differently
to distinguish them. Our convention for accessors that bypass business rules
is to prefix them with "doSet." Similarly, get accessors that return raw data
values, such `getPrivileges`, are prefixed with "doGet." For more on why
we have these `doSet` methods and why they are public, see in the following
chapter, "Methods for Enforcing Property Rules."

In the Java code, static variables (shown in all capital letters) contain the possible values for the role and privileges properties[19] (see Listing 7.31).

```
// ACCESSORS - test for property values
public boolean isRoleAdmin()
{
  return this.role.equals(ROLE_ADMIN);
}

public boolean isRoleChair()
{
  return this.role.equals(ROLE_CHAIR);
}

public boolean isRoleMember()
{
  return this.role.equals(ROLE_MEMBER);
}

public boolean hasNominatePrivilege()
{
  return (this.privileges & PRIVILEGES_NOMINATE_MASK) > 0;
}

public boolean hasDeletePrivilege()
{
  return (this.privileges & PRIVILEGES_DELETE_MASK) > 0;
}
// ACCESSORS - set properties to special values
public void doSetRoleAdmin()
{
  this.role = ROLE_ADMIN;
}
```
                                                    (continued)

LISTING 7.31
Java property value accessors for TeamMember.

_____

19. See the code listing on the CD available with this book.

```java
public void doSetRoleChair()
{
  this.role = ROLE_CHAIR;
}
public void doSetRoleMember()
{
  this.role = ROLE_MEMBER;
}

// CONDUCT BUSINESS

public void makeMember() throws BusinessRuleException
{
  this.doSetRoleMember();
  this.privileges = PRIVILEGES_DEFAULT_MASK;
}

public void makeAdmin() throws BusinessRuleException
{
  this.doSetRoleAdmin();
  this.grantNominatePrivilege();
  this.revokeDeletePrivilege();
}

public void makeChair() throws BusinessRuleException
{
  this.doSetRoleChair();
  this.grantNominatePrivilege();
  this.grantDeletePrivilege();
}

public void grantNominatePrivilege()
{
  this.privileges |= PRIVILEGES_NOMINATE_MASK;
}

public void grantDeletePrivilege()
{
  this.privileges |= PRIVILEGES_DELETE_MASK;
}

public void revokeNominatePrivilege()
{
  if (this.hasNominatePrivilege())
      this.privileges ^= PRIVILEGES_NOMINATE_MASK;
}
```

(continued)

LISTING 7.31

Java property value accessors for TeamMember. (continued)

```
public void revokeDeletePrivilege()
{
  if (this.hasNominatePrivilege())
      this.privileges ^= PRIVILEGES_DELETE_MASK;
}
```

LISTING 7.31
Java property value accessors for TeamMember.

In the Squeak code, additional instance methods that are not shown here return the possible values for the role and privileges properties[20] (see Listing 7.32).

TeamMember methodsFor: 'accessing'

isRoleAdmin
   ↑ self doGetRole = self roleAdmin

isRoleChair
   ↑ self doGetRole = self roleChair

isRoleMember
   ↑self doGetRole = self roleMember

TeamMember methodsFor: 'testing'

hasDeletePrivilege
   ↑self getPrivileges anyMask: self privilegeDeleteMask

hasNominatePrivilege
   ↑self getPrivileges anyMask: self privilegeNominateMask

TeamMember methodsFor: 'domain services'

makeAdmin
   self doSetRoleAdmin.
   self grantNominatePrivilege.
   self revokeDeletePrivilege

makeChair
   self doSetRoleChair.
   self grantNominatePrivilege.
   self grantDeletePrivilege

makeMember
   self doSetRoleMember.
   self doSetPrivileges: self privilegeDefaultMask

(continued)

LISTING 7.32
Squeak property value accessors for TeamMember.

---

20. See the code listings on the CD available with this book.

grantDeletePrivilege
    self doSetPrivileges: (self doGetPrivileges bitOr: self privilegeDeleteMask)

grantNominatePrivilege
    self doSetPrivileges: (self doGetPrivileges bitOr: self privilegeNominateMask)

revokeDeletePrivilege
    self hasDeletePrivilege
    ifTrue: [self doSetPrivileges: (self doGetPrivileges bitXor: self privilegeDeleteMask)]

revokeNominatePrivilege
    self hasNominatePrivilege
    ifTrue: [self doSetPrivileges: (self doGetPrivileges bitXor: self privilegeNominateMask)]

TeamMember methodsFor: 'private'

doSetRoleAdmin
    role ← self roleAdmin.
    self changed: #role

doSetRoleChair
    role ← self roleChair.
    self changed: #role

doSetRoleMember
    role ←self roleMember.
    self changed: #role

doSetPrivileges: bits
    privileges ← bits.
    self changed: #privileges

LISTING 7.32
Squeak property value accessors for TeamMember.

Accessing: Collaborations

Since a child cannot exist without its parent object, only the get and set accessors are written for the person collaborator. In Listings 7.33 and 7.34 the code is not checking collaboration rules. Can a team member change its person? No, but we will enforce that along with other business rules when we implement them in the next chapter.

Print

Using the "Most Specific Carries the Load" principle (74), a team member has the responsibility of printing its properties and asking its generic collaborations to print it (see Listings 7.35 and 7.36).

```
// ACCESSORS - collaborators

public IPerson getPerson()
{
  return this.person;
}


public void addPerson(IPerson aPerson) throws BusinessRuleException
{
  if (aPerson == null)
    throw new BusinessRuleException("Tried to add null person");
  this.person = aPerson;
}
```

LISTING 7.33
Java collaboration accessors for TeamMember.

> *TeamMember methodsFor: 'collaboration-accessing'*
>
> **person**
>   ↑person
>
> **addPerson: aPerson**
>   aPerson
>   ifNil: [BusinessRuleException signal: 'Tried to add nil person.'].
>   person ← aPerson.
>   self changed: #person

LISTING 7.34
Squeak collaboration accessors for TeamMember.

```
// PRINT

public String toString()
{
  StringBuffer buffy = new StringBuffer(60);
  buffy.append("Team Member: ");
  buffy.append("\nRole: " + this.role);
  buffy.append("\n" + this.securityLevel);
  buffy.append(this.person.toString());
  return buffy.toString();
}
```

LISTING 7.35
Java method for printing a team member.

TeamMember methodsFor: 'printing'

printOn: aStream
    aStream nextPutAll: 'TeamMember:'.
    aStream cr; nextPutAll: self doGetRole value.
    self securityLevel printOn: aStream cr.
    self person printOn: aStream cr.
    self team printOn: aStream cr

LISTING 7.36
Squeak method for printing a team member.

Equals

Using the "Most Specific Carries the Load" principle (74), a `specific` team member has the responsibility of checking equality for itself and asking its `generic` collaborator, person, to check itself (see Listings 7.37 and 7.38).

```
// EQUALS

public boolean equals(Object anObject)
{
   if (anObject instanceof TeamMember)
     {
       TeamMember other = (TeamMember)anObject;
       if (!this.role.equals(other.role)) return false;
       if (this.person == null && (other.person != null)) return false;
       if (this.person != null && (!this.person.equals(other.person)))
          return false;
     return true;
     }
   else return false; // not instance of TeamMember
}
```

LISTING 7.37
Java method for checking for equal TeamMembers.

TeamMember methodsFor: 'comparing'

= anObject
    self species = anObject species ifFalse: [↑ false].
    self doGetRole = anObject doGetRole ifFalse: [↑ false].
    self person = anObject person ifFalse: [↑ false].
    ↑ true

LISTING 7.38
Squeak method for checking for equal TeamMembers.

Run: Test Objects

Specific test objects require generic test objects. TeamMember test objects use Person test objects. The following TeamMember test objects are created:

- A team member with chair role status and a high security level
- A team member with admin role status and default (low) security level
- A team member with member role status, default security, and no nominate privileges
- A team member with member role status, nominate privileges, and secret security level

Code for only one test object is shown in Listings 7.39 and 7.40. See the CD for the others.

```
// RUN

public static TeamMember testChair() throws BusinessRuleException
{
  TeamMember aTeamMember = new TeamMember(Person.testPerson());
  aTeamMember.makeChair();
  SecurityLevel sLevel = aTeamMember.getSecurityLevel();
  sLevel.setLevelHigh();
  return aTeamMember;
}
```

LISTING 7.39
Java test object for TeamMember.

TeamMember class methodsFor: 'examples'

testChair
    "TeamMember testChair"
    | aTeamMember |
    aTeamMember ←self newWith: Person testPerson and: Team testTeam.
    aTeamMember makeChair.
    aTeamMember securityLevel setLevelHigh.
    ↑ aTeamMember

LISTING 7.40
Squeak test object for TeamMember.

Whole – Part Object Definitions _____

Collaboration patterns described by the `whole - part` pattern are:

- `container - content`
- `assembly - part`
- `group - member`
- `outer place - place`

Building `whole - part` collaborations is very similar to building `generic - specific` collaborations if the `whole` is considered like the `generic` and the `part` is considered like the `specific`. In fact, coding the `whole - part` requires only these few modifications to the `generic - specific` DIAPER:

- Profile interfaces are unnecessary.
- The `whole` always allows for multiple `parts`.
- A `part` may have multiple `wholes` (e.g., `group - member` collaborations).
- A `part` may exist without a `whole`.

Putting the work in the `specific` was a major determinant in coding `generic - specific` collaborations. Applying that same principle when coding `whole - part` collaborations impacts these steps in the DIAPER:

- Printing — A `part` asks its `whole` to print itself.
- Comparing — A `part` asks its `whole` to compare itself.
- Testing — A `part` test object uses a `whole` test object.

PRINCIPLE 76
PART CARRIES THE LOAD

When work requires cooperation between a `whole` collaborator and a `part` collaborator, encapsulate the majority of the effort within the `part` collaborator.

Unlike the `generic - specific` collaborations, profile interfaces are unnecessary in `whole - part` collaborations because `whole - part` does not use object inheritance. Conduct business interfaces are still recommended when flexibility and extensibility are desired.

Whole – Part Example

This example continues the implementation of the domain we started in the previous section. Here we are implementing the `group - member` collaboration.

> EXAMPLE—A team member belongs to exactly one team. Each team has a description and format, which can be one of the following: no chair, single chair, or multiple chairs (see Figure 7.6). The team's format defines the following collaboration rule: A team member cannot be added to a team if the team member has a chair role and the team's format cannot support a chair being added to the team.

In the Team – TeamMember object model, the team member object is playing the `specific` in a `generic - specific` collaboration and it is playing the `part` in a `whole - part` collaboration.

Team: Java & Squeak DIAPER

In terms of implementation, the interesting aspects of the `Team` class are the format property and the collection of team member collaborators.

The format property is implemented like the role property of the `TeamMember` class, by encapsulating its representation inside the class, and providing special property value accessors. The team member collaboration is implemented similarly. The object definition has an instance variable for a collection object

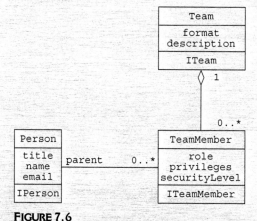

FIGURE 7.6
Team – TeamMember object model.

and accessors for adding and removing team members. A get accessor returns a view on the collection, and a special get accessor returns a single team member for a person, assuming the person is on the team.

Define: Conduct Business Interface

Determine mine services are included in this conduct business interface because no profile interface is implemented. See Listing 7.41.

```java
public interface ITeam
{
  // ACCESSING - get /set properties
  public String getDescription();
  public void setDescription(String newDescription)
    throws BusinessRuleException;

  // ACCESSING - get property values
  public boolean isFormatMultipleChair();
  public boolean isFormatSingleChair();
  public boolean isFormatNoChair();

  // ACCESSING - set property values
  public void setFormatNoChair() throws BusinessRuleException;
  public void setFormatSingleChair() throws BusinessRuleException;
  public void setFormatMutlipleChair() throws BusinessRuleException;

  // ACCESSING -- collaborations
  public List getTeamMembers();
  public void addTeamMember(ITeamMember aTeamMember)
    throws BusinessRuleException;
  public void removeTeamMember(ITeamMember aTeamMember)
    throws BusinessRuleException;

  // DETERMINE MINE
  public List getChairs();
  public ITeamMember getTeamMember(IPersonProfile aPerson);
}
```

LISTING 7.41
Java conduct business interface for Team.

Define: Team Class

The Team class has an instance variable to hold the collection of team members, plus instance variables for the description and format properties.

For the Java version, a static inner class, TeamFormat, which is not shown here but is in the CD code listings, is used to represent the three format values—no chair, single chair, and multiple chairs (see Listing 7.42).

```
public class Team extends Object implements ITeam
{
  // DEFINE
  private String description;
  private ArrayList teamMembers;
  private TeamFormat format;
}
```

LISTING 7.42
Java class specification for Team.

```
Model subclass: #Team
  instanceVariableNames: 'description teamMembers format '
  classVariableNames: ''
  poolDictionaries: ''
  category: 'Collaboration-Examples'
```

LISTING 7.43
Squeak class definition for Team.

Initialize

Team initialization code creates the collection object and sets the format to the default of "multiple chairs."

In Java, the initialization of the array list object and setting the format to the default occurs in the default constructor. See Listing 7.44. No other constructors are needed. In Squeak this initialization occurs in the `initialize` method. See Listing 7.45.

```
public Team()
{
  this.description = new String();
  this.format = FORMAT_MULTIPLE;
  this.teamMembers = new ArrayList();
}
```

LISTING 7.44
Java constructor for Team.

Accessing: Properties

The description instance variable has the usual get and set methods, returning and taking a string value, respectively. The format instance variable has get property value accessors of the form "isFormatX" for each X value of the format, and has set property value accessors of the form "setFormatX" for each X value of the format. Both the Java and Squeak code examples are very straightforward, so the code is not included here. As usual, the code is on the CD.

Team class methodsFor: 'instance creation'

new
> ↑super new initialize

Team methodsFor: 'initialize-release'

initialize
> description ← String new.
> format ← self setFormatMultipleChair.
> teamMembers ← OrderedCollection new

LISTING 7.45
Squeak methods for creating and initializing a team.

Accessing: Collaborations

The team has two get accessors for the team member collaboration: one returns a view containing all the team members, and the second returns a team member for a given person.

The Java methods for managing the team member array list are the same as in person. A public method returns an "unmodifiable" version of the array list, and a protected method returns a list iterator on the array list. Methods to establish and dissolve a team member collaboration add and remove the team member from the array list, respectively. These methods are listed on the CD.

What is new in this Java implementation is the method that locates the team member of the team for a given person. Searching a collection for the first element that returns true for a given test is such a routine occurrence that we created our own utility class, CollectionDetector, with a detect method containing code that iterates through a collection. For each element in the collection or list, the detect method calls the detectBlock method with the list element and the value that is the subject of the search. If the detect-Block returns true for any list element, then the search stops and that list element is returned as the result. To use the CollectionDetector, define a subclass implementing the detectBlock method with the code needed to locate the desired object in the list. Next, create an object in the subclass, and ask that object to detect within a given list for a given object. The getTeam-Member method defines the CollectionDetector subclass as an anonymous inner class, and creates an object in this class to detect a person within the list of team members (see Listing 7.46). Code for the CollectionDetector class is included on the CD.

```
public ITeamMember getTeamMember(IPersonProfile aPerson)
{
  CollectionDetector personDetector = new CollectionDetector()
  {
    public boolean detectBlock(Object listElement, Object keyValue)
    {
      return ((ITeamMember)listElement).getPerson().equals(keyValue);
    }
  }; // end anonymous inner class definition
  return (ITeamMember)personDetector.detect(this.teamMembers, aPerson);
}
```

LISTING 7.46
Java getTeamMember for person collaboration accessor for Team.

In Squeak, collections can be asked to find and return an object that satisfies some test; the message to the collection is **detect:ifNone:**, and it returns nil if no object within the collection satisfies the test (see Listing 7.47).

Team methodsFor: 'collaboration-accessing'

teamMemberFor: aPerson
  ↑self teamMembers
    detect: [:aTeamMember | aTeamMember person = aPerson]
    ifNone: [ ]

LISTING 7.47
Squeak get teamMemberFor person collaboration accessor for Team.

Printing

Using the "Part Carries the Load" principle (76), a team does not ask its parts to print. Instead, the team prints only its own properties.

In Java, Team implements the usual toString method to print the description and format properties of a team. In Squeak, Team implements the printOn: method to do the same. Code listings are on the CD.

Equals

Using the "Part Carries the Load" principle (76), a team compares only its own properties and does not try to compare its team members to those of the other team.

In Java, the equals method compares the properties of a team. Squeak allows using the = operator for this comparison. Code listings are on the CD.

Run: Test Objects

By default, a team allows multiple chairs, so two other test objects are required, one for each remaining format value. Code is shown for the single chair team test object in Listings 7.48 and 7.49. Code for other test objects is shown on the CD.

```java
public static Team testSingleChairTeam() throws BusinessRuleException
{
    Team aTeam = new Team();
    aTeam.setFormatSingleChair();
    aTeam.setDescription("Executive Strategy Team");
    return aTeam;
}
```

LISTING 7.48
Java test object for a team with a single chair.

```
Team class methodsFor: 'examples'

testSingleChairTeam
    "Team testSingleChairTeam"
    | aTeam |
    aTeam ← Team new.
    aTeam setFormatSingleChair.
    aTeam description: 'Executive Strategy Team'.
    ↑aTeam
```

LISTING 7.49
Squeak test object for a team with a single chair.

Team Member: Java & Squeak DIAPER (Updated) ____

This section shows only the parts of the TeamMember implementation that need to be updated to support the TeamMember – Team collaboration.[21]

Team Member Initialization Rules

Because a team member represents a person's participation in a particular team, a team member cannot exist without both a person and a team. Team-Member thus requires an additional initialization rule: A team member must have a team to exist.

---

21. These updates are necessary because we implemented the collaborations one-by-one. Normally, we would look at all the collaborations of TeamMember before starting to code, and therefore would not need to change existing methods.

Define: TeamMember Class

Give `TeamMember` an instance variable to reference its team collaborator.

Using the "How I See You" principle (71), the team instance variable in the Java implementation is typed with the team conduct business interface (see Listing 7.50).

In Squeak, we just add a new instance variable to the TeamMember definition (see Listing 7.51).

```
public class TeamMember extends Object implements ITeamMember
{
  // DEFINE
  private IPerson person;
  private ITeam team;
  private TeamRole role;
  private byte privileges;
  private SecurityLevel securityLevel;
}
```

LISTING 7.50
Java revised class specification for TeamMember.

```
Model subclass: #TeamMember
  instanceVariableNames: 'person team role privileges securityLevel '
  classVariableNames: ''
  poolDictionaries: ''
  category: 'Collaboration-Examples'
```

LISTING 7.51
Squeak revised class definition for TeamMember.

Initialize

The new initialization rule changes how team member objects are created. The team member object inherits some of its properties from its person. The team checks collaboration rules for the team member that may include these object inherited properties, so the collaboration between team member and person must be set before the Team – TeamMember collaboration is established.

Object creation methods that establish two or more collaborations need some extra care. While the first collaboration may pass the rules and be established, the second could fail, in which case, the first must be dissolved, too. In this example, the team member must be removed from the person object if the team member cannot be a part of the team.[22]

---

22. Because of initialization failure, rolling back the established collaborations should not require business rule checking as was discussed in p. 57, "Rolling Back Entity Collaborations." In the next chapter, we'll show how to bypass the business rule checking for this case.

PRINCIPLE 77
PUTTING PARENTS FIRST

> When an object must establish two or more collaborations to be valid, parent collaborations must be established first.

The team object is added to the parameter list of the `TeamMember` Java class constructor, and code is added to break the person collaboration if the team collaboration fails (see Listing 7.52).

```
public TeamMember(IPerson aPerson, ITeam aTeam)
                  throws BusinessRuleException
{
  this.makeMember();
  this.securityLevel = new SecurityLevel();
  this.addPerson(aPerson);
  try {this.addTeam(aTeam);}
  catch(BusinessRuleException anException)
  {
    aPerson.removeTeamMember(this);
    throw anException;
  }
}
```

LISTING 7.52
Java revised constructor for TeamMember.

The existing Squeak object creation method needs to be converted into a method that takes two parameters: a person and a team. Code is added to dissolve the person collaboration if the team collaboration fails (see Listing 7.53).

TeamMember class methodsFor: 'instance creation'

newWith: aPerson and: aTeam
```
| aTeamMember |
aTeamMember ← super new initialize.
aTeamMember addPerson: aPerson.
[aTeamMember addTeam: aTeam]
   on: BusinessRuleException
   do: [:ex|
     aPerson removeTeamMember: aTeamMember.
     ex signal].
↑ aTeamMember
```

LISTING 7.53
Squeak revised method for creating a team member.

Accessing

The new collaboration requires new accessors to get, add, and remove the collaborator.

The Java accessors are similar to those for the person collaborator, so only the method signatures for the accessors are shown in Listing 7.54.

The Squeak methods in Listing 7.55 are added to the "collaboration-accessing" message category.

```
public ITeam getTeam();
public void addTeam(ITeam aTeam) throws BusinessRuleException;
public void removeTeam(ITeam aTeam) throws BusinessRuleException;
```

LISTING 7.54
Java method signatures for team collaborator accessors of TeamMember.

```
team
addTeam: aTeam
removeTeam: aTeam
```

LISTING 7.55
Squeak method signatures for team collaborator accessors of TeamMember.

Printing

Applying the "Part Carries the Load" principle (76), a team member prints its own details, and asks its team to print its own details as well. Code should be added to the Java toString method and the Squeak printOn: method to print the team. These methods are on the CD.

Equals

Applying the "Part Carries the Load" principle (76), a team member compares its team to that of another team member. The Java equals method and the Squeak = operator are modified to compare the teams. See Listings 7.56 and 7.57.

```java
public boolean equals(Object anObject)
{
  if (anObject instanceof TeamMember)
  {
    TeamMember other = (TeamMember)anObject;
    if (!this.role.equals(other.role)) return false;
    if (this.person == null && (other.person != null)) return false;
    if (this.person != null && (!this.person.equals(other.person)))
      return false;
    if (this.team == null && (other.team != null)) return false;
    if (this.team != null && (!this.team.equals(other.team)))
      return false;
    return true;
  }
  else return false; // not instance of TeamMember
}
```

LISTING 7.56
Java revised method for checking for equal TeamMembers.

TeamMember methodsFor: 'comparing'

= anObject
    self species = anObject species ifFalse: [↑false].
    self getRole = anObject getRole ifFalse: [↑false].
    self person = anObject person ifFalse: [↑false].
    self team = anObject team ifFalse: [↑false].
    ↑true

LISTING 7.57
Squeak revised method for checking for equal TeamMembers.

Run: Test Objects

Applying the "Part Carries the Load" principle (76), a team member test object uses the team test object. The purpose of the test object is to test the collaboration, not to create a team filled with lots of team members for extensive testing. Tests of that magnitude require more sophisticated test techniques and test harnesses. For our purposes, we need to update all the test methods in both TeamMember classes to create team members with the new constructor and using the person and team test objects. See Listings 7.58 and 7.59.

```
public static TeamMember testChair() throws BusinessRuleException
{
  ITeam aTeam = Team.testTeam();
  TeamMember aTeamMember = new TeamMember(Person.testPerson(),aTeam)
  aTeamMember.makeChair();
  SecurityLevel sLevel = aTeamMember.getSecurityLevel();
  sLevel.setLevelHigh();
  return aTeamMember;
}
```

LISTING 7.58
Java test object for TeamMember as chair of team.

TeamMember class methodsFor: 'examples'

testChair
   "TeamMember testChair"
   | aTeamMember |
   aTeamMember ←self newWith: Person testPerson and: Team testTeam.
   aTeamMember makeChair.
   aTeamMember securityLevel setLevelHigh.
   ↑ aTeamMember

LISTING 7.59
Squeak test object for TeamMember as chair of team.

Transaction – Specific Object Definitions _____

Collaboration patterns described by the transaction - specific pattern are:

- transaction - role
- transaction - specific item
- transaction - place
- follow-up transaction - transaction
- line item - specific item

Transaction - Specific vs. Generic – Specific

Transaction - specific collaborations look deceptively like generic - specific collaborations; however, a transaction is a more active collaborator than a generic. A single transaction often unites multiple collaboration patterns (see Figure 7.7). Because transactions coordinate between many collaboration patterns, they are called the "glue" of the object model.

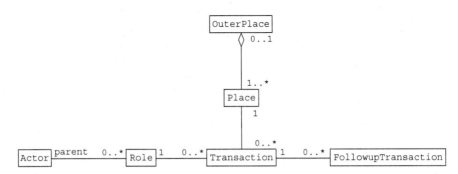

FIGURE 7.7
A transaction coordinates between many collaboration patterns.

Transaction - Specific Implementation Guidelines

Here are the important facts about transaction - specific collaborations that shape how they are implemented:

- No object inheritance is involved.
- No collaborator is more "specific" than another.
- A transaction can have multiple specifics, but each is of a different type.
- A specific can have multiple transactions of the same type.
- A specific can have different types of transactions.

As with whole - part, profile interfaces are not necessary; conduct business interfaces are always recommended.

The specific work principle does not apply with transaction - specific. Instead, the relevant rule of thumb arises from the fact that a transaction exists to record the interaction of a person and a thing at a given place. This implies that a transaction cannot exist without its specifics, namely its role, specific item, and place.[23] The reverse is clearly not true because a person, place, and thing can exist independently of any transactions.

PRINCIPLE 78
LET THE COORDINATOR DIRECT

When different types of objects are united by a single common coordinator and must work toward a common goal, allow the coordinator to direct the actions.

---

23. Some systems do not track the location of a transaction, a few do not require a role, and even fewer transactions do not require a specific.

Read that principle carefully. It does not say to put all the work into a central controller object. Each object is still responsible for performing its own share of the work, but only when cued from the coordinator.

Here is how the directing coordinator principle applies to the `transaction - specific` DIAPER:

- Printing   – A `transaction` asks its `specifics` to print themselves.
- Comparing   – A `transaction` asks its `specifics` to compare themselves.
- Testing   – A `transaction` test object uses `specific` test objects.

A `transaction` brings other objects, `specifics`, together. The `specifics` are not usually of the same type. Rather than forcing the different types into one collection of `specifics`, the recommended approach is to define a separate instance variable for each type.

Multiple `transactions` for a `specific` record that object's history of interactions. Also, analyze transactions services do work across the `transactions` of a `specific`. The natural implementation defines an instance variable within the `specific` to hold the `transactions`.

Transaction – Specific Example

This example illustrates the `transaction - role` and `transaction - specific item` collaborations.

> EXAMPLE—A team member can nominate documents for publication on the corporate Web site. Using object think, a document nominates itself for a team member. The document nominate service creates a nomination (`transaction`) with the team member (`role`) and itself (`specific item`).[24] See Figure 7. 8.

Team member collaboration rules:

- A team member must have nominate privileges to nominate a document.

---

24. A document is an instance of a document template. To keep the object model small, the document template was not included. Had it been included, the document would object inherit from the document template, and the document interface would extend the document template profile interface.

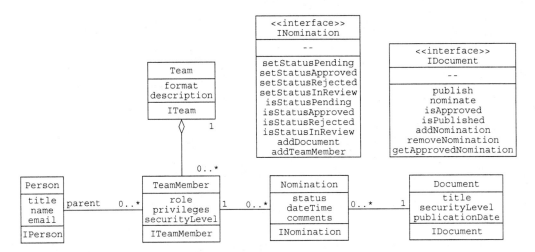

FIGURE 7.8
TeamMember – Nomination – Document object model.

- A team member can only nominate a fixed number of times per 30 days:
  - Five times for a team member whose role is member or admin.
  - Ten times for a team member whose role is chair.

Document collaboration rules:

- A document must have a title to be nominated.
- A document cannot be nominated after it is published.
- A document cannot be nominated while it has a pending nomination.
- A document cannot be nominated by a team member with a security level less than the document's security level.

With the addition of TeamMember – Nomination – Document to our object model, the team member object is now playing in three collaboration patterns. It is playing as the `specific` in a `generic - specific` collaboration, as the `part` in a `whole - part` collaboration, and as a `specific` in a `transaction - specific` collaboration.

Document: Java & Squeak DIAPER _____

Interesting implementation aspects of the document are the security level, publication date properties, and the collection of nominations. We have seen the security level before. This is the same security level object used in the

TeamMember class implementation. Every document is created with an initial security level of "low."

Publication date is only set if the document is published; otherwise, the date is null. When the state of the object determines whether a property exists or is accessible, it is a business rule violation to request the property when the object is not in the proper state. Accordingly, asking an unpublished document for its publication date is a business rule violation, and so the get accessor throws an exception.

Use a collection to hold collaborators. This collection will be searched to find the approved nomination and to tally the number of nominations within a range of dates. A document has an analyze transactions service to return its approved nomination, because while the document may have any number of pending, in review, and rejected nominations, it can only have one approved nomination. Also, once a document has an approved nomination, its behavior changes. However, asking an unapproved document for its approved nomination is similar to asking an unpublished document for its publication date; it generates a business rule violation.

A document has the following initialization rules:

- A document must have a title property to exist.
- A document by default has its security level set to "low."

Define: Conduct Business Interface

This interface is fairly straightforward. Because there is no profile interface, the conduct business interface has the accessors, determine mine services, and analyze transactions service. It also provides the conduct business services to publish and nominate a document. See Listing 7.60.

```
public interface IDocument
{
  // ACCESSORS -- get properties
  public String getTitle();
  public SecurityLevel getSecurityLevel();
  public Date getPublicationDate() throws BusinessRuleException;

  // ACCESSORS -- get collaborators
  public List getNominations();
```

(continued)

LISTING 7.60
Java conduct business interface for Document.

```java
// ACCESSORS -- set properties
public void setTitle(String newTitle) throws BusinessRuleException;

// DETERMINE MINE
public boolean isPublished();
public boolean isApproved();

// ANALYZE TRANSACTIONS
public INomination getApprovedNomination()
throws BusinessRuleException;

// CONDUCT BUSINESS
public void publish() throws BusinessRuleException;
public void nominate(ITeamMember aTeamMember)
throws BusinessRuleException;
}
```

LISTING 7.60
Java conduct business interface for Document. (continued)

Define: Document Class

The Java code keeps the nominations sorted by storing them in a TreeSet, which is a standard Java class that exhibits the SortedSet interface. A TreeSet sorts itself in ascending order with the lowest ordered elements first.

```java
public class Document extends Object implements IDocument
{
  private String title;
  private Date publicationDate;
  private SecurityLevel securityLevel;
  private TreeSet nominations;
}
```

LISTING 7.61
Java class specification for Document.

```
Model subclass: #Document
    instanceVariableNames: 'title publicationDate securityLevel nominations '
    classVariableNames: ''
    poolDictionaries: ''
    category: 'Collaboration-Examples'
```

LISTING 7.62
Squeak class definition for Document.

Initialize

Document initialization code creates the collection object, sets the security level to the default, sets the string property to an empty string, and sets the publication date to null. A string title is required for the document to exist, and the set title accessor throws an exception if the title is null. See Listings 7.63 and 7.64.

```
public Document(String newTitle) throws BusinessRuleException
{
  this.setTitle(newTitle);
  this.publicationDate = null;
  this.securityLevel = new SecurityLevel();
  this.nominations = new TreeSet();
}
```

LISTING 7.63
Java constructor for Document.

Document class methodsFor: 'instance creation'

new
  BusinessRuleException signal: 'Cannot create document without a title.'

newWith: aTitleString
  | aDocument |
  aDocument ← super new initialize.
  aDocument title: aTitleString.
  ↑aDocument

Document methodsFor: 'initialize-release'

initialize
  title ← String new.
  publicationDate ← nil.
  securityLevel ← SecurityLevel new.
  nominations ← OrderedCollection new

LISTING 7.64
Squeak methods for creating and initializing a document.

Accessing: Properties

The usual suspects apply here. The publication date has some interesting accessors. The get accessor throws a business exception if the property is not set. To avoid this unhappy event, an additional property value accessor tests if the publication date is set. These accessors are shown in Listings 7.65 and 7.66; the others are on the CD.

```java
public Date getPublicationDate() throws BusinessRuleException
{
  if (this.publicationDate == null)
    throw new BusinessRuleException("Document is unpublished.");
  else return this.publicationDate;
}

public boolean isPublished()
{
  try {this.getPublicationDate();}
  catch(BusinessRuleException ex){return false;}
  return true;
}
```

LISTING 7.65
Java publicationDate property accessors for Document.

Document methodsFor: 'accessing'

publicationDate
    publicationDate ifNil: [BusinessRuleException signal: 'Document is unpublished.'].
    ↑ publicationDate

Document methodsFor: 'testing'

isPublished
    ↑ publicationDate notNil

LISTING 7.66
Squeak publicationDate property accessors for Document.

Accessing: Collaborations

A document's nominations help determine its state. A document is "approved" for publication when it has an approved nomination. Along with the usual collaboration accessors, there is a service to return the approved nomination. This service raises an exception if the document lacks an approved nomination. To guard against this exception, the document includes an "is approved" service that checks whether the document has an approved nomination without raising an exception.

For the Java version, four collaboration accessors are needed: (1) a `public` accessor to return an "unmodifiable" list of nominations, (2) a `protected` accessor to return a list iterator for the nominations, (3) a `public` method to return the approved nomination, and (4) a `public` method to ask if a document is approved. The first two accessors are left to the reader. The "get approved nomination" method locates an approved nomination in the list of nominations by using an anonymous inner class programmed to detect an approved nomination. This technique was explained earlier (see Listing 7.46). The "is approved" method provides a check before trying to get the approved nomination (see Listing 7.67).

The Squeak version requires similar accessors as shown in Listing 7.68.

```java
public INomination getApprovedNomination() throws BusinessRuleException
{
   INomination aNomination = null;
   CollectionDetector approvedDetector = new CollectionDetector()
   {
     public boolean detectBlock(Object listElement, Object keyValue)
     {
       return ((INomination)listElement).isStatusApproved();
     }
   };
   aNomination = (INomination)approvedDetector.detect(this.nominations);
   if (aNomination == null)
     throw new BusinessRuleException("No approved nomination.");
   return aNomination;
}

public boolean isApproved()
{
   try { this.getApprovedNomination(); }
   catch(BusinessRuleException ex) { return false; }
   return true;
}
```

LISTING 7.67
Java collaboration accessors for the approved nomination of a document.

Document methodsFor: 'collaboration-accessing'

approvedNomination
   ↑ self nominations
   detect: [:aNomination | aNomination isStatusApproved]
   ifNone: [BusinessRuleException signal: 'Document has no approved nomination.']

Document methodsFor: 'testing'

isApproved
   ↑self nominations anySatisfy: [:aNomination | aNomination isStatusApproved]

LISTING 7.68
Squeak collaboration accessors for the approved nomination of a document.

Finishing Up the DIAPER

Printing and comparison (equals) are implemented using the "Let the Coordinator Direct" principle (78): the document prints and compares its own properties, but not those of its nominations. See the CD for the Java and Squeak code.

For testing, we want to be thorough. We will create at least two document test objects: one with a default security level, and another with a secret security level. Only the secret document test object is shown in Listings 7.69 and 7.70.

```java
public static Document testSecret() throws BusinessRuleException
{
  Document aDocument =
      new Document("Food and Beverage Industry Surveillance Tips" );
  SecurityLevel sLevel = aDocument.getSecurityLevel();
  sLevel.setLevelSecret();
  return aDocument
}
```

LISTING 7.69
Java test object for a document with secret security.

```
Document class methodsFor: 'examples'

testSecret
    "Document testSecret"
    | aDocument |
    aDocument ← self newWith: 'Food and Beverage Industry Surveillance Tips'.
    aDocument securityLevel setLevelSecret.
    ↑aDocument
```

LISTING 7.70
Squeak test object for a document with secret security.

Nomination: Java & Squeak DIAPER _____

A nomination goes through various lifecycle states:

- Pending
- In review
- Approved
- Rejected

A nomination's lifecycle state transitions are governed by business rules. A nomination cannot:

- Transition to the "pending" state unless in review or already pending
- Transition to the "in review" state unless pending or already in review
- Transition to the "approved" state unless in review or already approved
- Transition to the "rejected" state unless in review or already rejected

These rules are enforced in the property value accessor methods, but we will defer rule checking until the next chapter.

The nomination has the following initialization rules:

- A nomination must have a document to exist.
- A nomination must have a team member to exist.
- A nomination has a nomination date set to the date and time when the nomination was created.

Define: Conduct Business Interface

To allow sorting of nominations by date in Java, a nomination must exhibit the `Comparable` interface as shown in Listing 7.71.

```
public interface INomination extends Comparable
{
// ACCESSORS -- get properties
public String getComments();
public Date getNominationDate();

// ACCESSORS -- get property values
public boolean isStatusApproved();
public boolean isStatusRejected();
public boolean isStatusPending();
public boolean isStatusInReview();

// ACCESSORS -- set properties
public void setComments(String newComments)
  throws BusinessRuleException;
```

(continued)

LISTING 7.71
Java conduct business interface for Nomination.

```
// ACCESSORS -- set property values
public void setStatusPending() throws BusinessRuleException;
public void setStatusInReview() throws BusinessRuleException;
public void setStatusApproved() throws BusinessRuleException;
public void setStatusRejected() throws BusinessRuleException;

// ACCESSORS -- get collaborators
public IDocument getDocument();
public ITeamMember getTeamMember();

  // ACCESSORS -- add collaborators
public void addTeamMember(ITeamMember aTeamMember)
  throws BusinessRuleException;
public void addDocument(IDocument aDocument)
  throws BusinessRuleException;

// DETERMINE MINE
public boolean isBefore(Date aDate);
public boolean isAfter(Date aDate);
}
```

LISTING 7.71
Java conduct business interface for Nomination. (continued)

Define: Nomination Class

In Java, a Date object is used to represent the nomination date property, and an inner class is defined to encapsulate the representation of the status property.[25] Both collaborator variables, document and team member, are referenced by their conduct business interfaces (see Listing 7.72).

```
public class Nomination extends Object implements INomination
{
  // DEFINE
  private NominationStatus status;
  private Date nominationDate;
  private String comments;
  private IDocument document;
  private ITeamMember teamMember;
}
```

LISTING 7.72
Java class specification for Nomination.

---

25. Since this static inner class implementation pattern is used repeatedly for status, role, and type variables it is a tempting candidate for a reusable component. Our goals in writing this code were readability and understandability. Both these goals are served by having the status, role, and type properties defined with domain specific names, such as TeamRole or NominationStatus, and by having the code defined right at the point at which it is used, inside the TeamMember or Nomination class.

A `Date` object is also used in Squeak to represent the nomination date property, and an association key-value pair is used to represent the status property (see Listing 7.73).

Model subclass: #**Nomination**
    instanceVariableNames: '**status nominationDate comments document teamMember** '
    classVariableNames: ''
    poolDictionaries: ''
    category: 'Collaboration-Examples'

LISTING 7.73
Squeak class definition for Nomination.

Initialize

A nomination requires two objects to exist. The implementation pattern here is similar to creating team members: if the second collaboration fails, then the first one must be dissolved.

In Java, there is no default constructor, and in Squeak, we override the default new operation to signal an exception. See Listings 7.74 and 7.75.

```
public Nomination(IDocument aDocument, ITeamMember aTeamMember)
                throws BusinessRuleException
{
   this.status = STATUS_PENDING;
   this.nominationDate = new Date();
   this.comments = new String();
   this.addTeamMember(aTeamMember);
   try { this.addDocument(aDocument); }
   catch(BusinessRuleException ex)
   {
     aTeamMember.doRemoveNomination(this);
     throw ex;
   }
}
```

LISTING 7.74
Java constructor for Nomination.

Accessing: Properties and Collaborations

Accessors include the regular get accessors, and a set accessor for the comments property. The nomination date cannot change, so it does not have a set accessor. There are also special property value accessors for the status, `isStatusApproved`, `setStatusApproved`, etc. These follow the conventions used to define the property value accessors for the team member role

Nomination class methodsFor: 'instance creation'

new
    BusinessRuleException
      signal: 'Cannot create nomination without a team member and a document.'

newWith: aTeamMember and: aDocument
    | aNomination |
    aNomination ← super new initialize.
    aNomination addTeamMember: aTeamMember.
    [aNomination addDocument: aDocument]
      on: BusinessRuleException
      do: [:ex|
        aTeamMember doRemoveNomination: aNomination.
        ex signal].
    ↑aNomination

Nomination methodsFor: 'initialize-release'

initialize
    status ←self statusPending.
    nominationDate ← Date today.
    comments ← String new.
    document ← nil.
    teamMember ← nil

LISTING 7.75
Squeak methods for creating and initializing a nomination.

property.[26] One difference is that these set property value accessors check the state transition rules and throw an exception if any rule is violated. Since these tests are implemented again with the rule checking in the next chapter, we omit the listings here.

For the team member accessor, only add accessors are needed because a nomination cannot exist without its team member and document. Nothing is different here from past collaboration accessors.

Printing

Applying the "Let the Coordinator Direct" principle (78), a nomination prints its own properties, and also directs its collaborators to print themselves. This is implemented in Java using the `DateFormat` class to format the nomination date for printing (see Listing 7.76).

In Squeak, instead of getting the printString of the collaborators, a slightly more efficient approach is to ask each collaborator to print on the same stream (see Listing 7.77).

---

26. See pp. 190–193.

```java
public String toString()
{
  DateFormat aDateFormat = DateFormat.getDateTimeInstance();
  StringBuffer buffy = new StringBuffer(30);
  buffy.append("Nomination on: ");
  buffy.append(aDateFormat.format(this.nominationDate));
  buffy.append("\nStatus: " + this.status);
  buffy.append("\n" + this.document);
  buffy.append("\n" + this.teamMember);
  return buffy.toString();
}
```

LISTING 7.76
Java method for printing a nomination.

```
Nomination methodsFor: 'printing'

printOn: aStream
    aStream nextPutAll: 'Nomination:'.
    self nominationDate printOn: aStream cr.
    aStream cr; nextPutAll: self doGetStatus value.
    self teamMember printOn: aStream cr.
    self document printOn: aStream cr
```

LISTING 7.77
Squeak method for printing a nomination.

Equals

Applying the "Let the Coordinator Direct" principle (78), a nomination compares its own properties, plus it directs its collaborators to compare themselves.

In Java, along with the `equals` method, a nomination has `compareTo` methods to support sorting by Java library classes. The `compareTo` method returns –1, 0, or 1 according to whether the receiver is more recent, at the same date and time, or after the other nomination, respectively. This implementation ensures nominations are sorted with the most recent first. The `compareTo` methods are shown in Listing 7.78; the `equals` method is listed on the CD.

The Squeak code is on the CD.

Run: Test Objects

As the coordinating collaborator, the nomination test object uses the other collaborator test objects. See Listings 7.79 and 7.80.

```java
public int compareTo(Object anObject)
{
  return this.compareTo((Nomination)anObject);
}

public int compareTo(Nomination aNomination)
{
  return aNomination.nominationDate.compareTo(this.nominationDate);
}
```

LISTING 7.78
Java methods for comparing Nominations.

```java
public static Nomination testNomination() throws BusinessRuleException
{
  ITeamMember aTeamMember = TeamMember.testTeamMember();
  Nomination aNomination =
    new Nomination(Document.testDocument(), aTeamMember);
  return aNomination;
}
```

LISTING 7.79
Java Nomination test object.

Nomination class methodsFor: 'examples'

testNomination
   "Nomination testNomination"
   | aNomination |
   aNomination ←self newWith: TeamMember testChair and: Document testNormal.
   ↑ aNomination

LISTING 7.80
Squeak Nomination test object.

Team Member: Java & Squeak DIAPER (Update II) ___

The `TeamMember` class needs the following definition updates to collaborate with nomination objects:

- Add a variable to the `TeamMember` class for holding the collection of nominations.
- Add to the team member profile interface a collaboration accessor for the team member's nominations.
- Add to the team member conduct business interface collaboration accessors to add and remove a nomination.

We will also update the constructor or initialize methods to create a collection object for the nominations when a team member is created.

Accessors must be added to get all nominations, add a single nomination, and remove a particular nomination.

Because `TeamMember` is not the coordinator (Principle 78 again), no changes are needed to allow for printing, comparing, or testing.

What's Next?

The next chapter completes the code started in this chapter by showing how to implement the business rules for the properties and collaborations.

Implementing Business Rules

The Big Pay-Off

This chapter shows how to implement business rules in programming code. In a sense, this chapter is what the whole book has been building toward. Previous chapters showed how to choose objects, define business rules, and code objects using the collaboration patterns. This chapter shows how to enforce real-world business rules with object methods organized by the collaboration patterns. Writing code without business rules is like solving physics problems without considering air resistance. This chapter considers air resistance. Sure, it takes a little more effort, but without it, your parachute would not work.

Recognizing Business Rules

Business rules come from domain experts; usually these are external clients, but they can be team members with specialized in-depth knowledge. Domain experts know the concepts behind the business being modeled, and say things like: "Some teams can only have one chair; other teams can have multiple chairs; and some teams do not require a chair at all." Business rules define domain-specified limits for property values and when two entities can collaborate. Logic rules come from the programmers or system developers. Programmers say things like: "The document get publication accessor throws an exception if the publication date is null."

PRINCIPLE 79
WHERE RULES COME FROM

> Business rules come from clients; logic rules come from good programming practices.

Both types of rules are important. Your project is unlikely to be called successful by the customer if there are glaring logic rule errors. However, your projects will definitely not be successful if there is no way to conduct business using the product. Because of this and because logic rules tend to be easier to determine, we will concentrate on the business rules.

Two Types of Business Rules

Before implementing a business rule, you must express the rule in object-centric terms and specify how the rule is to be enforced. Rules expressed in object-centric terms fall into one of the following categories:

- Property rules   – Used by objects to decide what values are valid for their properties
- Collaboration rules – Used by objects to decide whether they can establish or dissolve collaborations

The rest of this chapter shows how objects enforce these business rules. Property rules are discussed first, because they are simpler. Also, many of the lessons learned for implementing property rules apply to the more complex and interesting collaboration rules.

Property Business Rules_____

Property rules specify domain-specific limits on a property's values. This section describes strategies and techniques for implementing business rule checking of property values.

Implementation Strategies

Property rules work in conjunction with property set accessors. Set accessors permit editing of an object's properties, while property rules verify that the new values are valid. Checking the property rule inside the property's set accessor ensures external methods cannot corrupt the property's value. Within the set accessor, the rule can be embedded directly as lines of code, or extracted out as a separate method to maximize method cohesiveness.

Method cohesiveness essentially means that a method should do only one thing. Setting a property involves doing three things: (1) checking the logical validity of the new value, (2) checking the business rule validity of the new value, and (3) assigning the new value. To maximize the method cohesiveness of the property set accessor, isolate the business rule check and the value assignment into separate methods. This method-cohesive implementation has distinct advantages. Isolating the business rule check allows subclasses to extend and override property rules by writing their own test methods.[1] Isolating the value assignment allows bypassing the business rules when necessary.[2] Logic rules tend to be the same for generalizations and specializations, so these do not merit isolation into their own method. Organizing code this way keeps you from having to refactor it later on.

PRINCIPLE 80
ISOLATE PROPERTY RULES

When a property has domain-specific limits on its values, define a separate method to enforce these limits, and call this test method from within the set property accessor.

PRINCIPLE 81
ISOLATE VALUE ASSIGNMENT

Define a separate method to assign a value into the property and bypass business rule checking when necessary. The set property accessor calls this method after checking the business rules.

---

1. The test method should not alter the object or produce any side-effects.
2. Be careful here; bypassing business rules is dangerous. Generally, only internal methods and data management classes have the right combination of information and authority to be allowed to do this.

Methods for Enforcing Property Rules

Using method cohesiveness to organize the property set accessor code produces the following three methods for every object property that can be externally set:

set (aValue)	Sets the designated value in the property of the object receiving this message ("this" or "self") if the business rules allow
testSet (aValue)	Tests the value against the receiver object's property rules; raises an exception if they fail
doSet (aValue)	Assigns the value into the object's property variable without rule checking

An extended version of this table, including methods for enumerated type properties, is shown in Appendix B.

The property set accessor generally goes in the conduct business interface, although the set accessor for the team member role property provided a good counter-example.[3] On the other hand, the "test set" and "do set" methods do not belong in the conduct business interface, since these methods are internal mechanisms for preserving object integrity and managing property storage. In Java, all these methods are declared `public`. Making the "do set" methods `public` allows data management classes in other packages to reconstitute the object from persistent storage. Since "test set" methods do not alter the object, making them `public` does no harm, and may prove useful when new collaborators are added to the system.

Property Categories

Different categories of properties give rise to different kinds of property rules and rule implementations. Recall the basic property categories from Chapter 5:

- Descriptive — Domain and tracking properties
- Time — Date or time properties
- Lifecycle state — One-way state transitions (e.g., nomination status: pending, in review, approved, rejected)
- Operating state — Two-way state transitions (e.g., sensor state: off, on)

---

3. See pp. 190–193, "Accessing: Property Values."

- Role   – Classifies people (e.g., team member role: chair, admin, member)
- Type   – Classifies places, things, and events (e.g., store type: physical, online, phone)

The following sections describe property rule implementations for the above property categories.

Descriptive and Time Property Business Rules _____

Descriptive properties are the "free-form" characteristics of an object, such as a person's name, title, and email, a team's description, or a document's title. Time properties have timestamp and date values. Logical rules prevent setting time and descriptive properties to bad values, such as an empty or null string, or bogus times (e.g., 25:63) and dates (e.g., March 33, 2000). Business rules for time and descriptive properties come in two flavors: (1) state transition rules that prevent properties from changing, and (2) value limit rules that constrain property values to specific sets.

PRINCIPLE 82
DESCRIPTIVE AND TIME PROPERTY BUSINESS RULES

> Descriptive and time properties are governed by business rules that define when the values can change and what ranges of values are possible.

Example: Document Title

This example shows a value limit rule for a descriptive property.

EXAMPLE—A document cannot have a title longer than 255 characters.

Limiting the size of the document title is a business rule to be checked by a separate test method. On the other hand, checking if the title is null or empty is a logical rule and is kept inside the set property accessor. Refer to Listing 8.1.

The test title method goes in the "accessing-rules" message category in Squeak (see Listing 8.2).

```
Document.java

// ACCESSORS - set properties

public void setTitle(String newTitle) throws BusinessRuleException
{
  if ((newTitle == null) || (newTitle.length() == 0))
    throw new BusinessRuleException(
              "Document cannot have null or empty title.");
  this.testSetTitle(newTitle);
  this.doSetTitle(newTitle);
}

// ACCESSORS - property rules

public void testSetTitle(String newTitle) throws BusinessRuleException
{
  if (newTitle.length() > 255)
    throw new BusinessRuleException(
              "Document title cannot exceed 255 characters");
}

// ACCESSORS - property do sets

public void doSetTitle(String newTitle){ this.title = newTitle; }
```

LISTING 8.1
Java methods for setting, testing, and assigning a descriptive property.

Document methodsFor: 'accessing'

title: aTitleString
    | aTrimmedTitleString |
    (aTitleString isNil or:
        [(aTrimmedTitleString ← aTitleString withBlanksTrimmed) isEmpty])
      ifTrue: [BusinessRuleException signal:
                    'Document cannot have nil or empty title.'].
    self testSetTitle: aTrimmedTitleString.
    self doSetTitle: aTrimmedTitleString

Document methodsFor: 'accessing-rules'

testSetTitle: aTitleString
    aTitleString size > 255
      ifTrue: [BusinessRuleException signal:
                    'Document title cannot exceed 255 characters.']

Document methodsFor: 'private'

doSetTitle: aTitleString
    title ← aTitleString.
    self changed: #title

LISTING 8.2
Squeak methods for setting, testing, and assigning a descriptive property.

Example: Document Publication Date

This example shows a state transition rule for a descriptive property.

> EXAMPLE—A document cannot set its publication date if it does not have an approved nomination.

Publication date is a write-once, read-only property that gets set when the document is published. It serves double duty by indicating whether the document is published and, if so, when.[4] These facts imply that the document does not have a property set accessor for the publication date, since this property cannot be externally edited. However, the document does have the following methods, which are shown in Listing 8.3:

- A test method to check if the publication date can be set
- An assignment method to put the value into the property
- A conduct business service that checks the property rule before assigning the publication date to the current date

```
Document.java
// CONDUCT BUSINESS

public void publish() throws BusinessRuleException
{
  this.testSetPublicationDate();
  this.doSetPublicationDate(new Date());
}

// ACCESSORS - property rules

public void testSetPublicationDate() throws BusinessRuleException
{
  if (this.isPublished())
    throw new BusinessRuleException("Document already published.");
  if (!this.isApproved())
    throw new BusinessRuleException(
            "Document not approved for publication.");
}

// ACCESSORS - property do sets

public void doSetPublicationDate(Date newDate)
{
  this.publicationDate = newDate;
}
```

LISTING 8.3
Java conduct business service and state transition rule test method.

---

4. Normally, using the "null" value to represent a business state is a bad thing to do. However, we encapsulated the "null-ness" from external methods by providing the "is published" accessor and raising an exception if the value was requested when it was null.

The Java "is published" and "is approved" services were shown in the previous chapter.[5]

Although there is no set accessor, the Squeak code includes a private method to consolidate in one place the property test, assignment, and change notification. As with the Java code, the property test calls a method that searches the nominations for an approved one and raises an exception if one is not found (see Listing 8.4). See the CD for all the code.

Document methodsFor: 'domain services'

publish
    self testSetPublicationDate.
    self doSetPublicationDate: Date today

Document methodsFor: 'accessing-rules'

testSetPublicationDate
    self isPublished ifTrue: [BusinessRuleException signal:
                'Document already published.'].
    self approvedNomination
      ifNil: [BusinessRuleException signal: 'Document not approved for publication.']

Document methodsFor: 'private'

doSetPublicationDate: aPublicationDate
    publicationDate ← aPublicationDate.
    self changed: #publicationDate

LISTING 8.4
Squeak conduct business service and state transition rule test method.

State, Role, and Type Property Business Rules

State, role, and type properties have fixed sets of legal values that are supplied by domain experts. Such properties with fixed sets of values are also known as enumerated types, and require special property accessors to encapsulate their implementation. In the previous chapter, these accessors were called property value accessors.

EXAMPLE—A nomination with a status property has get accessors that ask if the status has a particular value: `isStatusPending`, `isStatusInReview`, `isStatusApproved`, `isStatusRejected`. It also has set accessors that request the status to take on a particular value: `setSta-`

---

5. See Listings 7.65 and 7.67.

tusPending, setStatusInReview, setStatusApproved, setStatusRejected.

For some enumerated type properties, the current property value can prohibit the property from taking on other values. This happens frequently with
lifecycle state properties; the current state value restricts the next acceptable
state value.

EXAMPLE—A nomination with a lifecycle state of "rejected" cannot
transition to a lifecycle state of "pending," "in review," or "approved."

PRINCIPLE 83
ENUMERATED PROPERTY BUSINESS RULES

Properties with enumerated types are governed by business rules that define
the set of legal values and the legal transitions from one value to another.

Example – Nomination Status

EXAMPLE—A nomination has a status property with the following
possible values:

- Pending
- In review
- Approved
- Rejected

A nomination's lifecycle state transitions are governed by business
rules. A nomination cannot:

- Transition to the "pending" state unless in review or already pending
- Transition to the "in review" state unless pending or already in review
- Transition to the "approved" state unless in review or already
  approved
- Transition to the "rejected" state unless in review or already rejected

Each lifecycle state transition rule is implemented by a distinct method. This
provides more flexibility for specialization classes that may want to selectively alter the transition rules.

The Java accessors and test methods for the "rejected" value of the status
property are shown in Listing 8.5. The other accessors and test methods are
listed on the CD.

In Squeak, the test methods for the state transition rules are placed in the
"accessing-rules" message category as shown in Listing 8.6.

Nomination.java

```
// ACCESSORS -- set property values

public void setStatusRejected() throws BusinessRuleException
{
  this.testSetStatusRejected();
  this.doSetStatus(STATUS_REJECTED);
}

// ACCESSORS - property value rules

public void testSetStatusRejected() throws BusinessRuleException
{
  if (this.isStatusInReview() || this.isStatusRejected()) return;
  else throw new BusinessRuleException(
              "Nomination cannot be rejected. Not under review");
}

// ACCESSORS - property do sets

public void doSetStatus(NominationStatus aStatus)
{
  this.status = aStatus;
}
```

LISTING 8.5
Java property value accessor and business rule test method.

Nomination methodsFor: 'accessing'

setStatusRejected
   self testSetStatusRejected.
   self doSetStatus: self statusRejected

Nomination methodsFor: 'accessing-rules'

testSetStatusRejected
   (self isStatusInReview or: [self isStatusRejected])
    ifFalse: [BusinessRuleException signal:
            'Nomination cannot be rejected. Not under review.']

LISTING 8.6
Squeak property value accessor and business rule test method.

Cross-Property Validation

Cross-property validation occurs when a property rule includes another property from the same or a different object.

EXAMPLE—A team member cannot become a chair (i.e., set its role property to "chair") if the team member belongs to a team whose format prevents it from having another chair.

When two objects are involved in a cross-property validation rule, each object requires its own test service. The first test is in the object trying to change its property value, and the second test is in the object capable of vetoing the property value. Often, this veto property test doubles as a property collaboration rule. For example, a team member cannot change its role property value to "chair" if its team cannot support another chair; however, it is also true that a team member cannot be added to the team if the team cannot support another chair. Isolating this veto test into its own method allows its use for cross-property validation and for collaboration rule checking. In the team member example, which is illustrated in Figure 8.1, the veto test is called from the test set method for the role property.

The team object definition includes a method for counting the number of chair team members. In Java, this method uses an anonymous inner class that tests elements from a list, selects those returning true, and returns them in another list. The test used here is whether a team member is a chair (see Listing 8.7). The code for the `CollectionSelector` class is on the CD.

TeamMember	Team	I am a team member.
		I set my role to chair by:
setRoleChair	testCanBeChair	⋏ testing if my role property can be set to the chair value.
testSetRoleChair		
doSetRoleChair		⋏ if the test succeeds then I set my role property to the chair value.
		I test if my role property can be set to chair by:
		⋏ asking my team to test if I can be a chair on it.

setRoleChair			(;) // no inputs or outputs
testSetRoleChair			(;)
	→	testCanBeChair	(aTeamMember;) // fails if team member cannot be chair
END DEFN			END TeamMember.testSetRoleChair
doSetRoleChair			(;) // sets role property to CHAIR value
END DEFN			END TeamMember.setRoleChair

FIGURE 8.1

TeamMember setRoleChair scenario.[6]

---

6. We prefer scenario views to other available collaboration or sequence diagrams because we find scenario views more readable. Coad, North, and Mayfield introduced scenario views in the *Object Models* book.

TeamMember.java

```java
// ACCESSORS -- set property value

public void doSetRoleChair() throws BusinessRuleException
{
  this.testSetRoleChair();
  this.doSet(ROLE_CHAIR);
}

// ACCESSORS - property value rules

public void testSetRoleChair() throws BusinessRuleException
{
  if (this.isRoleChair()) return;
  if (this.team != null)
    this.team.testCanBeChair(this);
}
```

Team.java

```java
// ACCESSORS - collaboration rules

public void testCanBeChair(ITeamMember aTeamMember)
              throws BusinessRuleException
{
  if (this.isFormatMultipleChair()) return;
  if (this.isFormatNoChair())
    throw new BusinessRuleException(
        "Cannot add chair team member to no chairs team.");
  if (this.getChairs().size() > 0)
    throw new BusinessRuleException(
        "Cannot add another chair team member to single chair team.");
}

// DETERMINE MINE

public List getChairs()
{
  CollectionSelector chairSelector = new CollectionSelector()
  {
    public boolean selectBlock(Object listElement, Object keyValue)
    {
      return ((ITeamMember)listElement).isRoleChair();
    }
  };
  return (List)chairSelector.select(this.teamMembers);
}
```

LISTING 8.7
Java set property accessor and cross-validation property test methods.

In Squeak, the two test methods belong in different message categories. Because it is validating a property, the team member test goes into the "accessing-rules" message category; and since it is validating for a collaborator, the team test method belongs in the "collaboration-rules" message category (see Listing 8.8).

TeamMember methodsFor: 'private'

setRoleChair
   self testSetRoleChair.
   self doSetRole: self roleChair

TeamMember methodsFor: 'accessing-rules'

testSetRoleChair
   self isRoleChair ifTrue: [↑ self].
   self team ifNotNil: [self team testCanBeChair: self]

Team methodsFor: 'collaboration-rules'

testCanBeChair: aTeamMember
   self isFormatMultipleChair ifTrue: [↑ self].
   self isFormatNoChair ifTrue: [BusinessRuleException signal:
    'Tried to add chair team member to no chairs team.'].
   self chairs size = 1 ifTrue: [BusinessRuleException signal:
    'Tried to add another chair team member to a single chair team.']

Team methodsFor: 'collaboration-accessing'

chairs
   ↑self teamMembers select: [:aTeamMember | aTeamMember isRoleChair].

LISTING 8.8
Squeak set property accessor and cross-validation property test methods.

Coordinating Collaboration Rules _____

Collaboration rules govern whether two objects can establish or dissolve a collaboration with each other. Because two objects are involved, the collaboration rule checking must be coordinated so that: (1) both objects can do rule checking, and (2) rule checking happens when either object establishes or dissolves the collaboration.

Dual Rule Checking

All the collaboration rules cannot be consolidated in one object. While putting all rules in one place may make the implementation easier in the short-term, it destroys pluggability, extensibility, and scalability.

Pluggability is the notion that an object in a collaboration can specify communication requirements between itself and its collaborator such that any other object meeting those requirements can collaborate with it. It also implies that different kinds of objects actually do meet the requirements.

Pluggability is lost if one collaborator takes on the responsibility of checking all the collaboration rules. This is because collaboration rules involve checking implementation level details—properties, state, and even other collaborators. By "knowing" the other's collaboration rules, the "manager" object doing all the work is assuming a particular implementation for its "dumb" collaborator. This constrains the manager object to collaborate only with this particular object implementation. Pluggability is discussed more extensively later in this chapter.

Extensibility is the notion that any object can add new properties, services, and collaborations without impacting other objects. Again, if one manager object is doing the work for both objects, then extensions to the implementation of the dumb object could change the collaboration rules, which are being handled by the manager object.

Scalability is the notion that the existing set of objects can easily accommodate and work with new types of objects. Once pluggability is lost, scalability becomes nearly impossible since each existing object is constrained to work with only one particular implementation for each of its collaborators.

> EXAMPLE—Consider these different implementations of the Team – TeamMember collaboration from the previous chapter.
>
> *Implementation 1:* Team checks both its own and the team member's collaboration rules.
>
> - If an expiration date is added to a team member to accommodate short-term contractors, then team collaboration rule checking is impacted because the team must now check whether a team member has expired before approving it for collaboration.
>
> *Implementation 2:* Team and team member both check their own collaboration rules.
>
> - In this scenario, adding an expiration date to a team member does not impact the team. Instead, the collaboration rule checking for the team member is expanded to check whether it has expired before agreeing to collaborate with a team.

PRINCIPLE 84
DUAL RULE CHECKING

To achieve pluggability, extensibility, and scalability, each object must check its own collaboration rules.

Commutative Rule Checking

Collaboration rules do not care how objects were brought together or pulled apart. Sometimes, conduct business services specify precisely how the object interactions occur, and the order in which the collaborations are created. Other times, user interfaces allow users to selectively associate or disassociate objects. Collaboration rules should be implemented without any assumptions about how or by whom they will be called.

> EXAMPLE—Consider the Team – TeamMember collaboration. Regardless of whether a team member is added to a team through the "add team member" accessor or a team is added to a team member through the "add team" accessor, all the collaboration rules need to be checked.

PRINCIPLE 85
COMMUTATIVE RULE CHECKING

> Implement collaboration rules so that either collaborator can request that the rules be checked.

Implementing Collaboration Rules _____

Establishing a collaboration between two objects is a scripted process during which each object is asked to check its own collaboration rules, and if these pass, then each object is asked to do whatever it takes to remember the other collaborator—set a collaboration variable or add the object reference to a collaboration collection.

Methods for Establishing a Collaboration

As with the property accessors, we want our collaboration accessors to be highly cohesive. When implementing collaboration accessors, we isolate the rule check and collaboration assignment into separate methods. Isolating the rule check allows subclasses to extend collaboration rules, and isolating the assignment allows bypassing the business rules when necessary.[7]

add (aCollaborator)   Adds the designated collaborator to the object receiving this message ("this" or "self") if the collaboration rules allow

---

7. As stated earlier, bypassing business rules is dangerous. Generally, only internal methods and data management classes need to do this.

testAdd (aCollaborator) Tests the collaborator against the receiver object's collaboration rules; raises an exception if they fail

doAdd (aCollaborator) Puts the collaborator into the receiver object's collaboration variable or collection without rule checking

An extended version of this table, including methods for dissolving collaborations, is shown in Appendix B ("Methods for Enforcing Collaboration Rules").

PRINCIPLE 86

ISOLATE COLLABORATION RULES

Define separate methods to enforce collaboration rules for establishing and dissolving a collaboration. Define the collaboration add and remove accessors to call the appropriate test method.

PRINCIPLE 87

ISOLATE COLLABORATION ASSIGNMENT

Define separate methods to assign and remove a reference to a collaborator and to bypass business rule checking when necessary. The collaboration add and remove accessors call the appropriate assignment method after checking business rules.

Unlike the property rule methods, all the methods for establishing a collaboration belong in the conduct business interface. The difference here is that two objects are involved in establishing a collaboration, and the process requires communication and cooperation between them. Since collaborators refer to each other through their conduct business interfaces, any methods used to communicate while establishing a collaboration must go into this interface. Putting the "do add" methods in the conduct business interface means they are also declared as `public` methods, but this is okay if your programmers are disciplined. Besides, these methods must be `public` to allow the object to be reconstructed from persistent storage through a data manager. Declaring these methods anything other than `public` constrains the data manager to reside in the same package as the business object. [8]

---

8. Remember that clutter is a bad thing. A package that is intended to contain only business classes should not be cluttered with data management or other "helper" classes.

Example: Establishing a Collaboration

Establishing a collaboration involves two collaboration add accessors, one for each collaborator. To satisfy the dual and commutative rule checking principles, both sets of collaboration rules must be checked by both collaboration add accessors.

EXAMPLE—Including collaboration rule-checking while establishing a Team – TeamMember collaboration requires the following steps in the collaboration add accessors:

Team >> add team member (a team member)
I test that "a team member" is logically valid (e.g., it is not null).
I test that I can add "a team member."
I ask "a team member" to test whether he can add me as a team.
I do add "a team member."
I ask "a team member" to do add me.

TeamMember >> add team (a team)
I test that "a team" is logically valid (e.g., it is not null).
I test that I can add "a team."
I ask "a team" to test whether he can add me as a team member.
I do add "a team."
I ask "a team" to do add me.

While the commutative rule checking principle requires both collaboration add accessors to perform rule checking and assignment, code duplication is reduced by allowing one add accessor to delegate the responsibility of establishing the collaboration to the other add accessor.

EXAMPLE—The streamlined version of the Team – TeamMember collaboration accessors has the team accessor delegating to the team member accessor:

Team >> add team (a team member)
I test that "a team member" is logically valid (e.g., it is not null).
I ask "a team member" to add team (me).

TeamMember >> add team (a team)
I test that "a team" is logically valid (e.g., it is not null).
I test that I can add "a team."
I ask "a team" to test whether he can add me as a team member.
I do add "a team."
I ask "a team" to do add me.

Follow the usual rules for assigning work: "Most Specific Carries the Load" principle (74), and "Let the Coordinator Direct" principle (78). Applying these workload principles to the three fundamental patterns yields the following assignments:

- `generic` delegates to `specific`
- `whole` delegates to a `part`
- `specific` delegates to a `transaction`

PRINCIPLE 88
STREAMLINING COLLABORATION ACCESSORS

> To streamline the collaboration accessors, allow one collaborator to delegate the process of establishing and dissolving the collaboration to the other collaborator.

PRINCIPLE 89
CHOOSING YOUR DIRECTOR

> To find the director of a streamlined collaboration, choose the `specific` of a `generic` - `specific`, choose the `part` of a `whole` - `part`, and choose the `transaction` of a `transaction` - `specific`.

Dissolving a Collaboration

The process for dissolving a collaboration between two objects is very similar to the process for establishing a collaboration. Again, the rule checking and collaboration assignment are isolated into separate methods, all the methods go into the conduct business interface, and the collaboration remove accessors are streamlined according to the "Choosing Your Director" principle (89).

remove (aCollaborator)	Removes the designated collaborator from the object receiving this message if the collaboration rules allow
testRemove (aCollaborator)	Tests the collaborator against the receiver object's collaboration rules; raises an error if they fail
doRemove (aCollaborator)	Clears a collaborator from the collaboration variable or removes from a collection without rule checking

An extended version of this table, including methods for establishing collaborations, is shown in Appendix B ("Methods for Enforcing Collaboration Rules").

Summary: Steps for Implementing Collaboration Rules

The previous chapter introduced the "DIAPER" process for implementing object definitions. This chapter expands the DIAPER process to include collaboration rule checking. Steps in the DIAPER process that are affected include the "Define" and "Accessing" steps.

In the "Define" step, collaboration rule checking requires including the "test add," "test remove," "do add," and "do remove" methods in the conduct business interface for the object's collaborations. Omitting the test methods is tempting when the object lacks collaboration rules; however, unless optimization is the preeminent goal, it is better to include the test methods and guarantee extensibility.

In the "Accessing" step, implement methods for testing collaboration rules and assigning the collaborator reference. Also, use the "Choosing Your Director" principle (89) to decide which collaborator directs and which delegates. Implement the directing collaboration accessor so that both collaborators check their collaboration rules and perform their assignments if the rules succeed.

Implementing Collaboration Rules Example _____

This section shows how to implement collaboration rules in Java and Squeak using the Person – TeamMember and Team – TeamMember collaborations coded in the previous chapter.

Person – Team Member – Team Collaboration Rules

As an `actor`, a person has no collaboration rules for its `roles`, which include team member.[9] The team member plays as a `specific` in a `generic - specific` collaboration with its person, and plays as a `part` in a `whole - part` collaboration with its team. Because it acts as these pattern players, the team member carries most of the load for checking the collaboration rules.

---

9. See p. 57, "Actor – Role Collaboration Rules."

Team member: Establish person collaboration rules.

1. A team member cannot collaborate with a person if the team member already has a person collaborator.
2. A team member cannot collaborate with a person who lacks a valid email.
3. A team member cannot collaborate with a person if the team member's team already includes another team member with the same person.

EXPLANATION

Rule #1 is a multiplicity rule. A team member can collaborate with only one person, and cannot exchange the person for another.

Rule #2 is a property rule. A person lacking a valid email property cannot collaborate.

Rule #3 is a conflict rule. A team member cannot collaborate with a person if the person conflicts with the team member's present team collaborator.

Team member: Dissolve person collaboration rules.

1. A team member cannot dissolve its collaboration with its person if the team member belongs to a team.

EXPLANATION

Rule #1 is a state rule. A team member on a team is in an improper state for dissolving its person collaboration.

Team member: Establish team collaboration rules.

1. A team member cannot collaborate with a team if the team member already has a team collaborator.
2. A team member cannot collaborate with a team if the team already includes another team member with the same person.

EXPLANATION

Rule #1 is a multiplicity rule.

Rule #2 is a conflict rule. This same conflict rule applies when establishing a person collaborator.

Team member: Dissolve team collaboration rules.

1. A team member cannot dissolve its collaboration with its team if the team member has nominations.

Rule #1 is a state rule. A team member with nominations is in an improper state for dissolving its team collaboration.

Team: Establish team member collaboration rules.

1. A team cannot collaborate with a team member if the team member is a chair, and the team's format will not allow it to add another chair team member.

EXPLANATION

Rule #1 is a property rule. This rule uses properties from both the team and team member. Because the team has the "standard" used for comparison, it owns the rule.[10] This rule also applies for cross-property validation and was used in a previous example (see p. 236).

Plan of Attack

The plan is to update the person, team member, and team object definitions to include the above collaboration rules. The following changes to the object definitions are applied where needed:

- Expand the conduct business interfaces
- Implement the "test" and "do" methods
- Revise the collaboration accessors

Expand Conduct Business Profiles

Update the person, team member, and team conduct business interfaces to include the "do" and "test" methods for collaborations (see Figure 8.2). Include the method signatures shown in Listing 8.9 in the person and team member conduct business interfaces.

Example: Person – Team Member – Team "Test" Methods

This section discusses the team member and team methods for checking collaboration rules (see Listing 8.10). Also included is a team member method to check for conflicts between the team member's team and person collaborators. This method does not go into the conduct business interface because

---

10. See p. 55, "Property Rules."

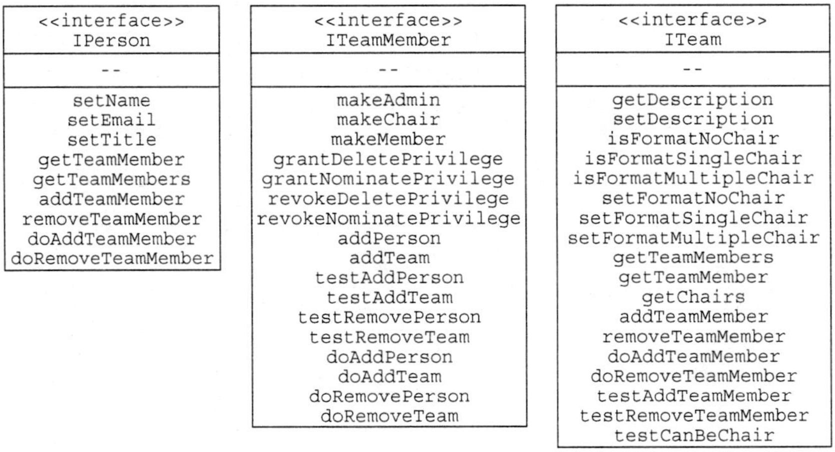

<<interface>> IPerson	<<interface>> ITeamMember	<<interface>> ITeam
--	--	--
setName setEmail setTitle getTeamMember getTeamMembers addTeamMember removeTeamMember doAddTeamMember doRemoveTeamMember	makeAdmin makeChair makeMember grantDeletePrivilege grantNominatePrivilege revokeDeletePrivilege revokeNominatePrivilege addPerson addTeam testAddPerson testAddTeam testRemovePerson testRemoveTeam doAddPerson doAddTeam doRemovePerson doRemoveTeam	getDescription setDescription isFormatNoChair isFormatSingleChair isFormatMultipleChair setFormatNoChair setFormatSingleChair setFormatMultipleChair getTeamMembers getTeamMember getChairs addTeamMember removeTeamMember doAddTeamMember doRemoveTeamMember testAddTeamMember testRemoveTeamMember testCanBeChair

FIGURE 8.2
Conduct business interfaces updated with collaboration "test" and "do" methods.

IPerson.java

```java
public interface IPerson extends IPersonProfile
{
  <<snip>>
  // ACCESSORS - collaboration do adds
  public void doAddTeamMember(ITeamMember aTeamMember);
  public void doRemoveTeamMember(ITeamMember aTeamMember);
}
```

ITeamMember.java

```java
public interface ITeamMember extends ITeamMemberProfile
{
  <<snip>>
  // ACCESSORS - collaboration rules
  public void testAddTeam(ITeam aTeam) throws BusinessRuleException;
  public void testRemoveTeam(ITeam aTeam) throws BusinessRuleException;
  public void testAddPerson(IPerson aPerson) throws BusinessRuleException;
  public void testRemovePerson(IPerson aPerson) throws BusinessRuleException;

  // ACCESSORS - collaboration do adds
  public void doAddTeam(ITeam aTeam);
  public void doAddPerson(IPerson aPerson);
  public void doRemoveTeam(ITeam aTeam);
  public void doRemovePerson(IPerson aPerson);
}
```

(continued)

LISTING 8.9
Java conduct business interfaces updated with collaboration rule test methods.

```
ITeam.java
public interface ITeam
{
  <<snip>>
  // ACCESSORS - collaboration do adds
  public void doAddTeamMember(ITeamMember aTeamMember);
  public void doRemoveTeamMember(ITeamMember aTeamMember);

  // ACCESSORS - collaboration rules
  public void testAddTeamMember(ITeamMember aTeamMember
              throws BusinessRuleException;
  public void testCanBeChair(ITeamMember aTeamMember)
              throws BusinessRuleException;
}
```

LISTING 8.9
Java conduct business interfaces updated with collaboration rule test methods. (continued)

it is internal to the team member. Conflict rules will be discussed more thoroughly later in this chapter. The team collaboration rule for adding a team member collaborator makes use of the method defined earlier during the cross-property validation example. This method confirms that a team member who is a chair can be added to the team (see Listing 8.7).

In Squeak, the collaboration test methods go in their own message category, "collaboration rules." See Listing 8.11.

Example: Person – Team Member – Team "Do" Methods

These methods assign or remove the collaborator reference without rule checking. The Java code is shown in Listing 8.12.

In Squeak, these methods are placed in the private message category to emphasize that only the collaboration accessors should use them (see Listing 8.13). These methods also handle change notification to dependents.

Example: Person – Team Member – Team Collaboration Accessors

Both person and team delegate to team member to direct the establishment or dissolution of the collaboration. Only the add accessors are shown in Listings 8.14 and 8.15 because the remove accessors so closely resemble them.

TeamMember.java

```java
public void testAddPerson(IPerson aPerson) throws BusinessRuleException
{
  if (this.person != null)
    throw new BusinessRuleException("Team member has a person.");
  if (!aPerson.hasValidEmail())
    throw new BusinessRuleException("Person has invalid email.");
  if (this.team != null)
    this.testAddPersonTeamConflict(aPerson, this.team);
}

public void testRemovePerson(IPerson aPerson)
              throws BusinessRuleException
{
  if (aPerson == null)
    throw new BusinessRuleException("Tried to remove null person.");
  if (!aPerson.equals(this.person))
    throw new BusinessRuleException("Tried to remove wrong person.");
  if (this.team !=  null)
    throw new BusinessRuleException("Team member on team cannot remove person.");
}

public void testAddPersonTeamConflict(IPerson aPerson, ITeam aTeam)
              throws BusinessRuleException
{
  ITeamMember aTeamMember = aTeam.getTeamMember(aPerson);
  if (aTeamMember != null)
    throw new BusinessRuleException("Person already on team.");
}
```

Team.java

```java
public void testAddTeamMember(ITeamMember aTeamMember)
              throws BusinessRuleException
{
  if (aTeamMember.isRoleChair())
    this.testCanBeChair(aTeamMember);
}
```

LISTING 8.10
Java "test" methods for checking collaboration rules.

TeamMember methodsFor: 'collaboration-rules'

testAddPerson: aPerson
  self person
   ifNotNil: [BusinessRuleException signal: 'Team member already has a person.'].
  aPerson hasValidEmail
   ifFalse: [BusinessRuleException signal: 'Tried to add person with invalid email.'].
  self team ifNotNil: [self testAddConflictBetween: aPerson and: self team]

LISTING 8.11
Squeak "test" methods for checking collaboration rules.

testRemovePerson: aPerson
  self person = aPerson
    ifFalse: [BusinessRuleException signal: 'Tried to remove different person.'].
  self team ifNotNil: [BusinessRuleException signal:
                    'Team member on team cannot remove person.'].

LISTING 8.11

Squeak "test" methods for checking collaboration rules. (continued)

Person.java

```java
public void doAddTeamMember(ITeamMember aTeamMember)
{
   this.teamMembers.add(aTeamMember);
}

public void doRemoveTeamMember(ITeamMember aTeamMember)
{
   this.teamMembers.remove(aTeamMember);
}
```

TeamMember.java

```java
public void doAddPerson(IPerson aPerson)
{
   this.person = aPerson;
}

public void doRemovePerson(IPerson aPerson)
{
   this.person = null;
}
```

Team.java

```java
public void doAddTeamMember(ITeamMember aTeamMember)
{
   this.teamMembers.add(aTeamMember);
}

public void doRemoveTeamMember(ITeamMember aTeamMember)
{
   this.teamMembers.remove(aTeamMember);
}
```

LISTING 8.12

Java low-level methods for connecting and disconnecting collaborators.

Person methodsFor: 'private'

doAddTeamMember: aTeamMember
    self teamMembers add: aTeamMember.
    self changed: #teamMembers

doRemoveTeamMember: aTeamMember
    self teamMembers remove: aTeamMember ifAbsent: [ ].
    self changed: #teamMembers

TeamMember methodsFor: 'private'

doAddPerson: aPerson
    person ← aPerson.
    self changed: #person

doRemovePerson: aPerson
    person ← nil.
    self changed: #person

LISTING 8.13
Squeak low-level methods for connecting and disconnecting collaborators.

```
Person.java

public void addTeamMember(ITeamMember aTeamMember)
  throws BusinessRuleException
{
  if (aTeamMember == null)
    throw new BusinessRuleException("Tried to add null team member.");
  aTeamMember.addPerson(this);
}

TeamMember.java

public void addPerson(IPerson aPerson) throws BusinessRuleException
{
  if (aPerson == null)
    throw new BusinessRuleException("Tried to add null person");
  this.testAddPerson(aPerson);
  this.doAddPerson(aPerson);
  aPerson.doAddTeamMember(this);
}

public void addTeam(ITeam aTeam) throws BusinessRuleException
{
  if (aTeam == null)
    throw new BusinessRuleException("Tried to add null team.");
  this.testAddTeam(aTeam);
  aTeam.testAddTeamMember(this);
  this.doAddTeam(aTeam);
  aTeam.doAddTeamMember(this);
}                                                          (continued)
```

LISTING 8.14
Java collaboration add accessors with collaboration rule testing.

```
Team.java
```

```java
public void addTeamMember(ITeamMember aTeamMember)
  throws BusinessRuleException
{
  if (aTeamMember == null)
    throw new BusinessRuleException("Tried to add null team member");
  aTeamMember.addTeam(this);
}
```

LISTING 8.14
Java collaboration add accessors with collaboration rule testing.(continued)

Person methodsFor: 'collaboration-accessing'

addTeamMember: aTeamMember
  aTeamMember
    ifNil: [BusinessRuleException signal: 'Tried to add nil team member.'].
  aTeamMember addPerson: self

TeamMember methodsFor: 'collaboration-accessing'

addPerson: aPerson
  aPerson
    ifNil: [BusinessRuleException signal: 'Tried to add nil person.'].
  self testAddPerson: aPerson.
  aPerson testAddTeamMember: self.
  self doAddPerson: aPerson.
  aPerson doAddTeamMember: self

LISTING 8.15
Squeak collaboration accessors with collaboration rule testing.

Implementing Conflict Collaboration Rules _____

Conflict rules come into play when business rules define restrictions between objects that collaborate through an intermediary object. In essence, conflict rules are collaboration rules between indirect collaborators, that is, in-laws. Conflict rules appear in all three of the fundamental patterns:

`Generic - Specific`	*Example*. Business rules prohibiting conflicting `roles` from belonging to the same `actor`.
`Whole - Part`	*Example*. Business rules preventing incompatible `parts` from joining the same `assembly`.
`Specific - Transaction`	*Example*. Business rules preventing a `role` from participating in events at restricted locations.

Implementing Conflict Rules

Conflict rules are implemented by following the same principles used for other collaboration rules: dual rule checking, commutative rule checking, and streamlined to a director. Conflict rules differ from collaboration rules in range and timing.

Conflict rules range over more objects than collaboration rules, which only involve two objects, a potential collaborator and a collaboration director. With conflict rules, a potential collaborator tests one or more existing collaborators of the collaboration director, and the existing collaborators test the potential one. Some conflict rules even depend on characteristics of the collaboration director. For maximum flexibility, methods for testing conflict rules should receive as input the directing collaborator and all its other collaborators.

Unlike collaboration rules, which must run before a collaboration is established, conflict rules may be deferred until the other collaborators are available for checking. Deferring conflict rules may be necessary, but it also introduces tricky considerations, such as determining which collaborators to roll back if the rules fail, and deciding how to gracefully kick out things that were accepted earlier. Generic - specific collaborations typically check conflicts immediately, when a potential specific is looking to collaborate with the generic. Rejection of the potential specific does not require rollback of the existing specifics, but is fatal to the rejected specific. Whole - part collaborations also tend to check conflicts immediately, and do not require rollback of other parts when a part fails. The exceptions may be certain assemblies that cannot exist if all parts are not present. As most parts can exist without a whole, rejection of a part is often not fatal to the part.

Deferred conflict rule checking occurs most commonly with transactions. A transaction cannot obtain a valid state until all its collaborators are present, and failure of the conflict rules is fatal to the transaction and results in the rollback of all its collaborators. On the other hand, composite transactions usually do not know when all their collaborators are available as they can have an unlimited number of line items with collaborating specific items. However, once a composite transaction knows its role and place, it can check conflict rules between these and its existing specific items or any specific items seeking to collaborate.

> EXAMPLE—A video rental transaction involving one or more video-tapes rejects a videotape with a restricted rating if the customer is underage. If the customer is required to show his credentials at the

beginning of the rental transaction then conflict rules can be run as soon a videotape attempts to collaborate with the rental, and a restricted videotape can be rejected immediately. Delaying the verification of customer information to the end means that a conflict with a restricted videotape is only detected after it is part of the rental transaction, and the restricted videotape must be rolled back out of the rental.

To satisfy the dual and commutative rule checking principles, conflict test methods must run whenever the collaboration director adds or removes a potentially conflicting collaborator.

> EXAMPLE—When a `transaction` (voter registration) adds a `role` collaborator (voter), it asks the `role` and its `place` collaborator (precinct) to check for conflicts ("test add voter registration conflict"). The same conflict checks are made when the voter is added first. In general, when a `transaction` adds a `place` collaborator, it checks it against its `role` collaborator and `specific item` collaborators, if they exist. The scenario in Figure 8.3 involves a `transaction` with only `role` and `place` collaborators, but the logic is the same when a `specific item` is involved. Regardless of the order in which the `place` and `role` are added to the `transaction`, the test conflict rules run once.

Methods for Checking Collaboration Conflicts

Conflict rules go into separate methods and are invoked by the appropriate "test add" or "test remove" method of the collaboration director.

testAddConflict (directCollaborator, indirectCollaborator, ...)	Checks receiving object's conflict collaboration rules using its direct collaborator and one or more indirect collaborators
testRemoveConflict (directCollaborator, indirectCollaborator, ...)	Checks receiving object's conflict collaboration rules using its direct collaborator and one or more indirect collaborators

Because they involve communication among collaborators, methods for checking conflict rules are `public` and belong in the conduct business interface.

Summary: Steps for Implementing Conflict Collaboration Rules

Conflict rules contribute to the test deciding whether a collaboration should be established or dissolved, and are invoked from the directing collaborator's test method.

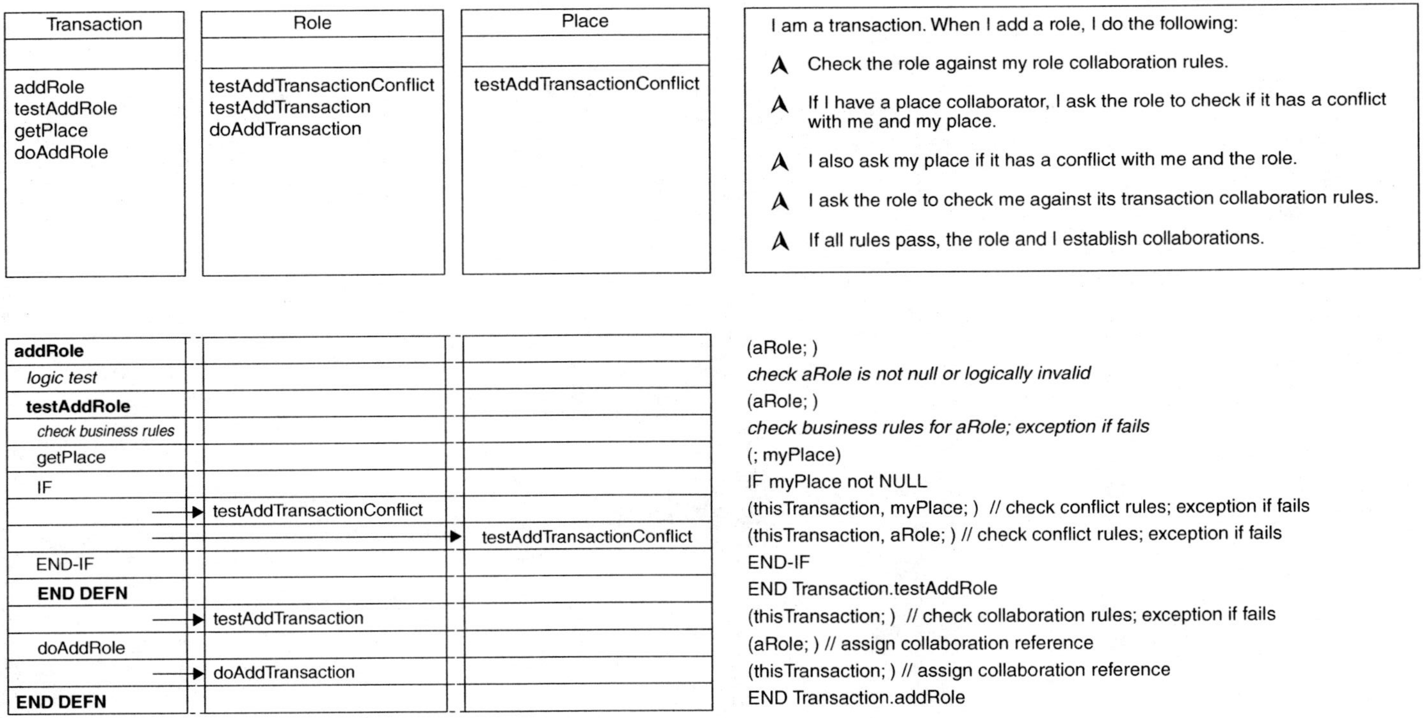

I am a transaction. When I add a role, I do the following:

▲ Check the role against my role collaboration rules.

▲ If I have a place collaborator, I ask the role to check if it has a conflict with me and my place.

▲ I also ask my place if it has a conflict with me and the role.

▲ I ask the role to check me against its transaction collaboration rules.

▲ If all rules pass, the role and I establish collaborations.

Transaction	Role	Place
addRole	testAddTransactionConflict	testAddTransactionConflict
testAddRole	testAddTransaction	
getPlace	doAddTransaction	
doAddRole		

```
addRole
  logic test                                                (aRole; )
                                                            check aRole is not null or logically invalid
testAddRole                                                 (aRole; )
  check business rules                                      check business rules for aRole; exception if fails
  getPlace                                                  (; myPlace)
  IF                                                        IF myPlace not NULL
    testAddTransactionConflict  testAddTransactionConflict  (thisTransaction, myPlace; )  // check conflict rules; exception if fails
                                                            (thisTransaction, aRole; )  // check conflict rules; exception if fails
  END-IF                                                    END-IF
END DEFN                                                    END Transaction.testAddRole
    testAddTransaction                                      (thisTransaction; )  // check collaboration rules; exception if fails
                                                            (aRole; )  // assign collaboration reference
  doAddRole                                                 (thisTransaction; )  // assign collaboration reference
    doAddTransaction
END DEFN                                                    END Transaction.addRole
```

FIGURE 8.3

Conduct business interfaces updated with collaboration "test" and "do" methods.

In the "Define" step, for each collaborator with conflict rules, include in its conduct business interface the relevant conflict test methods.

In the "Accessing" step, for objects with conflict rules, implement the appropriate test conflict methods for establishing and dissolving collaborations. Also, revise the test collaboration methods of the directing collaborator to include conflict rule checking with its existing and potential collaborators. If conflict rule checking is deferred, then each test method tests whether the potential collaborator is the last to be added, and if so, checks the conflict rules of its existing collaborators and the potential one.

Implementing Conflict Rules Example _____

This section shows how to implement conflict collaboration rules in Java and Squeak using the TeamMember – Nomination – Document collaboration coded in the previous chapter.

Team Member – Nomination – Document Example

In this example, a document nominates itself with a team member. Applying the "do it myself" principle to this business process transforms it into a conduct business service of the document that creates a nomination with the document and participating team member (see Figure 8.4).

Team Member – Nomination – Document Collaboration Rules

In this example, there are no remove collaboration rules because this document management system requires a historical record of all nominations, even failed ones. Also for this reason, there are no methods to remove nominations from a team member or document.

Team member: Add nomination collaboration rules.

1. A team member must have nominate privileges to nominate a document.
2. A team member can only nominate a fixed number of times per 30 days:

• Five times for a team member whose role is member or admin
• Ten times for a team member whose role is chair.

I am a document. When I nominate myself for a team member I do the following:

✗ Create a nomination for myself and the team member.

I am a nomination. When I am created for a document and team member I do the following:

✗ Add the team member as a collaborator. If fails then raise an exception.

✗ Add the document as a collaborator. If fails then remove my team member and raise an exception.

```
(aTeamMember; )
(aDocument, aTeamMember; aNomination ) // creates aNomination
(aTeamMember; ) // See Figure 8.6; exception if fails
(aDocument; ) // exception if fails
IF addDocument fails
(aNomination; )
Nomination.new RAISES EXCEPTION
END-IF
END Nomination.new
END Document.nominate
```

Document
nominate

Nomination
new
addTeamMember
addDocument

Document
doRemoveNomination

nominate

new
addTeamMember
addDocument
I F
RAISE EXCEPTION
END-IF
END DEFN

doRemoveNomination

END DEFN

FIGURE 8.4

Conduct business interfaces updated with collaboration "test" and "do" methods.

Rule #1 is a property rule. Team members know what privileges they need to nominate. Rule #2 is an example of a dynamic multiplicity rule; its limits are not fixed but dependent on the state of the team member.

Document: Add nomination collaboration rules.

1. A document must have a title to be nominated.
2. A document cannot be nominated after it is published.
3. A document cannot be nominated again while it is pending.

EXPLANATION

Rule #1 is a property rule. Rule #2 is a state rule. A document with a published status cannot be nominated. Rule #3 is also a state rule.

Document: Add team member conflict rules.

1. A document cannot be nominated by a team member whose security level is less than the document's security level.

EXPLANATION

Rule #1 is a conflict rule that evaluates a team member according to his security level property. The document owns this rule because it has the standard of comparison.

Plan of Attack

In this example, the collaboration accessors are critical to a conduct business service because they contain the necessary collaboration and conflict rules. To implement the conduct business service, do the following:

- Expand conduct business interfaces
- Implement "test" and "do" methods for collaborations
- Revise collaboration accessors
- Implement conduct business services

As the `transaction` and the coordinator between the two `specifics`, the nomination is best suited to direct the testing for all the collaboration and conflict rules. In the implementation, the nomination will call the "test" and "test conflict" methods from its own "test" method (see Figure 8.6).

Expand the Conduct Business Interface

Listing 8.16 uses the minimalist approach, only adding test methods when the domain has an actual rule. Only the additional methods required are shown.

Update the three interfaces by adding the relevant "test" and "do" methods (see Figure 8.5).

ITeamMember.java

```
public interface ITeamMember extends ITeamMemberProfile
{
    <<snip>>
    public void testAddNomination(INomination aNomination)
                throws BusinessRuleException;
    public void doAddNomination(INomination aNomination);
}
```

INomination.java

```
public interface INomination extends Comparable
{
    <<snip>>
    public void testAddDocument(IDocument aDocument)
                throws BusinessRuleException;
    public void testAddTeamMember(ITeamMember aTeamMember)
                throws BusinessRuleException;
    public void doAddDocument(IDocument aDocument);
    public void doAddTeamMember(ITeamMember aTeamMember);
}
```

IDocument.java

```
public interface IDocument
{
    <<snip>>
    // ACCESSORS -- collaboration rules
    public void testAddNomination(INomination aNomination)
                throws BusinessRuleException;
    public void testAddNominationConflict(
                INomination aNomination, ITeamMember aTeamMember)
                throws BusinessRuleException;
    // ACCESSORS - do add
    public void doAddNomination(INomination aNomination) ;
    public void doRemoveNomination(INomination aNomination) ;
}
```

LISTING 8.16

Java updates to conduct business interfaces.

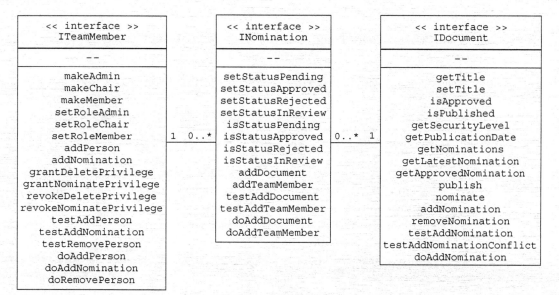

FIGURE 8.5
Conduct business interfaces updated with collaboration "test" and "do" methods.

Example: Team Member – Nomination – Document

Listings 8.17 and 8.18 show the document method for checking conflicts with a team member within a nomination. The conflict rule compares the security levels of the team member and documents. In both the Java and Squeak implementations, the security level is an object that implements a "greater than" method for comparing levels. See the CD for code specifics.

Document.java

```
public void testAddNominationConflict(
                INomination aNomination, ITeamMember aTeamMember)
                throws BusinessRuleException
{
   if (this.securityLevel.greaterThan(aTeamMember.getSecurityLevel()))
      throw new BusinessRuleException(
                "Security violation. Team member has improper security.");
}
```

LISTING 8.17
Java conflict collaboration rule method.

Document methodsFor: 'collaboration-rules'

testAddNominationConflict: aNomination with: aTeamMember
 (self securityLevel > aTeamMember securityLevel)
  ifTrue: [BusinessRuleException signal:
            'Security violation. Team Member has improper security.']

LISTING 8.18
Squeak conflict collaboration rule method.

Example: Nomination "Test" Method

As the director of the conflict rules, the nomination is responsible for asking the document if it conflicts with the team member. To ensure commutativity, this check is included in both the "test add document" and "test add team member" methods, but it runs only when both document and team member collaborators are present. These "test" methods also enforce the nomination's multiplicity rules of having only one team member and one document. See Listings 8.19 and 8.20.

```
Nomination.java
public void testAddTeamMember(ITeamMember aTeamMember)
                throws BusinessRuleException
{
  if (this.teamMember != null)
    throw new BusinessRuleException("Team member already exists.");
  if (this.document != null)
    this.document.testAddNominationConflict(this, aTeamMember);
}
public void testAddDocument(IDocument aDocument)
                throws BusinessRuleException
{
  if (this.document != null)
    throw new BusinessRuleException("Document already exists.");
  if (this.teamMember != null)
    aDocument.testAddNominationConflict(this, this.teamMember);
}
```

LISTING 8.19
Java collaboration rule "test" method using collaboration conflict "test" method.

Example: Team Member "Test" Methods

The team member's "test" methods enforce the restrictions that a team member cannot nominate if its lacks the nominate privilege or if it has exceeded its maximum number of allowed nominations.

In Java, static variables define a length of time and the maximum number of documents allowed during that time for a chair and a non-chair team member.

Nomination methodsFor: 'collaboration-rules'

testAddDocument: aDocument
    self document ifNotNil: [BusinessRuleException signal: 'Document already exists.'].
    self teamMember ifNotNil: [aDocument testAddNominationConflict: self
        with: self teamMember]

testAddTeamMember: aTeamMember
    self teamMember
     ifNotNil: [BusinessRuleException signal: 'Team member already exists.'].
    self document
     ifNotNil: [self document testAddNominationConflict: self with: aTeamMember]

LISTING 8.20
Squeak collaboration rule "test" method using collaboration conflict "test" method.

The service that counts nominations within a given period of days uses a
`CollectionSelector` object to select a sub-list of nominations occurring
within the date range. The size of this sub-list determines the number of nominations within the date range. See Listing 8.21.

```
TeamMember.java
public void testAddNomination(INomination aNomination)
                throws BusinessRuleException
{
  if (!this.hasNominatePrivilege())
    throw new BusinessRuleException(
                "Security violation. Team member cannot nominate.");
  if (this.countNominationsPerPeriod() >= this.maxNominationsAllowed())
    throw new BusinessRuleException(
                "Team member cannot nominate. Too many nominations.");
}

public int maxNominationsAllowed()
{
  if (this.isRoleChair()) return MAX_CHAIR_DOCUMENTS;
  else  return MAX_DOCUMENTS;
}

public int countNominationsPerPeriod()
{
  return this.countNominationsPerDays(NOMINATIONS_TIME_PERIOD);
}

public int countNominationsPerDays(int daysInPeriod)
{
  if (this.nominations.isEmpty()) return 0;
```

(continued)

LISTING 8.21
Java TeamMember "test" methods for adding a nomination.

```
Calendar myCalendar = Calendar.getInstance();
myCalendar.add(Calendar.DATE, -1 * daysInPeriod);
Date endDate = myCalendar.getTime();

CollectionSelector selectList = new CollectionSelector()
{
  public boolean selectBlock(Object listElement, Object keyValue)
  {
    return ((INomination)listElement).isAfter((Date)keyValue);
  }
};
Collection nomsInRange = selectList.select(this.nominations, endDate);
return nomsInRange.size();
}
```

LISTING 8.21
Java TeamMember "test" methods for adding a nomination. (continued)

In the Squeak version, instance methods in the "constants" message category return the values used for defining the length of the nomination period and the maximum number of documents allowed during that nomination period for a chair and a non-chair team member (see Listing 8.22). These methods are shown on the book CD.

TeamMember methodsFor: 'collaboration-rules'

testAddNomination: aNomination
  self hasNominatePrivilege
   ifFalse: [BusinessRuleException signal: 'Team member cannot nominate.'].
  self countNominationsPerPeriod >= self maxNominationsAllowed
   ifTrue: [BusinessRuleException signal:
          'Team member cannot nominate. Too many nominations.']

TeamMember methodsFor: 'accessing'

maxNominationsAllowed
  self isRoleChair
   ifTrue: [↑self maxChairDocuments]
   ifFalse: [↑self maxDocuments]

TeamMember methodsFor: 'domain services'

countNominationsPerPeriod
  ↑self countNominationsPerDays: self nominationsTimePeriod

countNominationsPerDays: anInteger
  | endDate |
  self nominations isEmpty ifTrue: [↑ 0].
  endDate ←Date today subtractDays: anInteger.
  ↑ (self nominations select:
         [:aNomination | aNomination nominationDate > endDate]) size

LISTING 8.22
Squeak TeamMember "test" methods for adding a nomination.

Example: Document "Test" Methods

The document "test" methods enforce the restrictions that a document cannot be nominated if it lacks a title, is already published, or already has an unresolved nomination.

Thanks to the sorted nature of the nomination collection, only the most recent nomination is checked to see if it is unresolved in Java (see Listing 8.23).

In Squeak, all nominations are searched to see if any are unresolved as shown in Listing 8.24.

Document.java

```java
public void testAddNomination(INomination aNomination)
                    throws BusinessRuleException
{
  if (this.isPublished())
    throw new BusinessRuleException("Document already published.");
  INomination lastNomination = null;
  try { lastNomination = this.getLatestNomination(); }
  catch(BusinessRuleException ex){ return; }
  if (lastNomination.isStatusPending() ||
      lastNomination.isStatusInReview())
  throw new BusinessRuleException("Document has unresolved nomination.");
}

public INomination getLatestNomination() throws BusinessRuleException
{
  if (this.nominations.isEmpty())
    throw new BusinessRuleException("Document has no nominations");
  return (INomination)(this.nominations.first());
}
```

LISTING 8.23
Java document test methods for adding a nomination.

```
Document methodsFor: 'collaboration-rules'

testAddNomination: aNomination
    self isPublished
      ifTrue: [BusinessRuleException signal: 'Document already published.'].
    self hasUnresolvedNominations
      ifTrue: [BusinessRuleException signal: 'Document has unresolved nomination.']
```

LISTING 8.24
Squeak document "test" methods for adding a nomination.

Example: Nomination Collaboration Accessors

The nomination collaboration accessors direct the rule checking as shown in
Listings 8.25 and 8.26 (see also Figure 8.6).

Nomination.java

```java
public void addTeamMember(ITeamMember aTeamMember) throws
                BusinessRuleException
{
  if (aTeamMember == null)
     throw new BusinessRuleException("Tried to add null team member");
  this.testAddTeamMember(aTeamMember);
  aTeamMember.testAddNomination(this);
  this.doAddTeamMember(aTeamMember);
  aTeamMember.doAddNomination(this);
}

public void addDocument(IDocument aDocument) throws
                BusinessRuleException
{
  if (aDocument == null)
     throw new BusinessRuleException("Tried to add null document");
  this.testAddDocument(aDocument);
  aDocument.testAddNomination(this);
  this.doAddDocument(aDocument);
  aDocument.doAddNomination(this);
}
```

LISTING 8.25
Java nomination methods for adding a team member and document.

Nomination methodsFor: 'collaboration-accessing'

addDocument: aDocument
    aDocument
     ifNil: [BusinessRuleException signal: 'Tried to add nil document.'].
    self testAddDocument: aDocument.
    aDocument testAddNomination: self.
    self doAddDocument: aDocument.
    aDocument doAddNomination: self

addTeamMember: aTeamMember
    aTeamMember
     ifNil: [BusinessRuleException signal: 'Tried to add nil team member.'].
    self testAddTeamMember: aTeamMember.
    aTeamMember testAddNomination: self.
    self doAddTeamMember: aTeamMember.
    aTeamMember doAddNomination: self

LISTING 8.26
Squeak nomination methods for adding a team member and document.

I am a nomination. When I add a team member, I do the following:

⋏ Check the team member against my team member collaboration rules.

⋏ If I have a document collaborator, I ask my document collaborator if it has a conflict with me and my team member.

⋏ I ask the team member to check me against its collaboration rules.

⋏ If all rules pass, the team member and I establish the collaboration.

Nomination	Team Member	Document
addTeamMember	testAddNomination	testAddNominationConflict
testAddTeamMember	doAddNomination	
getDocument		
doAddTeamMember		

Nomination	Team Member	Document	
addTeamMember			(aTeamMember;)
logic test			*check a TeamMember is not null or logically invalid*
testAddTeamMember			(aTeamMember;)
check business rules			*check business rules for a TeamMember; exception if fails*
getDocument			(; myDocument)
IF			IF myDocument not NULL
		testAddNominationConflict	(thisNomination, aTeamMember;) //check conflict rules; exception if fails
END-IF			END-IF
END DEFN			END Nomination.testAddTeamMember
	testAddNomination		(thisNomination;) //check collaboration rules; exception if fails
doAddTeamMember			(aTeamMember;) // assign collaboration reference
	doAddNomination		(aNomination;) // assign collaboration reference
END DEFN			END Nomination.addTeamMember

FIGURE 8.6

Scenario for Nomination addTeamMember.

Collaboration Pluggability

Toward Pluggable Business Objects

The goal here is a pluggable object model for a particular domain. Clients do not usually want a reusable class library for handling systems beyond the scope of their business domain, but they do want a model that scales and grows along with their business. Keeping an eye on the domain and business constraints gives focus to the refactoring efforts and defines the limits of reuse.

> EXAMPLE—In the TeamMember – Nomination – Document system, only persons with memberships on corporate teams can nominate documents, but the system may scale and evolve to multiple types of teams, team memberships, and documents. Less probable, but possible, are other types of nominations.

With these business constraints and assessments delivered from the client, the object modelers have limits and direction for refactoring the TeamMember – Nomination – Document object model. Nominations, as the most stable object in the model, need pluggable collaborations to accommodate new types of team members and documents.

Pluggable Collaborations

A collaboration is pluggable if different types of objects can be fitted into one or both of the collaborator slots and still satisfy the communication requirements between the two. Communication requirements are diagrammed in object models by drawing an interface for each pluggable collaborator, listing the methods required of it by the other.

This book uses interfaces to highlight and contrast different types of services. Through its placement in an interface, a service is identified as object inherited, conduct business, or returning required information. Services not in an interface are inessential to collaboration and reflect design decisions.[11] As a result, the TeamMember – Nomination – Document object model in Figure 8.5 represents collaborations with interfaces that include set property accessors for the team member, nomination, and document objects. Under this model, a nomination is constrained to work only with team members that have security level, role, and privilege properties, and that is not very pluggable.

---

11. Methods shown in profile interfaces are object inherited; methods shown in conduct business interfaces are public, but not object inherited; and methods not listed in interfaces but coded in the object definition are design-level.

To make the TeamMember – Nomination – Document object model more pluggable, the essential communication requirements must be factored out of conduct business interfaces and into separate collaboration interfaces. Communication requirements express essential properties as well as services.

> EXAMPLE—The client for the TeamMember – Nomination – Document model has stipulated team memberships will always be individual people and that for legal reasons all team memberships and documents must include security levels that are checked during the nomination process.

The first step in moving the object model toward a more pluggable design is to re-express these property requirements in terms of interfaces.

Pluggable Team Member Essential Properties

The requirement that all team members must be individuals is restated as, "All team members exhibit the person profile."[12] Asserting that team members exhibit the person profile ensures that all team members have name, title, and email properties, but does not mandate any particular implementation or representation of those properties.

The requirement that all team members must have a security level is restated as, "All team members exhibit an interface with a security level accessor." Other properties implemented in the example for the team member, namely role and privileges, reflect a particular mechanism for granting people the ability to nominate documents; other mechanisms are possible as long as they conform to the constraint that a team member possess the appropriate security level.

Extracting both these requirements into a single interface and plugging this interface into the nomination object establishes the essential properties of a nomination's team member, but also allows any number of team member variations and implementations (see Figure 8.7).

Pluggable Team Member Collaboration Rules

Of course, the heart of collaboration is in the business rules, and this chapter has already shown a clear and simple pattern for implementing business rules as part of the process of adding and removing collaborations. Any refactoring of collaborations must include the methods to ensure rule checking is

---

12. Recall that the person profile interface has all the object inheritable determine mine services for a person, including the get accessors for the person properties.

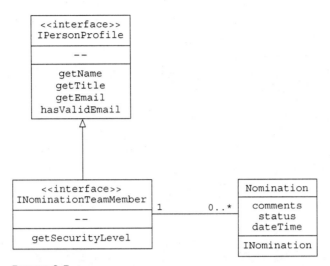

FIGURE 8.7

Essential properties of a TeamMember collaborating with a Nomination object.

enforced for every variation of object plugged into the collaboration.[13] Again, we look to the client to establish the limits of the collaboration methods.

> EXAMPLE—The client for the TeamMember – Nomination – Document model has stipulated that nomination history must always be preserved, even for rejected and unresolved nominations.

Here, the client has given a firm rule that nominations will not be removed from team members or documents, so only the "add" collaboration methods need be included in the collaboration interface (see Figure 8.8).

The final step is to check the team member conduct business interface for any additional services required for the nomination collaboration, and extract these into the collaboration interface. This example has no other required services.

---

13. In fact, the collaboration methods already support multiple implementation versions and specializations. The "add" and "remove" methods assume nothing about multiplicity, thus allowing different versions to have different multiplicities. The "test add" and "test remove" methods extract rule checking, allowing each version or specialization to establish its own business rules for the collaboration. Lastly, the "do add" and "do remove" methods allow different implementations for referencing the collaborators.

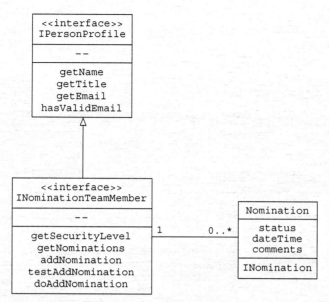

FIGURE 8.8
The pluggable TeamMember collaboration for a Nomination object.

PRINCIPLE 90
PLUGGABLE MEANS INTERFACES

To make a collaboration pluggable, factor the essential communication requirements out of the current conduct business interfaces and into separate collaboration interfaces.

PRINCIPLE 91
ESSENTIAL CHARACTERISTICS

Extract from business requirements any properties, services, and collaboration methods that are essential across many variations of a pluggable collaborator; include these in the pluggable collaboration interface.

Note that while refactoring further might satisfy the design goals of the developers, it is unnecessary to support the business requirements, and begins to conflict with a higher priority: understandability of the model by the client. The collaboration interface shown here allows pluggability, scalability, and extensibility of the business object model while preserving its clarity. The team member implementation coded in this chapter and the previous chapter

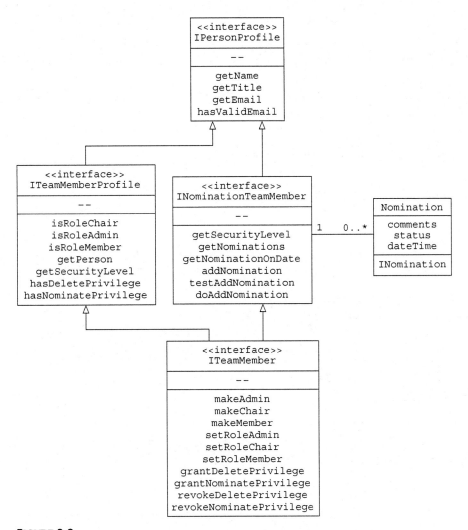

FIGURE 8.9

A TeamMember implementation refactored with the collaboration interface.

can easily be re-expressed in terms of the pluggable collaboration interface (see Figure 8.9).

Tackling Pluggability

Making collaborations pluggable while simultaneously respecting business constraints is a tall order because it involves allowing two parameters, the collaborators, to vary independently. If, however, one collaborator is fixed and the other varying, as was done in the previous TeamMember – Nomination example, then a desirable level of pluggability can be achieved without sacrificing model integrity. The trick is in deciding which collaborator should be fixed.

The solution is to fix the collaborator that is expected to vary the least. In other words, make pluggable the collaborator that is most likely to be specialized or change over time. Lacking firm guidelines from the client, the next best solution is to use good object sense. With `generic - specific`, make the `specific` pluggable. With `transaction - specific`, it is not as clear which varies the most, but events are rarely specialized. If you want new history against a thing, create a new kind of history, but don't specialize an old kind. `Whole - part` is similar. `Assemblies` don't get specialized; instead, new kinds of `assemblies` are created. `Containers` are the same; they vary less than their `parts`. `Group - member` can go either way.

PRINCIPLE 92
PLUGGABILITY WITH INTEGRITY

To allow pluggability without sacrificing model integrity, design pluggable collaborations by fixing one collaborator and creating a pluggable interface for the other collaborator.

PRINCIPLE 93
SELECTING PLUGGABLE COLLABORATORS

Make pluggable the collaborator that varies the most. Lacking guidelines from the client, plug `specifics` into a `generic`; plug `specifics` into a `transaction`; plug `parts` into `containers` and `assemblies`; and, allow `groups` and `members` to go either way.

Combining Collaboration Patterns

> When we try to pick out anything by itself, we find it hitched to everything else in the Universe.
>
> *John Muir*

Patterns as Molecules

Every pattern-based methodology has as its ultimate goal the construction of object models from patterns. The popular metaphor compares patterns to "building blocks" that connect and snap together to build larger structures. Streamlined object modeling takes a different approach by starting with the elements of the patterns instead of the patterns themselves. This approach proposes elementary pattern players, similar to chemical elements, and pairs them up to form "molecules." Which pattern players can pair up and form molecules depends on their individual characteristics. Ultimately, only 12 pairs of the pattern players form stable molecules called collaboration patterns. This chapter takes the chemical analogy to the next level and shows how to create compound collaboration molecules from the original 12 collaboration patterns.

Because collaboration patterns reflect real-world relationships between objects that are the stable over time, they form sturdy molecules for constructing object models. By placing one of the two collaborating pattern players into another collaboration pair, two collaborations are combined, making a bigger but still stable molecule.[1] Compound collaboration molecules come in two varieties: snap-togethers and overlays. Snap-together collaboration molecules connect two or more collaboration patterns into a larger structure. Overlay collaboration molecules merge pattern players from two or more collaboration patterns, creating new kinds of pattern players, with new characteristics derived from the originals.

Understanding Pattern Players

Since combining collaborations depends on the pattern players involved, it is essential to understand what the pattern players represent in the real world and how they participate in collaborations. To this end, every pattern player can be categorized into an empirical category and one or more fundamental pattern categories.

Empirical Categories

The empirical categories indicate what an object represents in the real world. An object represents either a single real-world entity or a collection of real-world entities.

Objects representing single real-world entities[2] fall into one or more of the following categories:

- People – Individuals or collections of individuals participating in contexts and events
- Places – Locations or hierarchies of locations where events happen
- Things – Tangible entities that are not people or a places
- Events – Point-in-time or time-interval interactions between people, places, and things

Objects representing collections of real-world objects are one of the following:

- Classification – A group of entities matching some criteria
- Receptacle – A container for receiving and storing entities
- Ensemble – A whole viewed as a collection of its parts[3]

---

1. Objects and their relationships provide a more stable representation of a real-world system than a functional or data description of it. See p. 8, "Stability Through Encapsulation."
2. Recall we use "entity" to denote a real-world something, and "object" to denote its representation or abstraction.
3. Definitions adapted from WordSmyth (*http://www.wordsmyth.net/*).

Fundamental Categories

The fundamental categories indicate how an object participates in its collaborations. Since all collaborations can be generalized into one of the fundamental patterns, an object can be categorized as one or more of the fundamental pattern players. As shown in previous chapters, putting an object in a fundamental category determines much of its implementation. An object participates in collaborations as one or more of the following:

- `generic`
- `specific`
- `transaction`
- `whole`
- `part`

Pattern Player Table

Table 9–1 summarizes the collaboration pattern players in terms of their empirical and fundamental categories.

People objects represent entities that can participate in contexts. Typically an `actor` is a person and a `role` is his description and behavior in a context; however, things and places can be `actors` and take on `roles`, too. A more precise category name might be "entity-context" objects, but since giving things and places `roles` is really making them anthropomorphic, plain "people" does just fine.

Pattern players in the `generic` row are parents to pattern players in the `specific` row. A people `specific` requires a people `generic`; a thing `specific` requires an thing `generic`; and an event `specific` requires an event `generic`.

> EXAMPLE—A truck can take on the role of delivery vehicle, and a person can take on the role of a customer. But a truck cannot be a customer, and a person cannot be a delivery vehicle.

Events record the interactions of people, places, and things. Pattern players with event interactions are specific people, specific things, or local places. When a `transaction` has interactions captured by a `follow-up transaction`[4] it is acting like a specific thing.

---

4. When a `composite transaction` has a `follow-up transaction`, it is acting like a `transaction`, which results from an overlay combination of the `composite transaction - line item` and `transaction - follow-up transaction` collaborations.

	1	2	3	4	5	6	7	
1	actor	item	composite					generic
2	role	specific	line item					specific
3			transaction					transaction
4			follow-up					transaction
5				outer	group	container	assembly	whole
6				place	member	content	part	part
	people	thing	event	place	classification	receptacle	ensemble	

Fundamental Categories

Empirical Categories

Legend:

Gray background	– event
Hatched background	– has interactions recorded by events

TABLE 9.1
Pattern Player Table.

Whole – Part Pattern Players.   Whole and part pattern players in the classification, receptacle, and ensemble categories represent collections of people, places, things, and events. Spatial containment for places is also handled by whole - part. The composite transaction - line item pattern has some aspects of the whole - part relationship, but the dominant relationship between the entities is object inheritance. Therefore, these go in the table as generic - specific.

Snapping Together Collaborations _____

The simplest forms of collaboration combinations are the "snap-togethers." Two collaborations snap together if they share a common pattern player, meaning that the same object acts as the same pattern player in both collaborations.

Transactions are the glue that brings people, places, and things together. As such, they are involved in many of the snap-together collaborations. Further, since the transaction is a sort of common denominator, all of the snap-together collaborations can then be snapped together themselves as shown in Figure 9.1.

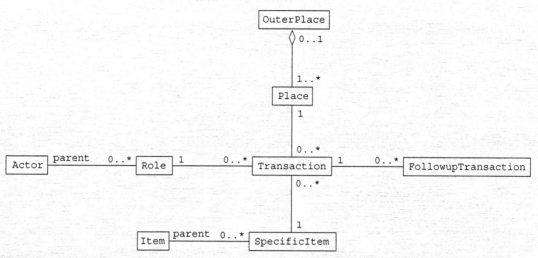

FIGURE 9.1
Transactions snap together many collaboration pairs.

Transaction – Role – Actor

The transaction - role - actor pattern represents people participating in a context and interacting with things and places that are recorded as events. The role pattern player represents the people object in the context and is the common pattern player between the collaboration patterns.

Transaction – Specific Item – Item

The transaction - specific item - item pattern represents an event involving a distinct individual thing that shares a common description with several related things.

Transaction – Place – Outer Place

The transaction - place - outer place pattern represents an event happening at a place that can be contained in a hierarchy of larger places.

Follow-up Transactions

Follow-up transactions happen after the original event recorded by a transaction, and they can involve the same people, places, and thing as the original, or they can involve new ones.

Snap-togethers for follow-up events involving the same people, places, and things are:

- `role - transaction - follow-up transaction`
- `place - transaction - follow-up transaction`
- `specific item - transaction - follow-up transaction`

Snap-togethers for follow-up events involving different people, places, and things are:

- `transaction - follow-up transaction - role`
- `transaction - follow-up transaction - place`
- `transaction - follow-up transaction - specific item`

EXAMPLE—A vehicle registration happens in a county of a state, and involves a particular vehicle and its owner. Each vehicle maps to a vehicle description that includes its make, model, year, and manufacturer. A registration can be renewed multiple times for the same owner and vehicle at the same or a different county. See Figure 9.2.

Composite Transaction – Line Item – Specific Item – Item

A `composite transaction` represents a complex event involving many things. `Line items` and `specific items` represent the involvement of the things in the event. See Figure 9.3.

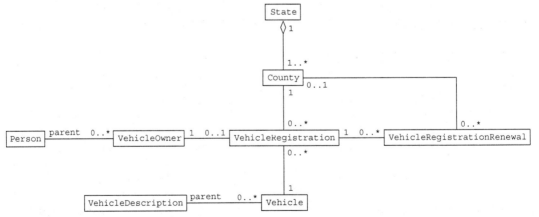

FIGURE 9.2
Example of a `follow-up transaction` that can happen at a different `place`.

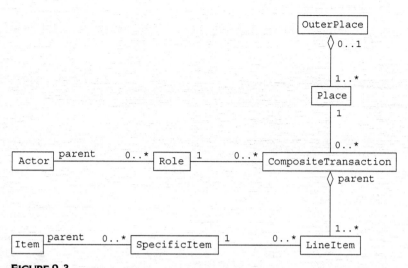

FIGURE 9.3
Composite transaction snap-together collaborations.

EXAMPLE—The infamous store order is an example of a composite transaction where the things involved are specific products with SKUs. For each specific product ordered, an order line item records the order quantity. To track sales regionally, each order remembers the store where it occurred, and each store belongs to a geographic region that is itself contained in zero to one geographic regions. See Figure 9.4.

Domain-Neutral Component

In their book, *Java Modeling in Color with UML*, Peter Coad, Eric Lefebvre, and Jeff De Luca[5] propose a "domain-neutral component" that resembles the snap-together collaborations shown in Figure 9.1. Coad and his co-authors use archetypes instead of pattern players as the basic units for object collaborations, but the resulting component has a similar structure: a central event with collaborating people, places, and things. The archetypes loosely map to the fundamental patterns players as shown in Table 9.2.

Even more intriguing, Coad and his co-authors show archetypal interactions (Table 9.3), which are typical interactions involving the archetypes in the domain-neutral component, and these match very nicely with the three types of services shown in this book.

---

5. *Java Modeling in Color with UML: Enterprise Components and Process*, Peter Coad, Eric Lefebvre, and Jeff De Luca, 1999, Prentice Hall.

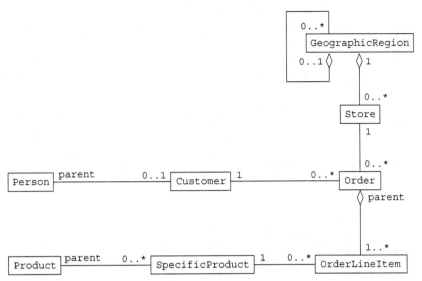

FIGURE 9.4
Example of a `composite transaction` snapping together several collaborations.

TABLE 9.2
Archetypes Compared to Pattern Players

Domain-Neutral Component Archetype	Fundamental Pattern Player
PartyPlaceThing	`specific`
Role	`specific`
Description	`generic`
MomentInterval	`transaction`
MIDetail	`transaction` (line item)

TABLE 9.3
Archetype Interactions Compared to Streamlined Services

Archetypal Interaction	Streamlined Object Modeling Service
Assess value to business	`specific` analyze transactions
Make moment interval	`specific` conduct business
Assess subsequent moment interval	`transaction` analyze transactions
Get custom else default	`specific` determine mine with object inheritance
Find available	`generic` determine mine

Overlay Collaborations_____

An overlay collaboration involves an object acting as different pattern players in multiple collaborations. This section shows some common overlapping collaborations, how they are derived, and an example of each. These are by no means the exhaustive set, just enough to give a general idea.

> EXAMPLE—In the nomination example, a team member is both a `role` for a `person` and a `member` of a `group` (see Figure 9.5).

Actor – Specific Role – Role Definition

Domains that use qualifications to schedule resources gather required qualifications in `role definitions`. Each `role definition` is a specific thing that can be classified, grouped, or sorted, and a generic thing that can have many specific instantiations. Project management and resource planning use `role definitions`.

This pattern combines the `actor - role` and `item - specific item` collaborations. Use this collaboration combination when an `actor` is assigned to take on a `role` with requirements described in a `role definition`. Record in the `specific role` the individual details of the `actor`'s assignment, and use the `specific role` as the `role` for `transactions` entered into while acting in that `role definition`. See Figure 9.6.

> EXAMPLE—A trucking company has trucks that can be configured to take on some number of the following delivery roles: non-food cargo, perishable food cargo, and non-perishable food cargo. The company creates scheduled cargo deliveries according to the delivery role types, and then assigns the actual cargo delivery to a truck with the appropriate delivery role. See Figure 9.7.

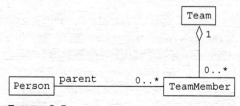

FIGURE 9.5
TeamMember is both a `role` and a `member` of a `group`.

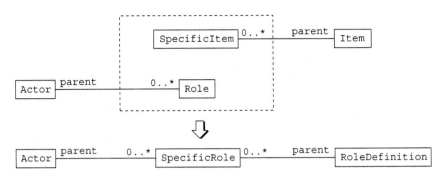

FIGURE 9.6

A specific role combines the role and specific item pattern players.

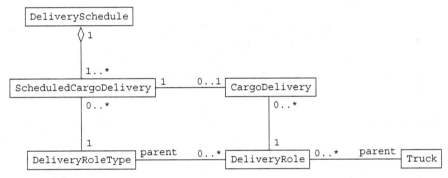

FIGURE 9.7

Using DeliveryRoleType to schedule deliveries and assign trucks.[6]

A specific role has two parents, its actor and its role definition, and it object inherits from both of them. To implement double object inheritance, the specific role implements the profile interfaces of both its parents (see pp. 161–162, "Define: The Parent Profile Interface"). Some care must be taken to avoid collision of service names

Actor - Fundamental Role - Subsequent Role

Subsequent roles appear in domains that include a context within a context. Nested contexts occur when a context of interactions includes a subset that requires additional information or qualifications for participation. A subsequent role captures the additional information required to participate in the more specific context.

---

6. Notice that ScheduledCargoDelivery is a line item in a composite transaction, and it is a transaction that gets assigned a role and has a follow-up transaction, CargoDelivery.

This pattern combines the `actor - role` collaboration with itself. The `fundamental role` represents the basic requirements for participation and is the parent to the `subsequent role` that contains the additional information required to participate in a specialized context. Use this pattern in a domain that offers different services to nested levels of memberships (see Figure 9.8).

> EXAMPLE—An airline frequent flyer program requires a member to travel 25,000 miles or more within a year to qualify for their elite services. Elite frequent flyers can obtain free first-class upgrades and bonus miles for flights. See Figure 9.9.

Item Actor - Member Role - Group

Domains that describe things differently based on context require items to become `actors`. An `item actor` is a description that can have further descriptions for different contexts.

This pattern combines the `item - specific item`, `actor - role`, and `group - member` collaboration patterns. The `member role` is the further description of the `item actor`. Use this pattern when the further description of the `item actor` can appear in multiple contexts. See Figure 9.10.

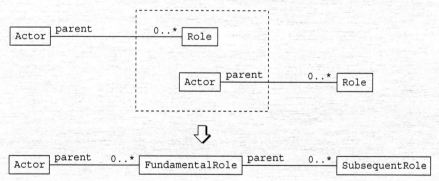

FIGURE 9.8
A fundamental role serves as an actor for a subsequent role.

FIGURE 9.9
An EliteFrequentFlyer is a subsequent role of a FrequentFlyer.

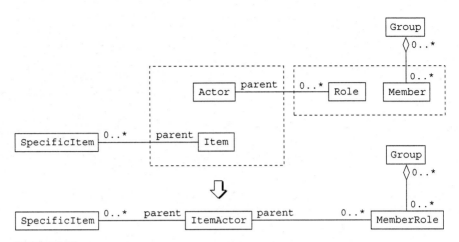

FIGURE 9.10

An item actor is a description that takes on roles.[7]

Item Actor - Content Role - Container.   This is another item actor
pattern. It combines the item - specific item, actor - role, and container
- content collaboration patterns. The content role is the further description
of the item actor. Use this pattern when the further description of the item
actor can appear in only one context.

> EXAMPLE—A retailer keeps multiple marketing descriptions for each
> of its products. A marketing description can be reused in many adver-
> tisements. The retailer also groups its products into categories and has
> a professional shopper assign a rank to each product in a category (see
> Figure 9.11). Here, the product rank is the container role, and the mar-
> keting description is the member role.

Composite Transaction – Composite Follow-Up Transaction

Domains tracking a sequence of events involving multiple things require
composite follow-up transactions. Just as a composite transaction
records the individual interactions of many things, a composite follow-up
transaction records the individual follow-up events for the many things in
the original event.

---

7. To obtain the item actor - content role - container pattern replace the group - member
   collaboration with the container - content collaboration.

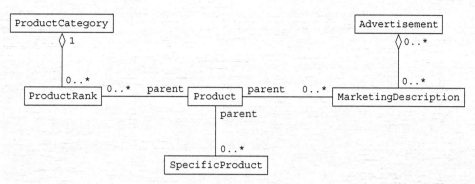

FIGURE 9.11
A Product collaborating as an `actor` with `content` and `member roles`.

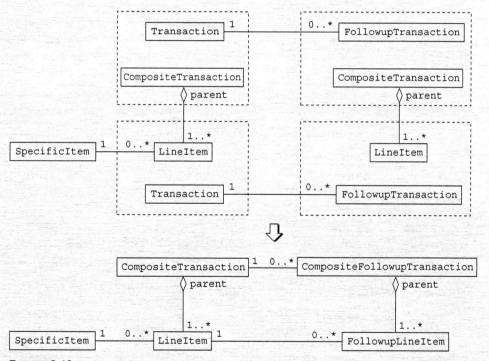

FIGURE 9.12
`Composite transactions` often require `composite follow-up transactions`.

This pattern combines the `composite transaction - line item` and `trans-action - follow-up transaction` collaborations. Use this combination only when follow-up details are needed for each `specific item` in the original `composite transaction`. See Figure 9.12.

Often, multiple follow-up events are required for a single composite event, and not all things handled in the original event are handled in each follow-up event. Together these explain why each line item in the original composite transaction has zero to many follow-up line items.

> EXAMPLE—An order is followed by some number of shipments. When more than one unit of a single product is ordered, it can be involved in multiple shipments to the same or different locations. Each shipment line item indicates the quantity shipped of the specific product, and collaboration rules prevent shipping more of the specific product than the quantity ordered. See Figure 9.13.

Item Assembly – Specific Assembly

Item assemblies appear in domains using templates to construct complex structures. An item assembly is a template whose parts are also templates or generic descriptions. Specific assemblies created from an item assembly contain parts created from part templates.

This pattern combines the assembly - part and item - specific item collaborations. As an assembly, the item assembly must have parts, and any structure created from it must have parts, too. Use this combination when complex structures are created from common templates. See Figure 9.14.

> EXAMPLE—A proposal generation system constructs proposals by selecting chapters from a proposal template. Subchapters are then chosen based on the selected chapters. To ensure the latest versions are always incorporated into the proposal, it contains references to chapters and subchapters, rather than copies of their text. The "paper" proposal is a report generated by extracting the text from the chapters and subchapters referenced in the proposal object. See Figure 9.15.

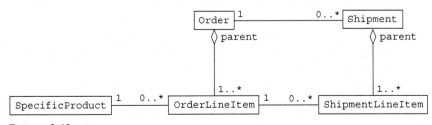

FIGURE 9.13
An Order followed by some number of Shipments.

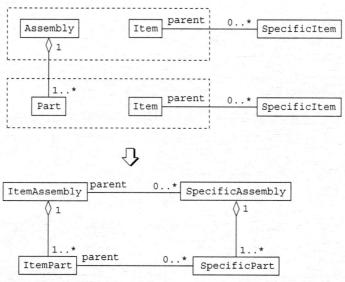

FIGURE 9.14
Item assemblies are templates for specific assemblies.

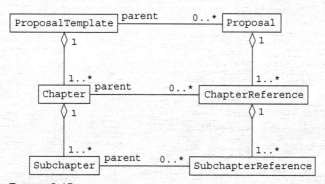

FIGURE 9.15
An assembly structure for creating Proposals.

Definite Generic – Transaction

Domains that allow generic descriptions to be used in events require definite generics. A definite generic acts as the parent description for a set of specific things, and can itself be involved in interactions. Typically, an event involving a definite generic is followed by an event involving one of its specific things.

This pattern combines the item pattern player in the item – specific item collaboration and the specific item in the specific item – transaction collaboration. The resulting pattern player, a definite generic, acts like a generic toward its child objects and like a specific that can interact in events. Transactions involving definite generics are object inheritable. See Figure 9.16.

> EXAMPLE—A video title can be reserved, and one of its videotapes can later be rented as a follow-up to the reservation (see Figure 9.17).

Plan – Plan Execution

Plan executions appear in domains that have templates for events. A plan execution records the details of an event described by a generic plan. Typi-

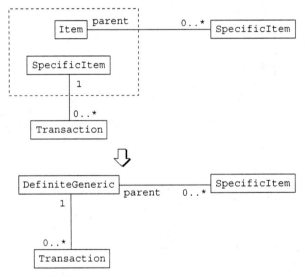

FIGURE 9.16
A definite generic is an item that has transactions and specific items.

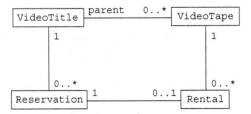

FIGURE 9.17
A VideoTitle has Reservations that are followed by Rentals of children.

cally, the plan describes a regularly scheduled event, and a plan execution records the details of one such event.

This pattern combines the item - specific item and transaction - specific item collaborations. In the same way that a specific item is a variation of its item, a plan execution is one particular run of its plan. Since this run is also an event, the plan execution acts like a transaction involving a specific thing, the plan. See Figure 9.18.

> EXAMPLE—A bottling plant has production lines that can be config-
> ured with different production plans. Each plan describes the package
> size, line speed, and fill rate of the line configuration. A production
> line execution records the actual line speed and fill rates, and how
> much was produced during the run. See Figure 9.19.

Process– Process Execution

Domains involving extensive or configurable workflows require process executions. A workflow is an ordered sequence of events. Simple, non-configurable workflows can be handled by successions of events, but when the chain of events is very lengthy or can be re-ordered, then it becomes necessary to model the sequence as a series of steps.

This pattern combines the plan - plan execution pattern and the assembly - part collaboration. A process is an assembly because, unlike a plan, which

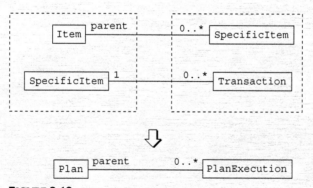

FIGURE 9.18
Plan executions are created from plan templates.

FIGURE 9.19
ProductionLineRuns are transactions created from plan templates.

is a single intended action, a process is made up of an ordered sequence of actions[8]. Like a plan, a process can run over and over again, and each run is modeled as a child execution; however, each process execution is itself made up of step executions for some or all of the steps within the parent process. See Figure 9.20.

> EXAMPLE—A construction company has multiple procurement processes for each type of component it procures during a project. When a specific construction component is to be procured, one of its type's processes is selected to generate a procurement schedule with the various steps needed to request, approve, and create purchases for that component. See Figure 9.21.

Membership Plan – Membership - Actor

Membership plans appear in domains where the enrollment of a person or thing in the system is tracked as history and governed by terms laid out in a plan, typically one plan of many. A membership records the details of an individual's participation, such as when the person or thing enrolled, the membership status, and the membership privileges. The membership object

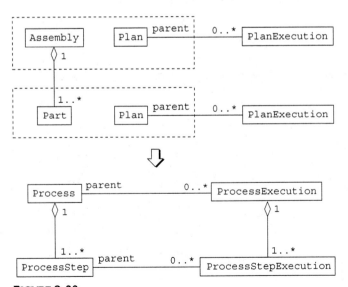

FIGURE 9.20
A process execution is created from a process assembled out of steps . .

---

8. Plan – an intended action; aim. Process – a systematic sequence of actions used to produce something or achieve an end. (WordSmyth, http://www.wordsmyth.net/)

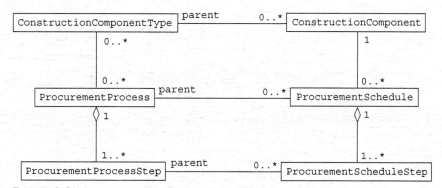

FIGURE 9.21
Generic ProcurementProcesses generate ProcurementSchedules for ConstructionComponents.

inherits the enrollment terms from its `membership plan`, including the length of the membership, fees, discount policies, and renewal methods.

This pattern combines the `plan – plan execution` pattern and `actor – role` collaboration. As a `role`, the `membership` and its `transactions` describe the `actor's` participation in the system; as a `plan execution`, the `membership` is one particular "run" of the `membership plan`, with a creation timestamp and usually an expiration date[9]. See Figure 9.22.

> EXAMPLE—An online application offers expert information and accredited training videos for credit to certified professionals who enroll as subscribers to the site. Individuals who join by responding to a promotion are enrolled under the subscription plan associated with

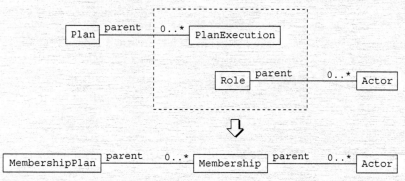

FIGURE 9.22
A `membership plan` has `plan executions` that are also `roles` for `actors`.

---

9. Expiration dates may be derived from the enrollment terms in the membership plan, or may be explicitly set in the membership if the membership plan can be revised after the membership is created.

FIGURE 9.23
A SubscriptionPlan generates time-limited Subscriber roles for Persons.

the promotion. Persons may renew as subscribers under the same or a different subscription plan. See Figure 9.23.

Parent – Parameterized Child

Parameterized children appear in domains where a thing can be described in multiple ways. Usually a thing is tightly bound to its description, but a parameterized child can be assigned to one or more descriptions, much like assigning a person or thing to one or more groups. Any interaction of the thing with other objects requires first specifying which description applies. Choosing a description is often modeled as a distinct event, followed by the interaction involving the thing.[10] Without that interaction tying it to a choice of a description, the thing cannot respond to certain requests for information; thus, many requests to the thing require a parameter to help disambiguate which description applies.

This pattern combines the group - member, item - specific item, transaction - specific item, and transaction - follow-up transaction collaborations. The group - member and item - specific item combination models the assignment of multiple descriptions to the parameterized child, and the nature of the parameterized child as a specialization of its descriptions. These combinations, along with the transaction collaborations, model the selection of a particular item as the relevant description and the follow-up interaction of one of its child objects. See Figure 9.24.

> EXAMPLE—A conference planning system schedules conferences for specific dates and times. Each conference can be described in multiple ways depending on the target demographic. An XML conference might target engineers and developers with a description like "XML Devcon." The same conference might then market itself to managers as

---

10. In some domains, the choice of the description and the interaction with the thing happen simultaneously and are combined into one event.

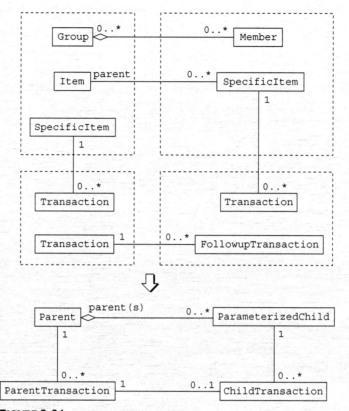

FIGURE 9.24

A parameterized child needs child transactions to determine its object inheritance.

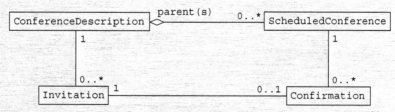

FIGURE 9.25

A Confirmation selects a parent for a ScheduledConference with multiple descriptions.

"XML for Dummies." An attendee receives an invitation for a particular conference description, and confirms he will attend one of the scheduled conferences. See Figure 9.25.

Two rules govern the behavior of `parameterized child` objects:

- **No `parent`, no interaction.** A `parameterized child` cannot interact with other objects, unless one of its `parents` is designated by the interaction.
- **No interaction, no object inheritance.** A `parameterized child` cannot perform object inheritance except in the context of an interaction that includes or follows the selection of one of the `parents`.

The "no `parent`" rule follows from `specific item` collaboration rules that prevent a `specific item` without a `parent` from collaborating with a `transaction`. This rule explains why a `child transaction` involving the `parameterized child` is always a follow-up to a `parent transaction` involving one of its `parents`. The exception is when the `parent` is selected simultaneously with the interaction involving the `child`, and the selection and interaction are captured in a single `transaction`.

The "no interaction" rule states the simple fact that without some context, a `parameterized child` cannot know which `parent` to use for object inheritance, and from the "no `parent`" rule, it follows that context is provided by a `child transaction`.

Two implementation approaches for `parameterized child` objects are recommended:

- Implement the non-parameterized `parent` profile interface plus a parameterized version that takes a `child transaction`.
- Implement a method that given a `child transaction` returns an object that implements the `parent` profile interface.

Object Model Documentation

The basic tool for the manipulation of reality is the manipulation of words. If you can control the meaning of words, you can control the people who must use the words.

Philip K. Dick

Documenting Your Work

Pictures may be worth a thousand words, but clients pay for words: words telling them what the system will do, what portions will be built now, and what portions will be built later. Developers need words, too: words describing collaboration rules, property values, and service definitions. This final chapter discusses creating supplementary documentation for an object model.

Components Description[1]

The "functional spec" is the traditional document for writing up the features and functionality of a system. Some people still argue that clients understand functional specs better than object models. We disagree. In our experiences, clients very easily comprehend object models because each model is a concise diagram of their business using names from their vocabulary; however, clients

---

1. For our purposes, a component is a portion of the system with a clearly defined purpose.

need a bridge to help them understand how that object model translates into a functioning system.

A components description is a form of functional specification that is based on an object model. Creating the specification from the model prevents conflicting views of the system, ensures the spec is written in the same vocabulary as the model, and provides a client-friendly textual supplement to the object model. All these benefits are not possible when the functional specification is created before the model. The next section of this chapter discusses some techniques and formats for creating a functional spec from the object model.

Object Model Description

The object model description is written for designers and programmers; it provides them the technical details necessary to understand the object model in-depth and to create a detailed design that incorporates off-the-shelf packages or the designer's own reusable custom solutions. Details provided include collaboration relationships, collaboration rules, high-level scripting for services, and property values and types. This final section of this chapter shows how to present this information.

Components Description

A Hybrid Deliverable

The components description is an object-centric functional spec. It is object-centric because it is organized around the object model and includes descriptions of the core objects; it is a functional spec because it describes features and functionality in the traditional language of a functional spec. In a pure object-oriented document, the features and functions would be explained as services provided by objects. Putting features and functions in the language of "the system shall" or "the component shall" makes the document more accessible and understandable to non-technical people.

The key advantage of the components description over the functional spec is its derivation from an object model. Object models reflect the client's business, incorporate the client's vocabulary, and are substantially more stable than functional decompositions. Creating the components description from the object model gives the components description a stable organization that reflects the client's business structure and goals and is expressed in a familiar vocabulary.

Multiple Uses

The components description serves multiple purposes for the client and the development team. For the client, the components description is a communication to the client that both explains the object model and presents the system features and functionality. Also, due to the structured format of the components description, an executive summary of the system can be extracted from it very quickly.

The development team reviews the components description to ensure all the team players agree on the features and functionality of the system. The approved business components description is then used to scope the project. The description of properties and collaborations in the components description are directly transferable to the object model description described later. However, features and functions are not. Features and functions must be re-expressed as business scenarios using object services.

Defining Components

A component is a portion of the system with a clearly identified purpose. Functional decompositions also include components; however, functional components are composed of functions, and require significant reorganization every time the business functionality changes.

An object model component is a named set of objects that work together to achieve a common purpose. Naming groups of objects improves the comprehension of the object model, especially when the names reflect business processes familiar to the client. Changes in business functionality usually result in changes within the component objects, but not a reorganization of the components.

Components come in many sizes, from individual objects to entire systems. One system may break product orders into multiple components such as "order placement," "order fulfillment," "order shipment," and "order returns." Another system may view all of these as features and functions within a single "order processing" component. How much a component encompasses depends primarily on system size and complexity. In general, large systems have large components, often subdivided into smaller ones.

EXAMPLE—An example component.

Lubricant Order Workflow – This component contains the functionality for processing orders for shipping vessel lubricant products, and includes the following features: routing orders to the proper agent work queues; agent approval, rejection, or editing of order line items for lubricant products; customer service approval, rejection, or editing of agent operations on order; and final order approval.

PRINCIPLE 94
LOOK FOR OBJECT GROUPS

Group together objects that work together to achieve a shared purpose; give them a name reflecting their shared purpose using the client's vocabulary.

PRINCIPLE 95
Object Group Providing a Feature

If a group of objects has a shared purpose that is only a small step toward achieving a larger goal, then consider the group as providing a feature or function for a component.

PRINCIPLE 96
OBJECT GROUP AS A COMPONENT

If a group of objects has a shared purpose that accomplishes a significant goal, then consider the group as a component.

PRINCIPLE 97
OBJECT GROUP AS A SUB-COMPONENT

If a group of objects has a shared purpose that involves many steps, but is too large to be a feature and too insignificant to be a component, then consider the group as a sub-component of a larger component.

Prioritizing Components

Object modeling excels at bringing out the client's long-term vision for the system, and knowing this vision early is essential to architecting a system that can stand the test of time. Components are an excellent mechanism for separating out the current requirements from the future ones, and for breaking down the overall system to do a more efficient and accurate cost/effort analysis. The trick is to concisely articulate the purpose of each component and to show how components interrelate and depend on each other. Core components are those that form a useful, working system; the rest are gravy.

> EXAMPLE—An oil company currently receives inquiries and orders for changing out the lubricants for large vessels by fax and telephone. The orders are entered into a mainframe and pass through a workflow approval loop and a delivery confirmation. A Web-enabled system to handle receiving and processing orders has three components:
>
> Lubricant Order Inquiry – Allows online customers to receive bids in response to inquires, and place orders from bids.
>
> Lubricant Order Workflow – Allows agents and customer service personnel to approve, reject, and edit orders.
>
> Lubricant Order Delivery – Allows port agents to enter the actual quantities of lubricant delivered.
>
> The order inquiry component cannot exist without the other two components; however, the order workflow and order delivery components can exist and provide value, by replacing the cumbersome mainframe screens, even if orders are still received by telephone or fax. A logical development plan for these components is:
>
> Phase One:
>   Lubricant Order Workflow
>   Lubricant Order Delivery
>
> Phase Two:
>   Lubricant Order Inquiry
>
> Building the order workflow and order delivery components first allows them to be debugged and in place before building the order inquiry component.

Components Description Format

The format of the components description follows its function—to organize and describe the system features and the objects involved in them.

A pure object model description also organizes a system as a collection of components. It focuses on describing the objects within each component, including their properties and services, how they collaborate together to achieve collective goals, and how the goals contribute to a common purpose.

The components description flips this view by putting the shared purpose first, and then listing the collective goals as features. Under each feature, the objects involved in that feature are described in terms of their properties and collaborations, and the system functionality involved in achieving that feature is listed. Object services are not discussed, but a good object thinker can easily spot the feature's system functionality as services of the feature's objects.

When an object appears in more than one component, it is fully described only once, in the component and under the feature for which it has the most significant contribution.

The components description format is shown in Listing 10.1.

System Components Description[2]

1. Component Name C1

    Description of component purpose.

    1. 1. Feature F1

        Description of feature purpose.

        1.1.1. Object O1

        object purpose.

        object properties. [optional]

        object collaborations

        1.1.2. Object O2

          ...   .

        1.1.m. Object O13

          ...   .

        1.1.n System functionality

        The component shall…

          ...   .

    1. 2. Feature F2

        1.2.1. Object O15

          ...   .

        1.2.N System functionality

LISTING 10.1
Components description format.

---

2. Indentations shown here are to highlight the nesting of the format levels, and most likely would not appear in an actual components description.

Creating an Executive Summary

The format of the components description allows it to be collapsed quickly into an executive summary. To create the executive summary, simply extract the component names and their high-level descriptions, and the component features and their high-level descriptions. If more detail is desired, include the high-level system functionality for each feature. To produce presentation slides, drop the textual descriptions.

The executive summary format is shown in Listing10.2.

System Executive Summary

1. Component C1

   Description of component purpose.

   1. 1. Feature F1

      Description of feature purpose.

   1. 2. Feature F2

      Description of feature purpose.

2. Component C2

   Description of component purpose.

   2. 1. Feature Fj

      Description of feature purpose.

   ...   .

LISTING 10.2
Executive summary format.

Components Description Example

This example shows how to express a portion of an object model using the components description format. The object model used comes from a previous example.

EXAMPLE—A Web-enabled application offers expert information and accredited training videos to professionals seeking certification who enroll as subscribers to the site. Individuals who join by responding to a promotion are enrolled under the subscription plan associated with the promotion. Persons may renew as subscribers under the same or a different subscription plan. See Figure 10.1.

The components description example is shown in Listing10.3.

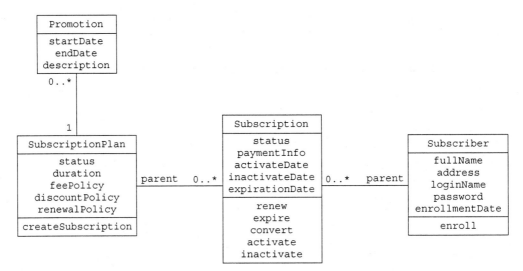

FIGURE 10.1

Objects involved in the subscriber management component[3].

System Components Description

1. Subscriber Management

The Subscriber Management Component allows site visitors to enroll as subscribers, renew their subscription, convert their subscription to a different plan, and update their personal information.

The Subscriber Management Component allows site administrators to create, delete, and edit subscription plans; create a promotion with a subscription plan; and access subscriber and subscription information.

1. 1. Subscriber Enrollment

The subscriber enrollment feature allows visitors to the site to enroll as subscribers either by:

responding to a promotion;

or selecting one of the standard subscription plans presented on the site.

(continued)

LISTING 10.3

Components description example.

---

3. Note that the object model follows the membership plan – membership – actor pattern, and that the SubscriptionPlan acts as a specific item for the Promotion transaction. Not shown is the Endorser, which is the role involved in the Promotion, and whose actor is an Organization. Also, because this is an analysis object model, several objects contain properties that in a design object model would be expanded to full-blown objects or multiple properties; notably, the SubscriptionPlan's policy properties and the Subscriber's payment information and address properties.

1.1.1. Promotion

A promotion allows a site visitor with the proper code to enroll under a special subscription plan.

Each promotion includes the following information:

Code – Visitor must enter to access promotion

Start date – When promotion becomes active

End date – When promotion expires

Each promotion involves exactly one subscription plan.

1.1.2. Subscription Plan

A subscription plan defines the enrollment terms for a subscriber.

Each subscription plan includes the following information:

Status – Active or inactive

Duration – Length in months of subscriber's enrollment

Fee policy – How much to charge for the subscription and how frequently payment is collected

Renewal policy – Whether subscriber can renew under this plan

Each subscription plan has some number of subscriptions. A subscription describes the exact terms of enrollment for an individual subscriber.

1.1.2. Subscription

A subscription records a subscriber's participation in the system under a given subscription plan. A subscriber gets a new subscription when they convert subscription plans or renew under the same or a different subscription plan. The collection of subscriptions associated to a subscriber show that individual's history of participation in the system.

Each subscription includes the following information:

Status – Active or inactive

Activate date time – When subscription activated for subscriber

Inactivate date time – When subscriber's participation in system through this subscription is turned off either by termination or renewal, which creates a new subscription

Expiration date – When subscriber access is scheduled to end under this subscription

Each subscription collaborates with:

a subscription plan that defines its enrollment terms;

a subscriber that defines the individual data for the subscription.

(continued)

1.1.3. Subscriber

...   <snip >   ...

1.1.4 Enrolling Subscribers Functionality

Visitors to the site can enroll as subscribers either by selecting one of the site subscription plans available or by responding to a promotion.

The system enrolls a visitor with a selected subscription plan by:

creating a subscriber object from information entered by the visitor;

using the selected subscriber plan to create a subscription and set the enrollment terms for the subscriber;

requesting and verifying payment information from the visitor;

and finally, associating the new subscription to the new subscriber object.

The system enrolls a visitor responding to a promotion by:

prompting the visitor for the promotion code;

verifying that the code is for an active promotion;

registering the visitor with the subscription plan associated with the promotion (see above).

Object Model Description_____

The object model description is a detailed, purely object-oriented explanation of the object model and the business requirements it represents. Its purpose is to describe each object in enough detail to allow implementation of a working prototype and creation of the design object model. While most clients do not completely read this document, some do forward it to a technical staff for evaluation and a recommendation on whether to proceed with development.

Documenting an object model is like documenting code—always recommended and seldom done. On the plus side, documenting an object model is an excellent review exercise, compelling the modeler to justify every part of the model, and producing a permanent record of the analysis results, which is extremely handy many months and many models later. On the downside, it can require considerable effort and precious time. From our past experiences, an object model description is essential when:

- The object model is large
- The collaboration rules are complex
- The object modelers are not available throughout the project lifecycle
- Formal reviews are required

PRINCIPLE 98
DOCUMENT THESE OBJECT MODELS

An object model description is necessary when: the object model is large or has complex collaboration rules or services; the object model is being handed off to a new team for design and development; or the object model is subject to a formal review process.

Scoping the Requirements

When preparing to write the object model description, remember: Documenting out-of-scope objects serves no one. Scope the requirements, and hence the object model, before writing more documentation. Get the entire development team—mangers, consultants, modelers, developers, and creative designers—involved in the process. To get these people from such diverse backgrounds on the same page, use the object model as the glossary of terms and repository of system entities, and use the components description as the specification of the high-level features.

Go through the components description with the team, using the object model as a reference, and prioritize features according to feasibility, time, budget, and client preferences. Sort these into categories: the "must-have" features, the "if-time-permits" features, and the "no-way-in-heck" features. Create a new version of the object model by whittling out objects, services, and collaboration rules identified as "no-way-in-heck." Keep an older version of the model with all features intact, for future development.

Iterative Development and Object Modeling

Building object models and writing documentation are not just for waterfall development. On the contrary, object modeling provides the best foundation for iterative development because the object model is the one system representation that remains stable even as new features and functionality are added. This is discussed more in the last section of this chapter.

Object Model Description Format

The object model description is an object-by-object description of the business requirements for the development team. By packaging the requirements around individual objects this document simplifies the task of doling out objects to individual developers. Quite simply, to specify business requirements for an object, list its property constraints, explain its business services, describe the nature of its collaborations, and specify its collaboration rules.

Like the components description document, the object model description is organized around the system components (see Listing 10.4).

Object Model Description[4]

1. Component Name C1

    Component purpose. [optional]

  1. 1. Object O1

    object purpose [optional]

    object properties

    object services

    object collaborations

    object collaboration rules

  1. 2. Object O2

    object purpose

    object properties

    object services

    object collaborations

    object collaboration rules

  1. 3. Object O3

    ...   .

2. Component Name C2

  2. 1. Object Oi

    ...   .

LISTING 10.4
Object model description format.

The properties section must describe the data types and legal values for each of the object's properties. Cross-validation rules among the object's properties should also be included here. Indications of whether a property is derived through a calculation or is read-only could go here, but often those sorts of decisions are best left to the object designers and developers. Also, note that a property in an object model description may become an object during design. For example, addresses, names, and policies are usually properties in analysis, but are "objectified" along with their logic rules during design.

---

4. Indentations shown here are to highlight the nesting of the format levels, and most likely would not appear in an actual object model description.

At a minimum, the service section describes the high-level business services of the object. These were typically described with less precision as "system functionality" in the components description. Interaction diagrams showing the dynamics involved in a service can be included, but only if the business logic insists that the service operate in a particular sequence. Otherwise, leave it to the object designers and developers. Because they are trivial, this section typically does not include descriptions of property or collaboration accessors.

Collaboration requirements can often be read straight from the diagram. This section is more to explain the nature of the collaboration. It also specifies the multiplicity of each collaboration using language such as "exactly one," "one or more," or "some number."

Collaboration rules must be documented since they are highly specialized to the client, and not available from the object model diagram. This section describes the rules that prevent collaborations between certain objects.

Object Model Description Example

This example shows the object model description for the subscriber management component described above. Two of the four objects in the original model are specified below.

> EXAMPLE—A Web-enabled application offers expert information and accredited training videos to professionals seeking certification who enroll as subscribers to the site. Individuals who join by responding to a promotion are enrolled under the subscription plan associated with the promotion. Subscribers may renew their subscriptions under the same or a different subscription plan. See Figure 10.1.

The object model description is shown in Listing10.5, on the next page.

Object Model Description

1. Subscriber Management

1. 1. Subscription Plan

```
┌─────────────────────────┐
│   SubscriptionPlan      │
├─────────────────────────┤
│        status           │
│       duration          │
│       feePolicy         │
│    discountPolicy       │
│     renewalPolicy       │
├─────────────────────────┤
│   createSubscription    │
└─────────────────────────┘
```

Properties

A subscription plan knows these properties:

 Status   – Pending, active, or inactive

 Duration   – Number of months subscription is valid

 Fee policy   – Policy for determining fee for subscriber

 Renewal policy – Policy for deciding if subscribers can renew

 Discount policy – Policy for determining discounts for subscribers

Services

A subscription plan knows how to create a subscription for a given subscriber.

- A new subscription object is created for the subscriber and associated with the subscription plan.
- The subscription is destroyed if any collaboration rules among subscription, subscriber, and subscription plan fail.

Collaborations

A subscription plan has collaborations with:

- Some number of subscriptions whose terms of participation in the system are defined by the subscription plan
- Some number of promotions

Collaboration Rules

A subscription plan has the following business rules with its collaborators:

- A subscription plan that is pending or inactive cannot collaborate with a subscription or promotion.
- A subscription plan has a collaboration conflict with a subscriber whose current subscription belongs to the subscription plan and the plan is not renewable.

(continued)

LISTING 10.5

Object model description example.

- A subscription plan has a collaboration conflict with a subscriber if the subscriber does not have valid or adequate payment information to cover the fee for the subscription.

1.2. Subscription

```
Subscription
───────────────
    status
  paymentInfo
  activateDate
 inactivateDate
 expirationDate
───────────────
    renew
    expire
    convert
    activate
   inactivate
```

Properties

A subscription knows these properties:

Status   – Pending: waiting to be activated

                 Active: activated and not yet expired

                 Expired: expiration date reached; in grace period for renewal

                 Inactive: can no longer participate

Activate date   – Date time when subscription is to be activated

Expiration date – Date time when subscription expires

Inactivate date – Date time when subscription made inactive

Services

A subscription knows how to activate itself.

- Fails if activate date not reached

- Fails if status is not "pending"[5]

- Sets status to "active"

A subscription knows how to inactivate itself.

- Fails if it is "inactive"

- Sets status to "inactive"

A subscription knows how to expire itself.

- Fails if expiration date not reached

- Fails if status is "inactive" or "expired"

- Sets status to "expired"   (continued)

---

5. These requirements prevent resetting an object's status to its current value so that objects are not gratuitously marked as changed.

A subscription knows how to renew itself.

- Fails if subscription is inactive
- Fails if its renewal policy (from subscription plan) does not allow renewal
- Asks its subscription plan to create a new subscription with its own subscriber
- If successful, sets the new subscription's activate date to its own expiration date

A subscription knows how to convert itself to a new subscription plan.

- Fails if subscription is inactive
- Asks new subscription plan to create a new subscription with its own subscriber
- If successful, inactivates itself

<u>Collaborations</u>

A subscription has collaborations with:

- Exactly one subscription plan that acts as a parent object
- Exactly one subscriber that acts as a parent object

<u>Collaboration Rules</u>

A subscription has the following business rules with its collaborators:

- A subscription cannot collaborate with a subscription plan if it already has one.
- A subscription cannot collaborate with a subscriber if it already has one.

Object Modeling and Iterative Development _____

The need for documentation during iterative development depends on how each iteration measures up against factors mentioned in Principle 98. Keep in mind that having documentation from an early iteration can be quite handy when circumstances change in later iterations. Here is a typical script for using an object model to go from business concept to code. Although numbered sequentially, some of these steps can be done in parallel, and steps can be repeated in an iterative process.

1. Object model the big picture.
2. Organize the object model into components.
3. Describe the purpose of each component.
4. Prioritize and select components for immediate development.

5. Object model the selected components in-depth.

6. Write a components description for the selected components.

7. Scope the components description.

8. Scope the object model.

9. Create the object model description.

10. Prototype selected objects.

11. Create the object model design.

12. Implement the object model design.

For a large system, start by object modeling the big picture. Focus on identifying the core objects, collaborations, and conduct business services. Save properties, collaboration rules, determine mine and analyze transactions services for later, during the in-depth object modeling (Step 5). Small projects, typically one or two simple components, may skip the first four steps and start with the in-depth object modeling in Step 5.

Steps 5–12 are the major steps in an object-oriented development lifecycle containing analysis, design, and implementation phases. Iterative development consists of repeatedly running through these steps on portions of the system, so that results learned while object modeling, designing, and implementing one portion of the system can feed back to improve the object modeling, designing, and implementing efforts for later portions of the system[6]. Key to iterative development is slicing the system into appropriately sized portions for the iterations.

Object model components are natural units for iterations. As discussed earlier, components can be readily prioritized according to their dependencies[7]. Use this prioritization along with client demands to choose one or more components for the first iteration. Developing components iteratively has the big advantage of progressively building on top of working components. Getting a small portion of the system tested, debugged, and working is always easier than testing and debugging the entire system at the end of the project. The other big advantage is the bonus points you score with clients when you can show them working functionality after a short time.

After the components in an iteration are object modeled in enough detail to move into design and implementation, the next step is to prioritize the objects. Here again, dependency is key. Design and build the objects on

---

6. See "baseball model" on pp. 11–13, *Object-Oriented Programming*, Coad and Nicola, 1993, Prentice Hall.

7. See pp. 300–301.

which other objects depend first. In the order workflow example, everything depends on first having an order, so you had better build it first.

Non-Business Requirements Gathering

In this book, the focus has been on business requirements. Interactive applications also include user interface, technical[8], and data persistence requirements. User interface and data persistence requirements should start after the object model has been scoped (Step 8). Waiting until after the object model is ready ensures the user interface designers are speaking to the client in the same vocabulary as the object modelers and business consultants, and are aware of the business rules in terms of the objects, properties, and services. While the object model should not drive the user interface design, all elements and functionality in the user interface design must map to something in the object model. The object model drives also data persistence requirements, since the object model defines the data. Technical requirements usually do not depend as heavily on the object model, especially if they are broad, such as calculating system load based on numbers of expected users. However, the object model can give a measure of the complexity of the system, which may have an effect on what is required to support the technical requirements.

---

8.   "We need a clustered system capable of failover to handle 24/7 availability."

Streamlined Object Modeling Principles

Object Modeling

PRINCIPLE 1
THE HOW OF WHY IS WHAT

Conceptual planning for an endeavor goes through three stages: why build, what to build, and how to build. How needs what to define its scope, and what needs why to define its purpose.

PRINCIPLE 2
THE OBJECT MODELING VIEWPOINT

Use object modeling to build group consensus by focusing on impersonal objects, not subjective users.

PRINCIPLE 3
OBJECT MODELING A NEW BUSINESS

Use object modeling with clients building a new business to flesh out details and issues, and document the proposed business in an impersonal and concrete manner.

PRINCIPLE 4
OBJECT MODELING FOR PROCESS RE-ENGINEERING

Use object modeling with clients re-engineering a business process to get them out of the current way of doing things and to help them see the big picture, so they can discover a better solution.

PRINCIPLE 5
OBJECT MODELING BEFORE USE CASES

For understanding a complex business process, use object modeling to bring out what needs to happen. Consider use cases afterward to illustrate how users interact with the objects in the system.

PRINCIPLE 6
MANAGING COMPLEXITY WITH OBJECT MODELING

Object modeling handles complexity by encapsulating information, rules, and behaviors within successive layers of objects. Each layer provides a stable intermediate form for building a larger system.

Finding Objects _____

Object Think

PRINCIPLE 7
PERSONIFY OBJECTS

Object model a domain by imagining its entities as active, knowing objects, capable of performing complex actions.

PRINCIPLE 8
GIVE OBJECTS RESPONSIBILITIES

Turn information about a real-world entity and the actions performed on it into responsibilities of the object representing the entity.

PRINCIPLE 9
OBJECT'S RESPONSIBILITIES

An object's responsibilities are: whom I know—my collaborations with others; what I do—my services; and what I know—my properties.

PRINCIPLE 10
TALK LIKE AN OBJECT

To scope an object's responsibilities, imagine yourself as the object, and adopt the first-person voice when discussing it.

Object Selection

PRINCIPLE 11
THE PEOPLE PRINCIPLE

Use an `actor` object to model individual people participating in a system. Also use an `actor` object to model an organization of people participating in a system as a single entity.

PRINCIPLE 12
THE CONTEXT PRINCIPLE

A context of participation exists whenever a person or organization undertakes actions that are tracked and recorded. Actions that require different permissions or information from the person or organization belong in different contexts.

PRINCIPLE 13
THE ROLE PRINCIPLE

For each context an entity participates in, create a separate `role` object. Put the information and permissions needed for that context into the `role`.

PRINCIPLE 14
THE PLACE PRINCIPLE

Model a location where recorded actions occur with a `place` object. Model a hierarchical location with an `outer place` containing a `place`. Model the uses of a `place` or `outer place` in different contexts with `role` objects.

PRINCIPLE 15
THE THING PRINCIPLE

Model a thing with two objects: an `item` that acts as a description defining a set containing similar things, and a `specific item` that distinguishes a particular thing from others in the set. Model the uses of a thing in different contexts with `role` objects.

PRINCIPLE 16
THE AGGREGATE THING PRINCIPLE

Model a receptacle of things as a `container` with `content` objects. Model a classification of things as a `group` with `member` objects. Model an ensemble of things with an `assembly` of `part` objects.

PRINCIPLE 17
THE EVENT PRINCIPLE

Model the event of people interacting at a place with a thing as a `transaction` object. Model a point-in-time interaction as a `transaction` with a single timestamp; model a time-interval interaction as a `transaction` object with multiple timestamps.

PRINCIPLE 18
THE HISTORY PRINCIPLE

To record historical or time-sensitive information about a person, place, or thing, use a time-interval `transaction`.

PRINCIPLE 19
THE COMPOSITE EVENT PRINCIPLE

Model people interacting at a place with multiple things as a `composite transaction`; for each thing involved, include a `line item` to capture specific interaction details.

PRINCIPLE 20
THE FOLLOW-UP EVENT PRINCIPLE

Model an event that follows and depends on a previous event with a `follow-up transaction`.

Collaboration Rules

Distributing Rule Checking

PRINCIPLE 21

MOST SPECIFIC, LOCAL, OR DETAILED OWNS THE RULE

For collaboration patterns involving people, places, and things, put the collaboration rules in the most specific, local, or detailed pattern players.

PRINCIPLE 22

INTERACTING ENTITY OWNS THE RULE

For collaboration patterns involving people, places, and things interacting with an event, each interacting pattern player that represents an entity owns its collaboration rules.

Services and Properties

Object Think Processes

PRINCIPLE 23

BE OBJECTIVE WITH PROCESSES

Be objective when asking about processes. Talk instead about the objects—people, places, things, and events—involved in the process and the actions on these objects, rather than asking clients how they "want to do it."

PRINCIPLE 24

DO IT MYSELF

Objects that are acted upon by others in the real world do the work themselves in the object world.

PRINCIPLE 25

DO IT WITH DATA

Objects encapsulate data representing an entity together with the services that act on it.

Distributing the Work

PRINCIPLE 26
DIRECTOR PRINCIPLE

Real-world actions on entities map to one of the objects representing that entity. This object is called the director of the action because it directs itself and its collaborators in carrying out the action.

PRINCIPLE 27
MOST SPECIFIC DIRECTS

When a real-world action maps to two collaborators representing a single entity or an aggregation of entities, the director is the most specific, local, or detailed pattern player.

PRINCIPLE 28
EVENTS DIRECT THE WORK

When an action requires cooperation among the collaborating entities of an event, the event directs the action.

Types of Services

PRINCIPLE 29
LET THE DIRECTOR CONDUCT

Use the "specific directs" and "event directs" principles to find the director of a process. Assign the director a conduct business service to initiate the process.

PRINCIPLE 30
MOST KNOWLEDGEABLE IS RESPONSIBLE

When a `role` acts on a `specific item` at a given place and the event is recorded, give the most knowledgeable or restrictive object a conduct business service that establishes the transaction.

PRINCIPLE 31
LET AN OBJECT DETERMINE MINE

Provide an object with determine mine services so it may answer requests for current information.

PRINCIPLE 32

LET AN OBJECT ASSESS EVENTS

Provide an object with analyze transactions services so it may assess its historical information, past events, and future scheduled events.

Descriptive Properties

PRINCIPLE 33

MAKE IT REAL AND RELEVANT

Descriptive properties come from an object's relevant real-world characteristics. Use domain experts, legacy databases, and information architectures to locate relevant descriptive properties.

PRINCIPLE 34

TRACK BUT DON'T KEY

Keep keys and object IDs off the diagram. Include identifying properties only if they come from the domain.

PRINCIPLE 35

HIDE REDUNDANT ACCESSORS

Assume each property listed in the object definition has a read and write accessor, but don't put them in the diagram.

PRINCIPLE 36

SHOW DERIVED ACCESSORS

Represent a derived property with a read accessor in the service section.

PRINCIPLE 37

ALWAYS DATE EVENTS

Transaction objects always include date and/or time properties.

PRINCIPLE 38
DATE OBJECTS WITH SPECIAL OCCURRENCES

Put date and/or time properties in non-transaction objects to record a non-repeatable occurrence or a repeatable occurrence that does not require history.

PRINCIPLE 39
HISTORICAL PROPERTIES NEED OBJECTS

Use history event objects to keep an audit trail of values for a property. Treat the property like a derived one; include a special accessor to read the property value for a given date.

State Properties

PRINCIPLE 40
KNOWING WHERE IN THE LIFECYCLE

In a person, place, or thing object, make the lifecycle state a property derived from event collaborators. In an event, make the lifecycle state a property, unless it is derived from follow-up events.

PRINCIPLE 41
KNOWING WHICH OPERATIONAL STATE

Put an operating state property in any person, place, or thing object that switches between different operational modes.

PRINCIPLE 42
CACHE WHEN FINAL

When an object reaches one of its final lifecycle states, consider caching its derived properties.

PRINCIPLE 43
ONLY CHANGE STATE WHEN CONDUCTING BUSINESS

Allow only conduct business services to change an object's lifecycle or operational state properties.

Complex Properties

PRINCIPLE 44
COLLAPSE CLUTTER OBJECTS

Collapse objects whose only purpose is to represent complex information into properties.

PRINCIPLE 45
CLASSIFY ROLES

Use a role classification property to distinguish different levels of participation only if the participation level requires no history and no additional properties, behaviors, or collaborations.

PRINCIPLE 46
CLASSIFY TYPES

Use a type classification property to distinguish different object types only if the type requires no history and has no additional properties, behaviors, or collaborations.

Object Inheritance

Parent – Child Responsibilities

PRINCIPLE 47
OBJECT INHERITANCE

Use object inheritance between two objects representing a single entity or event when the entity participates in multiple contexts, when the entity comes in many variations, or when the event involves multiple interactions.

PRINCIPLE 48
PARENT RESPONSIBILITIES

In object inheritance, the parent object contains information and behaviors that are valid across multiple contexts, multiple interactions, and multiple variations of an object.

PRINCIPLE 49
CHILD RESPONSIBILITIES

In object inheritance, the child object represents the parent in a specialized context, in a particular interaction, or as a distinct variation.

PRINCIPLE 50
CHILD ASSUMES THE PARENT'S PROFILE

In object inheritance, the child object assumes its parent's profile, enabling it to answer read-only requests for information about properties and collaborators of the parent.

Object Inheritance vs. Class Inheritance

PRINCIPLE 51
OBJECTS NOT CLASSES

Object inheritance relates two objects, each representing different views of the same entity or event. Class inheritance relates two classes, one extending the structure defined in the other.

PRINCIPLE 52
REPRESENTATION VS. SPECIALIZATION

Use object inheritance to represent multiple views of an entity. Use class inheritance to specialize an existing class of objects.

PRINCIPLE 53
VALUES VS. STRUCTURE

Object inheritance is the sharing of actual property values from a parent object. Class inheritance is the sharing of the structure for holding property values from an existing class definition.

PRINCIPLE 54
DYNAMIC VS. STATIC

Object inheritance is dynamic since shared property values often change their state during the course of a parent object's lifetime. Class inheritance is static because the structure for holding property values rarely changes during a class definition's lifetime.

Object Inheritance of Properties

PRINCIPLE 55
VALUES THROUGH SERVICES

Use object inheritance to allow a child to share property values with its parent. Add a read accessor in the child for each property value it object inherits from its parent.

PRINCIPLE 56
READ BUT NO WRITE

Never allow a child object to change property values in its parent.

PRINCIPLE 57
ONLY PUBLIC PROPERTIES

Properties of the parent that are not publicly accessible cannot be object inherited by a child object.

PRINCIPLE 58
NO DESIGN, JUST BUSINESS

Don't allow a child to object inherit design properties that were added to the parent to improve efficiency, support persistence storage, allow interactive display, or satisfy programming practices.

PRINCIPLE 59
QUERIES NOT STATES

Don't allow a child to object inherit read accessors for state, type, or role properties. Do allow the child to object inherit related property value services, such as "isPublished," "isCancelled," "isAdmin," etc.

Object Inheritance of Collaborations

PRINCIPLE 60
IN MY PARENT'S GROUPS

Always allow a child to object inherit its parent's group, assembly, and container collaborations.

PRINCIPLE 61
REMEMBERING MY PARENT'S EVENTS

Always allow a child to object inherit its parent's historical and event `transactions`.

PRINCIPLE 62
FAMILY TIES

Always allow a child to object inherit its parent's parent, but do not allow a child to object inherit other child objects belonging to its parent.

PRINCIPLE 63
SHARE AND SHARE ALIKE

Allow a child to object inherit `follow-up transactions` for its parent's events if and only if the `follow-up transactions` are valid for all the parent's children.

PRINCIPLE 64
MY PARENT THE EVENT

Allow a line `item child` to object inherit the `role` and `place` collaborations of its `composite transaction` parent.

Object Inheritance of Services

PRINCIPLE 65
DETERMINE MINE, TOO

A determine mine service of a parent is object inheritable if every child object could be asked the question the determine mine service answers.

PRINCIPLE 66
ANALYZE ONLY WHAT YOU KNOW

An analyze transactions service of a parent is object inheritable if the child object can object inherit the `transactions` being analyzed.

PRINCIPLE 67
CHILDREN CANNOT CONDUCT BUSINESS

A conduct business service of a parent is never object inheritable because the child cannot alter the parent or the context of the parent.

Child vs. Strategy Objects

PRINCIPLE 68
IT'S A CHILD NOT A FUNCTION

Use internal, stateless Strategy objects to encapsulate pluggable functionality for Context objects. Use external, stateful child objects to model another view of parent objects.

Implementing Collaboration Pairs

Object Definition Interfaces

PRINCIPLE 69
SHOWING YOUR PROFILE EVERYWHERE

To implement object inheritance, describe the parent's object inheritable services with a profile interface, and require all child objects to exhibit the profile interface.

PRINCIPLE 70
CONDUCT BUSINESS INTERFACES

A conduct business interface includes all the business services of an object, either directly or by extending the object's profile interface.

PRINCIPLE 71
HOW I SEE YOU

Collaborators refer to one another using their conduct business interfaces.

PRINCIPLE 72
MAKE THE CHILDREN PARENT-READY

To allow future system growth, define profile interfaces for child objects so they can later become parents.

Implementing Objects

PRINCIPLE 73
MINIMUM PARAMETER RULE

Only properties and collaborations necessary for an object to exist should be passed into the object's construction method.

PRINCIPLE 74
MOST SPECIFIC CARRIES THE LOAD

When work requires cooperation between two collaborators, encapsulate the majority of the effort within the most specific collaborator.

PRINCIPLE 75
PROPERTIES BEFORE COLLABORATIONS

Object construction methods initialize properties before establishing collaborations because collaboration rules may check property values.

PRINCIPLE 76
PART CARRIES THE LOAD

When work requires cooperation between a `whole` collaborator and a `part` collaborator, encapsulate the majority of the effort within the `part` collaborator.

PRINCIPLE 77
PUTTING PARENTS FIRST

When an object must establish two or more collaborations to be valid, parent collaborations must be established first.

PRINCIPLE 78
LET THE COORDINATOR DIRECT

When different types of objects are united by a single common coordinator and must work toward a common goal, allow the coordinator to direct the actions.

Implementing Business Rules

PRINCIPLE 79
WHERE RULES COME FROM

Business rules come from clients; logic rules come from good programming practices.

Implementing Property Business Rules

PRINCIPLE 80
ISOLATE PROPERTY RULES

When a property has domain-specific limits on its values, define a separate method to enforce these limits, and call this test method from within the set property accessor.

PRINCIPLE 81
ISOLATE VALUE ASSIGNMENT

Define a separate method to assign a value into the property and bypass business rule when necessary. The set property accessor calls this method after checking the business rules.

PRINCIPLE 82
DESCRIPTIVE AND TIME PROPERTY BUSINESS RULES

Descriptive and time properties are governed by business rules that define when the values can change and what ranges of values are possible.

PRINCIPLE 83
ENUMERATED PROPERTY BUSINESS RULES

Properties with enumerated types are governed by business rules that define the set of legal values and the legal transitions from one value to another.

Implementing Collaboration Rules

PRINCIPLE 84
DUAL RULE CHECKING

To achieve pluggability, extensibility, and scalability, each object must check its own collaboration rules.

PRINCIPLE 85
COMMUTATIVE RULE CHECKING

Implement collaboration rules so that either collaborator can request to be checked.

PRINCIPLE 86
ISOLATE COLLABORATION RULES

Define separate methods to enforce collaboration rules for establishing and dissolving a collaboration. Define the collaboration add and remove accessors to call the appropriate test method.

PRINCIPLE 87
ISOLATE COLLABORATION ASSIGNMENT

Define separate methods to assign and remove a reference to a collaborator and to bypass business rule checking when necessary. The collaboration add and remove accessors call the appropriate assignment method after checking business rules.

PRINCIPLE 88
STREAMLINING COLLABORATION ACCESSORS

To streamline the collaboration accessors, allow one collaborator to delegate the process of establishing and dissolving the collaboration to the other collaborator.

PRINCIPLE 89
CHOOSING YOUR DIRECTOR

To find the director of a streamlined collaboration, choose the `specific` of a `generic - specific`, choose the `part` of a `whole - part`, and choose the `transaction` of a `transaction - specific`.

Collaboration Pluggability

PRINCIPLE 90
PLUGGABLE MEANS INTERFACES

To make a collaboration pluggable, factor the essential communication requirements out of the current conduct business interfaces and into separate collaboration interfaces.

PRINCIPLE 91
ESSENTIAL CHARACTERISTICS

Extract from business requirements any properties, services, and collaboration methods that are essential across many variations of a pluggable collaborator; include these in the pluggable collaboration interface.

PRINCIPLE 92
PLUGGABILITY WITH INTEGRITY

To allow pluggability without sacrificing model integrity, design pluggable collaborations by fixing one collaborator and creating a pluggable interface for the other collaborator.

PRINCIPLE 93
SELECTING PLUGGABLE COLLABORATORS

Make pluggable the collaborator that varies the most. Lacking guidelines from the client, plug `specifics` into a `generic`; plug `specifics` into a `transaction`; plug `parts` into `containers` and `assemblies`; and allow `groups` and `members` to go either way.

Object Model Documentation _____

Components Description

PRINCIPLE 94
LOOK FOR OBJECT GROUPS

Group together objects that work together to achieve a shared purpose; give them a name reflecting their shared purpose using the client's vocabulary.

PRINCIPLE 95
OBJECT GROUP PROVIDING A FEATURE

If a group of objects has a shared purpose that is only a small step toward achieving a larger goal, then consider the group as providing a feature or function for a component.

PRINCIPLE 96
OBJECT GROUP AS A COMPONENT

If a group of objects has a shared purpose that accomplishes a significant goal, then consider the group as a component.

PRINCIPLE 97
OBJECT GROUP AS A SUB-COMPONENT

If a group of objects has a shared purpose that involves many steps, but is too large to be a feature and too insignificant to be a component, then consider the group as a sub-component of a larger component.

PRINCIPLE 98
DOCUMENT THESE OBJECT MODELS

An object model description is necessary when: the object model is large or has complex collaboration rules or services; the object model is being handed off to a new team for design and development; or the object model is subject to a formal review process.

Streamlined Object Modeling Summary

12 Collaboration Patterns

Actor —parent—— 0..* —Role

Use to model the participation of a person, organization, place, or thing in a context.

- An actor knows about zero to many roles, but typically takes on only one of each kind.
- A role represents a unique view of its actor within a context. The role depends on its actor and cannot exist without it.

OuterPlace ◇—0..1——1..*—Place

Use to model a hierarchy of locations where events happen.

- An outer place is the container for zero or more places.
- A place knows at most one outer place. The place's location depends on the location of its outer place.

Item —parent—— 0..* —SpecificItem

Use to model a thing that exists in several distinct variations.

- An item is the common description for zero to many specific items.
- A specific item knows and depends on one item. The specific item's property values distinguish it from other specific items described by the same item.

Assembly ◇—0..1——1..*—Part

Use to model an ensemble of things.

- An assembly has one or more parts. Its parts determine its properties, and the assembly cannot exist without them.
- A part belongs to at most one assembly at a time. The part can exist on its own.

Use to model a receptacle for things.

- A container holds zero or more content objects. Unlike an assembly, it can be empty.
- A content object can be in at most one container at a time. The content object can exist on its own.

Use to model a classification of things.

- A group contains zero or more members. Groups are used to classify objects.
- A member, unlike a part or content objects, can belong to more than one group.

```
Role ─1──────0..*─ Transaction
```

Use to record participants in events.

- A transaction knows one role, the doer of its interaction.
- A role knows about zero or more transactions. The role provides a contextual description of the person, organization, thing, or place involved in the transaction.

```
Place ─1──────0..*─ Transaction
```

Use to record where an event happens.

- A transaction occurs at one place.
- A place knows about zero to many transactions. The transactions record the history of interactions at the place.

```
SpecificItem ─1──────0..*─ Transaction
```

Use to record an event involving a single thing.

- A transaction knows about one specific item.
- A specific item can be involved in zero to many transactions. The transactions record the specific item's history of interactions.

Use to record an event involving more than one thing.

- A composite transaction must contain at least one line item.
- A line item knows only one composite transaction. The line item depends on the composite transaction and cannot exist without it.

Use to record the particular involvement of a thing in an event involving multiple things.

- A specific item can be involved in zero to many line items.
- A line item knows exactly one specific item. The line item captures details about the specific item's interaction with a composite transaction.

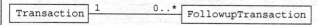

Use to record an event that occurs only after a previous event.

- A transaction knows about some number of follow-up transactions.
- A follow-up transaction follows and depends on exactly one previous transaction.

Three Fundamental Patterns

Generic – Specific	• actor - role • item - specific item • composite transaction - line item
Whole – Part	• outer place - place • assembly - part • container - content • group - member
Specific – Transaction	• role - transaction • place - transaction • specific item - transaction • transaction - follow-up transaction • specific item - line item

Five Kinds of Collaboration Rules

Type	• Is the potential collaborator the right type for me? • In entity collaborations, the most specific collaborator owns the rule. • In event collaborations, the interacting entity owns the rule.
Multiplicity	• Do I have too many collaborations to establish another? • Will I have too few collaborations if I remove one? • Each collaborator checks its own multiplicity rules.
Property	• Verify my property values or the potential collaborator's property values against a constant standard. • The collaborator who knows the standard owns the rule. • Compare my property values with a potential collaborator's property values. • The collaborator who knows the acceptable range of values owns the rule
State	• Am I in the proper state for establishing or dissolving a collaboration? • Each collaborator checks its own state rules.
Conflict	• Do any of my collaborators conflict with the potential collaborator? • Since conflict rules are just collaboration rules between indirect collaborators, the same principles for deciding who owns the collaboration rule apply.

Pattern Player Collaboration Rules

	Type	Multiplicity	Property	State	Conflict
Actor					
Role	✓	✓	✓	✓	✓
Outer Place		✓	✓	✓	
Place	✓	✓	✓	✓	✓
Item		✓		✓	
Specific Item	✓	✓	✓	✓	✓
Assembly		✓	✓	✓	
Part	✓	✓	✓	✓	✓
Container		✓	✓	✓	
Content	✓	✓	✓	✓	✓
Group		✓	✓	✓	✓
Member	✓	✓	✓	✓	✓
Role	✓	✓	✓	✓	✓
Transaction		✓			
Place	✓	✓	✓	✓	✓
Transaction		✓			
Specific Item	✓	✓	✓	✓	✓
Transaction		✓			
Composite Transaction		✓			
Line Item	✓	✓			
Specific Item		✓			
Line Item		✓			
Transaction	✓	✓	✓	✓	✓
Follow-up Transaction		✓			

Three Kinds of Services

Conduct Business	• A service that kick offs processes and accomplishes an action rather than answers a question. • A service that creates new objects or changes objects' states. • Typical conduct business services include creating new objects, establishing collaborations, and setting property values. • In entity collaborations, the most specific collaborator directs the process. • In event collaborations, the transaction directs the process.
Determine Mine	• A service that satisfies requests for current information about the object's properties, state, and collaborations. • A service that should never alter the states of any objects. • Typical determine mine services include returning property values and collaborators, working with collaborators to determine an aggregate value, and performing a search.
Analyze Transactions	• A service that assesses historical or future information captured in associated events. • A service that should never alter the states of any objects. • Typical analyze transactions services compute summary results from past transactions, compute summary results from collaborators of past transactions, and locate future scheduling conflicts.

Six Kinds of Properties

Descriptive	• Domain-specific and tracking properties
Time	• Date or time properties
Lifecycle State	• Status of one-way state transitions (e.g., nomination status: pending, in review, approved, rejected)
Operating State	• Status of two-way state transitions (e.g., sensor state: off, on)
Role	• Classification of people (e.g., team member role: chair, admin, member)
Type	• Classification of places, things, and events (e.g., store type: physical, online, phone)

Methods for Enforcing Collaboration Rules

add (aCollaborator) **remove** (aCollaborator)	• Adds or removes the collaborator if the collaboration rules allow. • Calls the corresponding "test" and "do" methods. • *Example*: `addNomination`
testAdd (aCollaborator) **testRemove** (aCollaborator)	• Tests the collaborator against the receiver object's collaboration rules and raises an exception if any rules fail. • *Example*: `testAddNomination`
testAddConflict (directCollaborator, indirectCollaborator, ...) **testRemoveConflict** (directCollaborator, indirectCollaborator, ...)	• Checks for conflicts with the direct collaborator and one or more indirect collaborators and raises an exception if any rules fail. • *Example*: `testAddNominationConflict`
doAdd (aCollaborator) **doRemove** (aCollaborator)	• Adds or removes the collaborator into or out of the receiver object's collaboration variable or collection without rule checking. • *Example*: `doAddNomination`

Methods for Enforcing Property Rules

set (aValue)
setValue( )
- Sets property to a given or enumerated value if property rules allow.
- Calls the corresponding "test" and "do" methods.
- *Example*: `setName`
- *Example*: `setStatusAccepted`

testSet (aValue)
testSetValue( )
- Tests the value against the receiver object's property rules and raises an exception if any rules fail.
- *Example*: `testSetName`
- *Example*: `testSetStatusAccepted`

doSet (aValue)
doSetValue( )
- Assigns a value into the object's property variable without rule checking.
- *Example*: `doSetName`
- *Example*: `doSetStatusAccepted`

Collaboration Rule Directors

Generic – Specific
- `specific`

Whole – Part
- `part`

Specific – Transaction
- `transaction`

Object Definition DIAPER

Define	• Name the class, indicate its superclass, and specify any interfaces exhibited. • Define variables for properties. • Define variables for collaborations.
Initialize	• Create construction method that has parameters for property values and collaborations necessary for the object to exist. • Construction method sets remaining properties to default or initial values. • Construction method creates collections for collective collaborations.
Access	• Write property accessors and collaboration accessors. • Write "test" methods for checking property and collaboration rules. • Write "do" methods for assigning and removing property values and collaborators.
Print	• Describe values of select properties and ask select collaborators to describe themselves. • The most specific collaborator asks generic collaborators to describe themselves. • An event asks interacting entity collaborators to describe themselves.
Equals	• Check if the receiving object is equal to another by comparing property values and select collaborators. • The most specific collaborator asks generic collaborators to compare themselves. • An event asks interacting entity collaborators to compare themselves.
Run	• Create sample objects with typical property values and sample objects for select collaborators. • The class of the most specific collaborator creates its sample objects by using sample objects from the classes of the generic collaborators. • The class of an event creates its sample objects by using sample objects from the classes of the event collaborators.

Object Inheritance Interfaces

Profile	• Specifies parent services that are object inherited by its child objects. • Includes most determine mine services, except when they summarize information about other child objects. • Includes analyze transactions services if the child object inherits the transaction collaborators analyzed. • Includes no conduct business services.
Conduct Business	• Specifies parent services that are not object inherited by its child objects. • Includes all public conduct business services, plus determine mine and analyze transactions services not in the profile interface. • Extends the profile interface. • When used to specify services of objects not involved in object inheritance, includes all public conduct business, determine mine, and analyze transactions services.

Bibliography

Beck, Kent. *Smalltalk Best Practice Patterns*. Upper Saddle River, NJ: Prentice Hall, 1997. ISBN: 013476904X.

Coad, Peter, and Edward Yourdon. *Object-Oriented Analysis*. (2nd ed.). Englewood Cliffs, NJ: Yourdon Press, 1991. ISBN: 0136299814

Coad, Peter and Jill Nicola. *Object-Oriented Programming*. Englewood Cliffs, NJ: Yourdon Press, 1993. ISBN: 013032616X

Coad, Peter, David North and Mark Mayfield. *Object Models : Strategies, Patterns, And Applications*. (2nd ed.). Upper Saddle River, NJ: Yourdon Press, 1997. ISBN: 0138401179

Coad, Peter, Mark Mayfield, and Jonathan Kern. *Java Design : Building Better Apps And Applets*. (2nd ed.). Upper Saddle River, NJ: Yourdon Press, 1999. ISBN: 0139111816.

Coad, Peter, Eric Lefebvre, and Jedd De Luca. *Java Modeling In Color With UML : Enterprise Components And Process*. Upper Saddle River, NJ: Prentice Hall PTR, 1999. ISBN: 013011510X

Eckel, Bruce. *Thinking in Java*. (2nd ed.). Upper Saddle River, NJ: Prentice Hall, 2000. ISBN: 0130273635

Flanagan, David. *Java In A Nutshell : A Desktop Quick*. (2nd ed.). Cambridge; Sebastopol, CA: O'Reilly, 1997. ISBN: 156592262X.

Gamma, Erich, et al. *Design Patterns : Elements Of Reusable Object-Oriented Software*. Reading, Mass.: Addison-Wesley, 1995. ISBN: 0201633612

Goldberg, Adele, and David Robson. *Smalltalk-80 : The Language And Its Implementation*. Reading, Mass.: Addison-Wesley, 1983. ISBN: 0201113716.

Goldberg, Adele. *Smalltalk-80 : The Interactive Programming Environment*. Reading, MA: Addison-Wesley, 1984. ISBN: 0201113724

Gosling, James, et al. *The Java Language Specification* (2nd ed.). Boston: Addison-Wesley, 2000. ISBN: 0201310082.

Guzdial, Mark. *Squeak : Object-Oriented Design With Multimedia Applications.* Upper Saddle River, NJ: Prentice Hall, 2000. ISBN: 0130280283

Kay, Alan C. "The Early History of Smalltalk." *The Second ACM SIGPLAN History of Programming Languages Conference (HOOPL-II), ACM SIGPLAN Notices* 28(3) (March, 1993): 69-75.

Lea, Douglas. *Concurrent Programming In Java: Design Principles And Patterns.* (2nd ed.). Reading, MA: Addison-Wesley, 2000. ISBN: 0201310090.

Neward, Ted. *Server-Based Java Programming.* Greenwich, CT: Manning, 2000. ISBN: 1884777716.

Quote References

Dick, Philip K. "How to Build a Universe That Doesn't Fall Apart Two Days Later." Undelivered speech written for an appearance at the University of Missouri in Rolla, May 5, 1978. (By permission of the Philip K. Dick Memorial Trust and its agents, Scovil Chichak Galen Literary Agency, Inc., New York, New York).

Jefferson, Thomas. "Schools and 'Little Republics.'" Letter to John Tyler, 1810.

Muir, John. *My First Summer In The Sierra.* Boston, New York: Houghton Mifflin, 1911.

Simon, Herbert Alexander. *The Sciences Of The Artificial.* (3rd ed.). Cambridge, MA: MIT Press, 1996. ISBN: 0262691914.

Yoda. *Star Wars: The Empire Strikes Back.* Dir. George Lucas. Lucasfilm Ltd., 1980.

Index

Pluggability with integrity principle, 273, 331
Pluggable collaborators, selecting, 273, 331
Pluggable means interfaces principle, 271, 331
process-process execution pattern, 291-92
Processes, being objective with, 319
Profile interface, 162, 342
    TeamMember, 184
Profile interface, defined, 162
Properties:
    object inheritance of, 325
    overriding, 148
    types of, 339
Properties before collaborators principle, 328
Property business rules, 228-31
    collaboration rules:
        conflict rules, implementing, 253-67
        coordinating, 239-41
        implementing, 241-53
    cross-property validation, 236-39
        Java set property accessor and cross-val-
            idation property test methods, 238
        Squeak set property accessor and cross-
            validation property test methods,
            238-39
    descriptive and time property business rules,
        231-34
        document publication date example,
            233-34
        document title example, 231-32
    enforcement methods, 230
    enumerated, 235
    implementation strategies, 229
    implementing, 329-30
    property categories, 230-31
    state, role, and type property business rules,
        234-36
        nomination status example, 235-36
Property rules, 55, 228-31, 336
    actor-role collaboration rules, 58-59
    assembly-part collaboration rules, 68
    container-content collaboration rules, 71
    group-member collaboration rules, 73
    isolating, 230
    item-specific item collaboration rules, 65
    methods for enforcing, 340
    outer place-place collaboration rules, 62
    transaction-follow-up transaction collabora-
        tion rules, 92
    transaction-place collaboration rules, 82
    transaction-role collaboration rules, 78
    transaction-specific item collaboration rules,
        84
Property value accessors, 190-94, 234

Publish-subscribe notification, 108
Putting parents first principle, 206, 328

Q
Queries not states principle, 138, 325

R
Re-engineering, 6
Read accessors, 109
Read but no write principle, 137, 325
Real-world modeling, 28
Remembering my parent's events principle, 143,
    326
remove, 244
Representation vs. specialization principle, 134,
    324
Role classifications, 121-22
Role classification accessors, 122
Role collaborations, and object inheritance, 139
role collaborations, overriding, 151
Role history, 122
role object, 18, 21
Role principle, 18, 317
Role properties, 339
Rolling back entity collaborations, 57

S
Selecting pluggable collaborators principle, 273,
    331
Service and property principles, 319-23
Service signature, 160
Services:
    analyze transactions services, 111-12
    collaboration accessor services, 106-7
    collaborators, notifying, 108
    determine mine services, 108-10
    and object inheritance, 144-47
        analyze transactions services, 145-46,
            338
        conduct business interface, 338
        conduct business services, 104-6, 147
        determine mine services, 144-45, 338
    types of, 103-104, 338
    write accessors, 108
Services and properties, 95-124

inform**IT**

www.informit.com

YOUR GUIDE TO IT REFERENCE

Articles

Keep your edge with thousands of free articles, in-depth features, interviews, and IT reference recommendations – all written by experts you know and trust.

Online Books

Answers in an instant from **InformIT Online Book's** 600+ fully searchable on line books. For a limited time, you can get your first 14 days **free**.

Catalog

Review online sample chapters, author biographies and customer rankings and choose exactly the right book from a selection of over 5,000 titles.